Andrew Gumbel is a British-born journalist, based in Los Angeles, who has won awards for his work as an investigative reporter, a political columnist, and a feature writer. For more than twenty years he worked as a foreign correspondent for Reuters and the British newspapers *The Guardian* and *The Independent*, covering stories in Europe, the Middle East, and the Americas. He covered the first democratic elections in East Germany after the fall of the Berlin Wall and has frequently reported on contested or suspect elections since in Bosnia, Serbia, Albania, Haiti, and, since 2000, in the United States. He writes frequently about the criminal justice system as well as politics for publications that have included *The Guardian*, the *Los Angeles Times*, the *Los Angeles Review of Books*, *The Nation*, *The Atlantic*, and *Vanity Fair*. He is the author of several books, including *Oklahoma City: What the Investigation Missed—And Why It Still Matters* (HarperCollins, 2012).

Also by Andrew Gumbel

Oklahoma City: What the Investigation Missed—
and Why It Still Matters

DOWN FOR THE COUNT

DIRTY ELECTIONS AND THE ROTTEN HISTORY OF DEMOCRACY IN AMERICA

ANDREW GUMBEL

THE NEW PRESS

NEW YORK
LONDON

To my children, the voters of the future

Requests for permission to reproduce selections from this book should be mailed to: Permissions Department, The New Press, 120 Wall Street, 31st floor, New York, NY 10005.

First published as *Steal This Vote* by Nation Books, New York, 2005
This revised and updated edition published in the United States by The New Press, New York, 2016
Distributed by Perseus Distribution

LIBRARY OF CONGRESS CATALOGING-IN-PUBLICATION DATA

Names: Gumbel, Andrew, author.
Title: Down for the count : dirty elections and the rotten history of
  democracy in America / Andrew Gumbel.
Other titles: Steal this vote
Description: Revised and updated edition. | New York : New Press, The, 2016.

| Revised edition of: Steal this vote. New York : Nation Books, c2005. |
  Includes bibliographical references and index.
Identifiers: LCCN 2015044836| ISBN 9781620971680 (paperback) | ISBN
  9781620971697 (e-book)
Subjects: LCSH: Elections--Corrupt practices--United States--History. |
  Voting-machines--United States--History. | BISAC: POLITICAL SCIENCE /
  Political Process / Elections.
Classification: LCC JK1994 .G87 2016 | DDC 324.973--dc23 LC record available at http://lccn.loc
  .gov/2015044836

The New Press publishes books that promote and enrich public discussion and understanding of the issues vital to our democracy and to a more equitable world. These books are made possible by the enthusiasm of our readers; the support of a committed group of donors, large and small; the collaboration of our many partners in the independent media and the not-for-profit sector; booksellers, who often hand-sell New Press books; librarians; and above all by our authors.

www.thenewpress.com

Book design and composition by Bookbright Media
This book was set in Minion Pro and Gotham

Printed in the United States of America

10 9 8 7 6 5 4 3 2 1

Not alone the triumphs and the statesmen; the defeats and the grafters also represent us, and just as truly. Why not see it so and say it?

—*Lincoln Steffens*

CONTENTS

AUTHOR'S NOTE

This is an updated and thoroughly revised version of a book that was first published under the title *Steal This Vote* by Nation Books in 2005. The clamorous events of the past ten years and the extraordinary backlash against voting rights in many parts of the country have required a shift in perspective away from the sense of puzzled incomprehension many Americans felt in the immediate aftermath of the 2000 election toward a more thorough contextualization of the country's dysfunctional electoral system, past and present.

There's less about voting machines this time, and more about money and the politics of voter suppression. It's gratifying to note that many of the judgment calls I made in the wake of the 2004 elections have proved correct, despite much sound and fury to the contrary at the time. Republicans *weren't* in cahoots with voting-machine companies to steal elections, as is now clear from their obvious focus on other things—redistricting, tightening the rules for third-party registration drives, cracking down on the invented problem of in-person voter fraud, and, as long as George W. Bush was president, aggressively politicizing the Justice Department. There *is* a persistent and continuing structural issue of race in the American political system; many of the recent laws passed to restrict ballot access and suppress minority votes have been sparked by modern versions of the Nativist impulses and racial backlash that drove voter suppression in the wake of the Civil War. If the story of suffrage rights in Western Europe is essentially a story of working-class empowerment and was largely settled by the end of the nineteenth century, the story of suffrage rights in the United States is uniquely focused on racial disparities and seems likely to be contested in those terms for the foreseeable future.

I've taken the opportunity not only to update the narrative but also to streamline the historical chapters and, in places, inject what I hope are more carefully considered political arguments. The book now includes endnotes, so readers can more easily track down my sources; the process has led to the correction of a number of small errors, mostly of attribution, and the addition of some new material. The conclusions are a little different too. One major change over the past decade has been the spike in interest in voting rights among serious scholars and academic institutions like the Brennan Center for Justice and the Moritz College of Law at Ohio State University. There have been some genuinely brilliant ideas, for example the National Popular Vote concept, which proposes a way to work around the electoral college without abolishing it. The legal record is also much richer; some of the best insights into the battles in Texas and North Carolina are to be gleaned from court documents. I've become, if anything, more pessimistic about the prospects for lasting and meaningful reform. But the work of many brilliant and passionate scholars and voting-rights activists has at least made it possible to understand what, theoretically, needs to be done—and why, regrettably, it will be so hard to get there.

INTRODUCTION:
"EVERYTHING IS A VIOLATION"

> The politicians in Washington have concluded that the system
> can't be all that bad because, after all, it produced *them.*
>
> —*DeForest Soaries, founding chair of
> the Election Assistance Commission*[1]

A few days before the 2004 presidential election, Jimmy Carter was asked what would happen if, instead of flying to Zambia, Venezuela, or East Timor, his respected international election-monitoring team turned its attention to the United States. His answer: the shortcomings of the system were so egregious that his colleagues at the Carter Center would never agree to such a thing. "We wouldn't think of it," he said. "The American political system wouldn't measure up to any sort of international standards."[2]

The former president reeled off four examples of what he meant: the lack of a nonpartisan central electoral commission to establish standards and approve voting equipment; the lack of uniformity in voting rules across the country, or even within individual states; the absence of a media environment in which candidates for office were offered equal air time free of charge, as happened routinely in most other mature democracies[3]; and the failure of much of the country's voting equipment to provide for meaningful recounts.

He could have added many more items to the list: the lack of accurate voter lists and the politicization of trying to amend them; the multiple obstacles to voter registration, leading to the disenfranchisement of tens of millions of eligible voters, including several million who want to cast a ballot in any given election season but find they cannot; the disenfranchisement of more than five million felons and ex-felons, in violation of the 1990 Copenhagen Document to which the United States is a signatory; the gross lack of competitiveness in congressional and state legislative races due to the distorting effects of campaign money, partisan gerrymandering, and the vast advantages of incumbency; the continuing pattern of discrimination and exclusion of African Americans, Native Americans, Hispanic Americans, new voters, students, and the poor; the lack of voting machines in many low-income neighborhoods, leading to impossibly long lines on Election Day and further de facto disenfranchisement; and the failure to police obvious conflicts of interest, to the point where election managers at county and state levels can be in charge of races in which they are themselves candidates or—as happened in Florida in 2000 and in Ohio in the year he was speaking—are entrusted with certifying the results of a presidential vote after playing a leading partisan role in the campaign.

Carter did in fact say more as soon as the 2004 election was over. The following year, he teamed up with James Baker, seasoned confidant to four Republican presidents, in a worthy but ultimately ill-fated effort to institute meaningful across-the-board reform that both major political parties could embrace. Sadly, the parties were in no mood to find common ground, on voting rights or anything else, and the only lasting legacy of the Carter-Baker commission was to help unleash a torrent of restrictive voter ID laws in Republican-controlled states—a development Carter came to abhor because of its discriminatory effect on African American voters.[4]

By 2015, the former president was so exasperated he described the United States in another radio interview as "just an oligarchy, with unlimited political bribery." He was talking, specifically, about the Supreme Court's 2010 *Citizens United* decision, which had lifted all limits on so-called independent expenditures by corporations, unions, and other special interests supporting candidates for office. "We've just seen a complete subversion of our political system as a payoff to major contributors who want and expect and sometimes get favors for themselves after the election's over," he said. "The incumbents, Democrats and Republicans, look upon this unlimited money as a great benefit to themselves. Somebody who's already in Congress has a lot more to sell to an avid contributor than somebody who's just a challenger."[5]

Not so long ago, the corruptions and inadequacies of the American electoral system were close to a taboo subject, rarely discussed by political candidates or the mainstream media and recognized only by insiders and by those voters—minorities and the poor—with firsthand experience of the obstacles routinely thrown in their path. Often it took an outsider with no illusions about some impossibly idyllic democratic American past to see things more clearly. "Absolutely everything is a violation!" the chair of South Africa's Independent Electoral Commission, Brigalia Bam, exclaimed during a tour of Florida in 2004. "All these different systems in different counties with no accountability. . . . It's like the poorest village in Africa."[6]

Dr. Bam was, admittedly, basing her judgment on the state long recognized as the basket case of America's election woes. She'd spent several days in Florida listening to stories of voter intimidation, attempted suppression of the black vote, slapdash polling station procedures, and substandard voting machines that lost or miscounted votes. Then again, 2004 was a relatively *good* year in Florida's recent electoral history, thanks to the introduction of provisional and early voting in response to the disasters of four years earlier, as well as some movement toward giving the vote back to ex-felons who had completed their probation and parole periods.

Had Bam returned eight or ten years later, she would have found that many of these progressive reforms had been either halted or reversed and that *more than 10 percent* of Florida's voting-age population were now excluded from voting because of a past criminal conviction. (The national average is about 2.5 percent.)[7] Many voting rights groups in the Sunshine State would have told her that instead of going out into the field and seeking to solve problems with registration or absentee balloting, as they had in 2004, they had all but given up fieldwork because of dizzying new restrictions that penalized even high school civics teachers seeking to register their eighteen-year-old students.

Regrettably, Florida is no longer an outlier. American democracy as a whole is experiencing its biggest backslide in more than a century. Where once it was the Democratic Party that perpetuated the most egregious inequalities and disregarded the civil rights of whole classes of voters, now it is an ascendant Republican Party that is using the language of reform and "commonsense" theft and fraud prevention to whip up its supporters and wage a furious war of attrition against voters it has identified as loyalists for the other side—minorities, recent immigrants, young people, and the poor. Some voters have allowed themselves to be buffeted by great gusts of partisan outrage and even to cheer on the malfeasance, as long as it benefits their side. Many more feel overwhelmed by apathy or disgust.

The backslide has only been exacerbated by some truly disastrous rulings by the U.S. Supreme Court, starting with the notorious *Bush v. Gore* decision that ended the 2000 election without resorting to anything so vulgar as counting the votes. *Citizens United* made it possible for special interests on both sides of the political aisle to buy candidates, poison the airwaves with distorted negative advertising, and effectively buy all but the highest-profile races at national, state, and local levels. *Shelby County v. Holder* (2013) dismantled a vital part of the Voting Rights Act that for almost half a century had given the Justice Department the power to police new election laws in states and counties with a track record of discrimination; the ruling has emboldened several states, especially in the South, to amp up their election laws to a degree of repressiveness unseen since the segregation era.

The aim of this book is not just to inspect the battered bodywork of American voting rights in the twenty-first century. By taking a long, hard look at history, it also asks why the United States, alone among the world's mature democracies, so clamorously has failed to manage its electoral process or live up to its own ardently espoused ideals. This was the first country in the world to embrace democratic rights as we now understand them, the first to see mass participation in the political life of its rural townships and emerging big cities. No country has been as vocal about the vibrancy of its democracy, or lectured the world more zealously about following its example. And yet, as we shall see, the health of that democracy has been repeatedly undermined by corrupt institutions, dirty elections, and extraordinary bursts of voter manipulation and suppression.

How come? The answer has a lot to do with the way racism was hardwired into the system from the beginning, and also a lot to do with the way those heady ideals have butted up at key moments against powerful economic and political forces with no interest in living up to them.

Most strikingly, the question of who gets to vote has never been fully settled and, for that reason, has never gone away.

The hit being taken to the cause of voting rights today is eerily reminiscent of the Gilded Age in the late nineteenth century, when the movement toward universal suffrage was stopped cold by self-proclaimed reformers using many of the same arguments we hear today about corruption, fraud, and the rogue influence of degenerates, criminals, and foreigners. Political leaders swayed by fear of mass political participation, and by the ascendancy of America's corporate might, abandoned the Lincolnian ideal of government "of the people, by the people, for the people" to wipe out populist movements, rein in the power of the big-city political machines, and give the former Confederate states free rein to cut blacks and poor whites out of the system altogether. The country essentially abandoned its early legacy as an experiment in the expansion of suffrage and instead became a world-class laboratory for vote suppression and election stealing.

In our new Gilded Age, the power of corporate money has, if anything, been allowed to run *more* rampant. Corporations now enjoy the same First Amendment rights as people and throw their weight behind political races in ways unimaginable even to Mark Hanna, President McKinley's free-marketeering campaign manager who more or less invented the corporate sponsorship of political candidates. While it's true we have more tools with which to combat brazen voter suppression (notably, the parts of the Voting Rights Act the Supreme Court has left intact), the fight is on to push back against ideologically driven laws that penalize minority voters and the poor in Texas, Florida, North Carolina, and elsewhere. The scale of the problem may no longer be the same—the ambition of modern-day Republicans is limited to shaving a few percentage points off the Democratic vote, not eliminating whole classes of voters. But the antidemocratic impulse and the slippery, deflective language in which it is couched have altered surprisingly little.

One of the heartbreaking aspects of the U.S. electoral system is that, in many quarters, there is in fact tremendous determination to get things right. More than half the states now either allow online registration or plan to do so soon.[8] Oregon, which already showed an experimental flair in 1998 when it switched to a 100 percent mail-in ballot system, has shifted the registration burden almost entirely from the voter to the state by enrolling anyone with a driver's license or other government ID. It expects to increase the number of eligible voters by three hundred thousand people, or almost 15 percent, for the 2016 electoral cycle. (As this book was going to press, California had just followed suit with similar legislation.)[9] Six states, appalled by the gerrymandering epidemic, have ended the practice of allowing elected politicians to carve up their own district boundaries and have established independent or bipartisan commissions.[10] An admirable number of state and county elections officials have seen through the shortcomings of electronic voting equipment and guided their jurisdictions to adopt optically scanned paper ballots, by far the most reliable, transparent, and cost-effective technology on the market. And they are generally avoiding the lure of Internet voting, which no computer scientist has yet figured out how to secure from undetectable hack attacks.[11]

The problem with all this reformist energy, much of it unleashed in the wake of the 2000 presidential election, is that the politics keep getting in the way. They get in the way from the top down, in the sense that even states with tolerably well-managed county elections offices—Wisconsin, or even Ohio—find themselves at the mercy of partisan decision making by state lawmakers and executives who have introduced voter ID laws, cut early voting, eliminated same-day registration, attempted to specify the weight of the paper on which online voter registration forms are printed (as Ohio's Republican secretary of state Kenneth Blackwell did in 2004), or attempted to reject absentee ballot requests from the other party on the grounds that a single box on the form was not checked correctly (as Ohio's Democratic secretary of state Jennifer Brunner did in 2008).[12]

The politics also get in the way from the bottom up, in the sense that election management in many cities and counties is a mess, and the two major parties have shown no serious interest in cleaning it up. On the contrary—they seem to prefer the mess because it enables them, in the event of a tight race in which one party has control over the process, to bend or break the rules, such as they are, and push the count in their direction. While elections officials have been known to pray before the first Tuesday in November that no race of theirs ends up being close, party managers seem quite comfortable with the fact that, in many parts of the country, there is no knowable way of producing a definitive result, only a fuzzy tangle of possible interpretations that can be manipulated and litigated as needed.

This relentless politicization, more than any other single factor, is what sets the American electoral system apart from its Western counterparts. In this book, I am significantly tougher on the modern-day Republicans than on the Democrats, for reasons that will be laid out in detail, but it's important to understand that the real blame lies with the *two-party system*, which has damaged the cause of representative democracy more gravely than either party on its own. In a better regulated environment, there would be no room for partisans on *either* side to compromise the country's electoral integrity.

The parties' default reaction to an election that has been bought or stolen is never to clamor for a fairer system. If the race is close and the stakes are high, the impulse is to fight like dogs to overturn the result—and, if that's not possible, to find more money and fight harder and dirtier next time. The United States is a country that thrives on ferocious competition—the sink-or-swim ethic of capitalist adventurism, forever flirting with the fringes of the permissible—and few competitive arenas are more cutthroat than elective politics. The political culture in this country is defined by what Lyndon Johnson's biographer Robert Caro once described as "the morality of the ballot box, in which nothing matters but victory and any maneuver that leads to victory is justified."[13] Only the means used to achieve that goal have changed over time.

No wonder there has never been a professional class of elections managers, or even the appetite to create one. Every recent election controversy has brought with it a blizzard of complaints about insufficient or nonfunctioning machines, poll workers who did not know how to fix them, voter identification procedures that were not followed correctly, voters who were given erroneous information about casting provisional ballots, and on and on. It has created a cottage industry for election protection lawyers, but has benefited almost nobody else.[14]

Regrettably, in many states, county elections offices are treated by both parties as a dumping ground for dimwits, timeservers, crooks, and small-time political appointees too incompetent to be given anything else to do. This is what Joseph P. Harris, a political scientist and onetime poll worker in Prohibition-era Chicago, found when he studied the question for the Brookings Institution in 1934:

> There is probably no other phase of public administration in the United States which is so badly managed as the conduct of elections. Every investigation or election contest brings to light glaring irregularities, errors, misconduct on the part of precinct officers, disregard of election laws and instructions, slipshod practices, and downright frauds. . . . The truth of the matter is that the whole administration—organizations, laws, methods and procedures, and records—are, for most states, quite obsolete.[15]

He could have written the same paragraph, more or less verbatim, at any time since. When John Bridges, a judge in rural Washington State, reviewed a contested gubernatorial election in 2004, he blasted the county elections office in Seattle—with cause—for its inertia, selfishness, irresponsibility, time-serving mentality, and refusal to be held accountable.[16] Two years later, an outspoken founding member of the Election Assistance Commission (EAC), the New Jersey Republican DeForest Soaries, complained loudly about the lack of training and standards guiding elections officials nationally. "If we were another country being analyzed by America," he said, "we would conclude that this country is ripe for stealing elections and for fraud."[17]

Administrators, in turn, rely on dozens, sometimes hundreds, of shoddily paid temporary workers and volunteers, who may come forward for the right reasons but are thrown into the job with inadequate training and little or no supervision. In the 1930s, the chief clerk of a big-city elections office complained, "It would be difficult to imagine a more incompetent and drunken lot of loafers anywhere than the nondescript outfit that was put on registration and election work, with a few exceptions."[18] Things have scarcely improved since, not least because of dwindling budgets and the disdain heaped since the Reagan era on the very concept of public office. In 2000, the *Los Angeles Times* interviewed a former county elections director in rural Washington State who quit to become a waitress at Sizzler because the money was better, and an elections commissioner in New York City who struggled to find competent voting machine technicians. "You make more money servicing laundry machines," he complained.[19]

Political influence is easier to exert, of course, if the bureaucrats are bumbling, inexperienced, and underpaid. So it's no coincidence if many of them are just that, or if the ones who take their jobs seriously risk being targeted for removal because they won't dance to the right political tune.[20] A county prone to the abuses of a tight local power network can conduct dirty elections more or less routinely with little or no accountability to higher authority. If an outsider candidate for school board or water board feels cheated, what, realistically, are the available remedies? Fraud is notoriously hard to prove under the best of circumstances, and next to impossible when the challenger's opponents control the elections office and, with it, access to materials needed to demonstrate official malfeasance or counting errors. Lawyers are expensive, and local watchdogs are often ineffectual. "I am 80 years old and I don't understand anything about computers," one canvassing board member from Waukesha County, Wisconsin, infamously said in 2011 after the county clerk claimed to have found fourteen thousand decisive extra votes on her laptop in a contentious election for the state supreme court.[21] At least in that instance there was a recount. In many jurisdictions, authorities simply refuse to conduct one. In others—in eleven states, as of 2015—the machines used on Election Day make recounts impossible.[22]

Away from the headlines and the high-profile partisan battles, the dysfunctions of the U.S. electoral system are as dismal as they are pervasive, driven by deeply local interests and concealed by money, influence peddling, and the quirks of a troubled past.

Take, as one particularly weird example, the industrial city of Vernon, California, which sits at the intersection of two freeways on the edge of downtown Los Angeles. For more than a century, a single family ran what was essentially a scam to rake in tax money from local businesses and pocket much of it for themselves in the form of vastly inflated salaries, benefits, and perks. They got away with it because they generated jobs, housed factories nobody else wanted (a stockyard, meatpacking, and an animal rendering factory), and kept their corruption quiet enough to stay out of the newspapers. None of that altered the fact that, in a sane political system, the city should never have been allowed to exist.[23]

Elections in Vernon have always been a joke, because the resident population is minuscule: just 112 souls, according to the 2010 Census. The ruling family—led by John Leonis, Vernon's founder, who remained in charge for forty-eight years, and Leonis Malburg, his grandson, who carried the torch for another fifty-six—kept strict tabs on who lived in city-controlled housing and who got to vote. Every four years, they would handpick candidates for mayor and city council and wave them through, often without the formality of an actual election.

Then, in 1980, the retiring police chief surprised the status quo by running for city council. He was evicted from his city-owned home and disqualified from the ballot, but that did not stop him. He moved in with the head of the city Chamber of Commerce, and together they mounted a challenge on *two* council seats. They would have won, too, except the city administrator found a way to invalidate six ballots, which was enough to overturn the results in a nail-biter race. Nobody outside Vernon—not the county district attorney, not the California secretary of state—said a word about it.

Twenty-six years later, a trio of challengers tried something similar, moving into Vernon just in time to file papers for the 2006 city election. The city, which had not been planning an election at all, responded by cutting off their electricity, sending eviction letters, and rescinding their voter registrations. But it was not enough. The courts took the side of the insurgents, and their candidacies were reinstated. Reluctantly, the city went ahead with the election, only to take the extraordinary step of refusing to count the votes on the unproven grounds that the outsiders were trying to steal the election and, with it, the city.

For six months, Vernon was in stalemate. The vote count, when it came, favored the city-backed candidates, but nobody knew whether it was trustworthy. In the end it was Malburg and his family who came under criminal investigation, because they didn't live in Vernon as required by the city charter; they occupied a mansion in an elegant residential neighborhood ten miles to the west. Malburg was stripped of his office and convicted of fraud, while his son was found to be a child molester and prosecuted accordingly. The state legislature came close to ending Vernon's status as a separate city, but it clung on with the help of millions in lobbying money and promises to open up the city and make $60 million in "good neighbor" contributions to programs for impoverished children in nearby communities. A disgusted John Pérez, California Assembly Speaker, said his legislative colleagues had "given Vernon a free pass to continue doing business as usual."[24]

A world away, on the Indian reservations of South Dakota and Montana, Native Americans have been continuing a decades-long fight—against elected officials of both parties—for minimal recognition of their rights. Where once they had to battle even for recognition as citizens (resolved by the Indian Citizenship Act in 1924), they still struggle to be accorded the same rights of representation and ballot access as the rest of the population. Since the introduction of early voting in the early 2000s, they have lobbied for satellite offices to be set up on reservations so tribal members don't have to drive—sometimes as far as 150 miles round-trip—to the nearest county seat and run through a gauntlet of discrimination and harassment when they get there to register and vote. In the early years, the answer was always no, ostensibly because of budgetary strictures. Then, in 2012, a private Native American rights group called Four Directions offered to put up the money needed to establish satellite offices on four Montana reservations. When the answer was still no, Four Directions sued.[25]

The political rationale for the refusal was clear. The counties wanted to keep Native Americans marginalized and out of local politics so officials would be under no pressure to lift them out of an unremitting cycle of poverty going back generations. And the state was more interested in accommodating the counties' interests than in standing up for civil rights. The counties argued in court that the satellite offices were a "convenience," not something to which Native Americans were entitled. But the tribes countered that denying them access to the vote was a clear and measurable form of discrimination outlawed under the Voting Rights Act. Voter turnout in Montana typically ran to 70 percent for tribal elections but only 30 percent for all other contests—not because members didn't want to vote in them, but because it was too difficult to register and get to the polls. "South Dakota is the Mississippi of the Great Plains," Tom Rodgers, a Blackfeet Indian and Washington lobbyist for Native American causes, suggested in 2013. "Montana is becoming the Alabama."

The lawsuit was initially rebuffed by a reactionary federal judge (who was forced into retirement shortly after because of a racist joke he cracked about President Obama).[26] But when the Justice Department weighed in on the plaintiffs' behalf, the tide turned, the parties settled, and the satellite offices were introduced in time for the 2014 midterms. Satellite offices have since cropped up on the Lone Pine reservation in South Dakota and elsewhere.

Still, many Native Americans living on reservations find it difficult to register to vote by mail, because the post office can be twenty or thirty miles away and they are afraid of being arrested on trumped-up charges of drunkenness and disorderly behavior if they stray too far from home. In states where mail-in voting is becoming more common, the issue has had a noticeably chilling effect on tribal participation.[27] "We love our country, we do," the lead plaintiff in the case, a Northern Cheyenne elder named Mark Wandering Medicine, said. "But when is our country going to love us back?"

Not so long ago, the relative obscurity of these stories was the norm in American public discourse. People needed reminding, if they ever knew, that the country's electoral contests tend to play out on a lopsided field and that pivotal close races have often been fought illegally, won unfairly, and lost ungraciously. Many Americans who lived through the protracted battle over Florida in 2000 felt instinctively that the country had sunk to some new low unseen since the dying days of Jim Crow and the Daley machine in Chicago. In fact, nothing has been more normal over the past two hundred years—including the past fifty—than for one side to push, shove, and strong-arm its way across the finish line, praising the strength and fairness of the process as it goes, while the other side stares forlornly at a defeat it can comprehend only as an outrageous theft threatening the fabric of democracy itself.

Once Florida blew the lid off the fantasy that all was for the best in the best of all possible democracies, these practices were at last laid bare, and the terms of the debate shifted accordingly. In theory, Florida was a wake-up call, spurring Congress and the White House to find a way to fix the system. Instead, elections turned into their own ferociously politicized battleground, in which neither major party trusted the other, violations routinely went unpunished, and no reliable mechanism existed to fix what was broken. The mistrust that had always existed between the parties extended rapidly to their supporters, many of whom came to see fraud and foul play lurking behind every polling station door, to the point where reasonable suspicion and anger about a dysfunctional system blurred into outright paranoia.

It's a two-party affliction. To this day, many Democrats are convinced that George W. Bush owed his 2004 election victory to some sleight of hand involving computer voting machines, sinister tabulation software operated on Republican servers in Tennessee, and a high-level GOP tech consultant who died in a plane crash before he could tell what he knew. No part of this scenario has garnered serious mainstream attention.[28] Likewise, plenty of Republicans are convinced that Barack Obama owed his landslide victory in 2008 to busloads of illegal immigrants, fraudulent registrations compiled by criminals and drug addicts on behalf of voting rights and community organizing groups, students illegally voting twice, and ghost voters raised from the dead.

Rank-and-file voters of both parties had every reason, after 2000, to make common cause and demand more transparent and accountable elections, but the implacable logic of the two-party system made such a thing inconceivable. It would have been like asking Yankee and Red Sox fans to mount a joint protest against poor umpiring. It wasn't just that the two sides could not stomach the idea of talking to one another; they were interested only in changing the decisions that went against *them*. And so party managers didn't push back against the paranoia—they tapped into it to stir up their base, which had the salutary effect of increasing overall turnout but also intensified the ugliness.

Without a doubt, the Republicans have been more effective at banging the drum of fraud and malfeasance, because they have placed it at the very center of their supporters' attention. They haven't just *invoked* the country's inglorious history of intimidation, kidnapping, bloodshed, bribery, embezzlement, intoxication, under-the-table bargaining, stuffed voter rolls, and creative vote counting, of ballots bought and sold, stolen, forged, spoiled, and tossed into lakes, rivers, and oceans. They have acted as though we were still stuck in some eternal 1868, when Boss Tweed's thugs roved the streets of New York, immigrants were naturalized en masse for the express purpose of voting in the Democrats, and the *Cincinnati Gazette* complained there were men "who would think no more of going to the polls and voting without being paid for it, than a cow does of going to her rack when there is no fodder in it."[29]

The tactical lure of the Republican focus on photo ID laws has been to tap into all the insecurities and prejudices of the party's overwhelmingly white base about a system out of control: the "otherness" of having a black man in the White House (was he even *born* in the United States?), of African Americans voting en masse and threatening the status quo in North Carolina, of demographic shifts in states like Texas, where the white population is on its way to being outnumbered by Latinos and other immigrant populations. "When you have a party that is almost exclusively white," the Republican strategist John Feehery said, "the pressure is to win with the white vote, not to find a way to reach out and expand your base."[30] Some Republicans, including Feehery and the former RNC chair Ken Mehlman, have sought to resist that pressure and find ways to diversify the party's support base. But they are pushing against a tide of extraordinary force and breadth. In 2005, Mehlman apologized to the NAACP for members of his party who "gave up on winning the African-American vote, looking the other way or trying to benefit politically from racial polarization."[31] Such an apology from the head of the party seems quite inconceivable now.

When they were first proposed, the new voter ID laws struck many voters as unimpeachable "commonsense" measures to make sure people casting a ballot were who they claimed to be—another reason why they caught on so rapidly. Party operatives pointed out, rightly, that in-person voter fraud was once a persistent feature of the electoral environment, but made no effort to explain that the days of "floaters" coming in from out of town to cast illegal ballots largely ended with the introduction of the secret ballot in the late nineteenth century. They didn't mention, either, that the most notorious instances of in-person vote fraud of the modern era—for example, the infamous two hundred names added to the voter rolls at the last minute in Alice, Texas, to give Lyndon Johnson an undeserved victory in his 1948 race for the U.S. Senate—occurred only because they were orchestrated by party operatives and corrupt elections officials, the very people responsible for checking voter eligibility in the first place. ID laws wouldn't have changed a thing in Alice, just as they wouldn't have deterred the Democratic Party machine in Chicago in the 1950s and 1960s. Contextualizing American history was not the point, of course; the goal was only to create an aura of illegality around the votes of likely Democrats, whose numbers the new laws were meant to suppress.

As a result, the burden of presumptive guilt in contested elections has been shifted onto individuals who have never, on their own, been a problem of any significance—except to those who, for reasons of partisan loyalty or racial prejudice, don't want them to be part of the process in the first place. The new laws do nothing to address the *real* problem, which is the risk of official malfeasance, especially in jurisdictions where one party exercises tight control. These days, anyone wanting to organize a fraudulent vote drive is more likely to do it through absentee ballots, which are subject to much looser administrative control than in-person voting. At least in recent history, far more election fraud prosecutions have arisen from absentee ballots than from any other source.

The last time in-person fraud was seriously considered as a factor of any consequence was in San Francisco in 1997, when a controversial ballot initiative asking voters to approve a $535 million football stadium passed by a narrow margin, possibly with the help of hundreds of people who had registered to vote more than once in the same neighborhood and 744 others recorded as being dead at the time they went to the polls. The malfeasance was widely attributed to Mayor Willie Brown and his well-oiled political machine, but the district attorney, a political ally of the mayor's, never found more than a single precinct captain to charge with a crime. The episode rocked the San Francisco Department of Elections, which had to contend with a panoply of reported problems beyond the alleged voter impersonation issue. These included thousands of ballots left unsecured in the rain and later dried off in microwave ovens, polling places in stadium-friendly neighborhoods that opened early, and polling places in stadium-hostile neighborhoods that experienced unexplained closures.[32]

Over the next four years, the elections office chewed through four chiefs and 80 percent of the staff quit. Ballot boxes were regularly found opened before they were counted, discrepancies in vote counts abounded, and, in one notorious episode, 240 valid ballots were discovered in a garbage can. By 2002, pressure had mounted to create an independent commission to clean things up—not before Brown's last handpicked elections chief, Tammy Haygood, had collected almost a year's salary beyond the date she was fired and qualified for a new health benefit to cover a sex change that her domestic partner was undergoing. It was a benefit introduced, so insiders said, with Haygood's situation specifically in mind.[33]

San Francisco is presumably the sort of place voter ID advocates think of when they talk about out-of-control fraud.[34] Back in 1975, the city saw an even more egregious onslaught of illegal in-person voting when hundreds of members of Jim Jones's Peoples Temple—yes, *that* Jim Jones—went from precinct to precinct casting repeat ballots for the Democratic mayoral candidate, George Moscone. Survivors of the Jonestown massacre later acknowledged they helped sway the election, but prosecutors made no headway in building a case against them. A voter fraud unit set up by the San Francisco district attorney was entrusted to Jones's personal lawyer, who took no action against Temple members and later said he had not been aware of any fraud. (Jones himself was appointed to run the city's housing authority.) Federal prosecutors fared no better once the city told them that the voter lists for the election had disappeared, along with four hundred precinct registration books. Moscone's Republican opponent, John Barbagelata, wanted to keep fighting, but he too gave up after a quarter stick of dynamite concealed in a box of See's Candy was delivered to two of his young children, addressed to "the people's choice."[35]

Could similar abuses happen today? Theoretically, yes, although it's worth remembering that political machines prefer to work quietly and would almost certainly choose other avenues. Would a strict voter ID law have helped remedy the fraud problem in 1975 or 1997? With that level of political control, not in the slightest.

One consequence of America's struggles with its democratic apparatus has been to dent its influence over election-monitoring and democratization overseas. Far from setting an example for others to follow, the United States has provided ample ammunition to Russia and other autocratic states in eastern Europe that want to cry foul whenever their own voting practices come under scrutiny. The bad blood has led to a revival of Cold War tensions within the fifty-six-member Organization for Security and Cooperation in Europe (OSCE), which played a critical role in the emergence of eastern bloc countries from the shadow of communist dictatorship in the 1990s but, since the Florida debacle, has been beset by internal divisions, budgetary woes, and a sharp decline in influence.

In 2003, the OSCE conducted a comprehensive review of its ground rules for election monitoring and urged member states to examine their commitment to such basic principles as transparency and accountability. The review pinpointed at least eleven areas where the United States, as a signatory to the original 1990 Copenhagen Document, could be said to fall short (a list similar to the points laid out at the beginning of this introduction). To the fury of the Russians and Belarusians, it had absolutely no effect on policy making, either federally or in the states.[36]

The following year, a Democratic congressman from Florida, Alcee Hastings, took over the presidency of the OSCE's parliamentary assembly and pushed the organization into an impossible position by calling for a full-scale monitoring mission to oversee every aspect of the Bush-Kerry presidential election. The OSCE realized there was no way to acquiesce without being seen to be out to get the Republicans, especially in Florida, so it settled instead for a short "targeted observation mission" restricted to a handful of states. Even that became a struggle, because the European Union wouldn't supply observers for fear of angering the Americans—they came up with just two, both Dutch—and several U.S. states, including Ohio, Florida, Pennsylvania, and Georgia, put up resistance to hosting the observers at all.[37]

The Russians erupted in fury at what they saw as political capitulation to the Americans and immediately pushed for an overhaul of the OSCE's election-monitoring practices—a none-too-subtle attempt to make them less effective, especially in the Russian sphere of influence. "The Organization is not only ceasing to be a forum uniting states and peoples but, on the contrary, is beginning to drive them apart," Russia's foreign minister, Sergei Lavrov, thundered at a ministerial meeting a month after the U.S. election. "Election monitoring is not only ceasing to make sense but is also becoming an instrument of political manipulation and a destabilizing factor."[38]

An unnerved OSCE delayed publication of its final report into the Bush-Kerry race for almost five months, afraid that even one misplaced turn of phrase might turn Lavrov's words into a self-fulfilling prophecy. But delaying had its own costs. The Russians threatened to pull their funding. The Belarusians accused the OSCE of being in the Americans' pocket. U.S. officials, afraid of the opposite, placed a number of what one OSCE official described as "inappropriate phone calls" in a nervous attempt to find out what the final report was going to say.

When the report came, it only inflamed the Russians and Belarusians further by diluting what little had been said in a preliminary draft put out on Election Day and reading like a long exercise in diplomatic cowardice. What were at first described as "allegations of electoral fraud and voter suppression" became, in the final version, "so-called voter suppression" of which monitors had been "unable to identify first-hand evidence" beyond what they read in the papers. Where the big 2002 reform bill, the Help America Vote Act, had been "a work in progress," now its impact was deemed to be "positive but limited."[39]

This kid-glove treatment of the OSCE's most powerful member made no difference in the United States—nobody cared either way—but it inflicted considerable harm on the overall credibility of the international election-monitoring business. Countries previously responsive to OSCE pressure noticed the Americans' blithe disregard for outside criticism and took it as an excuse to follow suit. One OSCE official said the Copenhagen Document risked turning into "Legoland, a virtual reality."[40] As budgets tightened, missions to countries where the OSCE stood even a chance of making a difference became shorter and were staffed by younger and less experienced observers, many of them from former Soviet countries whose governments had little interest in criticizing other people's shortcomings.

Thereafter, the OSCE sent monitoring missions back to the United States every two years, quietly pointing out the same flaws that fell on the same deaf ears. Then, in 2012, OSCE observers in Texas and Iowa ran into a buzz saw of Tea Party activists and elected officials who raved about a United Nations takeover and threatened to arrest any OSCE monitor within three hundred yards of a polling station.[41]

That set a familiar pattern in motion: the OSCE backed off, claiming—with a straight face—that it didn't really need to enter polling stations to observe the election, and the Russians, still aggrieved by a critical report on Vladimir Putin's reelection as president the previous spring, raged once again about double standards. "It is strange," the Russian foreign ministry said, "why the U.S. authorities, who often accuse other countries of being not democratic enough, prefer not to notice such violation of democracy in their own country."[42]

It was, unfortunately, a fair point.

1

THE ANTIDEMOCRATIC TRADITION AND THE NEW RIGHT

You gotta remember the smartest thing the Congress did was to limit the voters in this country. Out of three and a half to four million people, two hundred thousand voted. And that was true for a helluva long time, and the republic would never have survived if all the dummies had voted along with the intelligent people.

—*Richard Nixon, to John Ehrlichman*
on the White House tapes (1971)[1]

If this were a dictatorship, it'd be a heck of a lot easier, just so long as I'm the dictator.

—*George W. Bush, six days after the*
Supreme Court made him president[2]

A week before the 2004 presidential election, Mona Charen of the *Washington Times* wrote a column arguing that the gravest threat to the American political system was its voters. At least a quarter of them were too ill-informed to be trusted, she asserted, and they were messing things up for everyone else. "If a person is utterly ignorant about matters of public policy, then he or she has a solemn obligation to refrain from voting," she said. Ignorance was a "choice"—not something the political parties or the public education system had an obligation to address.[3]

Drew Avery, a student writing in the *Seattle Times*, felt similarly. "Stop talking about voter quantity and start focusing on voter quality," he said. "I know people who don't vote and, frankly, I'm glad they don't. Not because their political philosophies don't match mine, but because they don't have passion and they can't be bothered to inform themselves."[4]

It was probably no coincidence that these pieces appeared on the eve of an election in which the Republicans were nervous that higher turnout might doom President George W. Bush's reelection chances, or that a mentality was already setting in among GOP operatives—more widespread now than it was then—that if voters preferred the Democratic Party there had to be something wrong with them.

But they also tapped into a longer tradition in American politics, one that has never been comfortable with the Lincolnian ideal of government "of the people, by the people, for the people." Adherents of this darker tradition believe in perpetuating a natural ruling class and see elections not as a validation but, at best, as a necessary inconvenience. They genuflect before the altar of representative democracy, as everyone must, but they don't truly believe in it. For them, the public interest and their own interest are one and the same; they see elections as exercises in salesmanship and obfuscation and have no interest in high-minded Socratic debate that can only derail their desired outcome. Better to rely on money and negative advertising to motivate the base and throw everyone else into confusion and disgust. If half the electorate stays home, so much the better.

There was a time, before the civil rights era, when sentiments like those expressed by Charen and Avery were part of the mainstream political conversation because they helped justify the segregationist policies of the South. But they have never fully gone away. In 1975, Michel Crozier, Samuel Huntington, and Joji Watanuki wrote a notorious book called *The Crisis of Democracy* in which they blamed the media and the antiwar movement for the American defeat in Vietnam. Popular participation had gone too far, they said; there was an "excess of democracy," and leaders needed to be more authoritarian, cultivate a more pliant media, and lull the masses into apathy and political disengagement.[5]

In a similar vein, George Will wrote a *Newsweek* column in 1983 arguing that people were not owed the right to vote per se, only the right to good government. Just because people voted in large numbers did not mean their best interests were being served, he said—just look at Weimar Germany and where it led.[6] Another example: Robert Kaplan, writing in *The Atlantic* in 1997, said voter apathy troubled him less than the idea of a volatile political system and a hyperactive, out-of-control electorate. "The last thing America needs," he argued, "is more voters—particularly badly educated and alienated ones—with a passion for politics."[7]

The flaw in such arguments is that they suggest the problem lies with democracy itself, that greater popular representation will invariably turn order into chaos. But democracy is almost by definition a messy, rowdy, unpredictable business, and it should be. There was nothing tidy about the Revolutionary War, or the movement to abolish slavery, or the battle for women's suffrage, or the march for civil rights. It's true that democracy will sometimes fail, as it did in Germany in the 1930s. But order and tranquility are not the answer, not in a country as diverse and restless as the United States. Order and tranquility almost always portend something sinister and authoritarian, as Crozier, Huntington, and Watanuki understood. If voters are ill-informed and apathetic, it means social and political tensions have been buried, not resolved. The answer is to educate and engage voters, not to freeze them out further.

The critics of democracy are correct about one thing: American voters are indeed among the most ill-informed and apathetic anywhere in the world. The International Institute for Democracy and Electoral Assistance routinely places the United States near the bottom of its turnout list, lower than any other industrialized country and roughly on par with Bangladesh, Mali, and Kyrgyzstan.[8] But this state of affairs is hardly the fault of the voters themselves. The immediate reasons for their disaffection are plentiful and easy to identify: the breathtaking lack of competitiveness in most congressional and state legislative races; disgust at politicians who spend more time raising campaign dollars than serving their non-donor constituents; the surfeit of lower-order races in which candidates address only highly targeted parts of the electorate; and the prevalence of personal, vituperative, deceptive campaigns that speak to the gut, not the head, and leave voters alienated and appalled.[9] With rare exceptions, more than 90 percent of Congress is reelected every two years without a meaningful fight; the same is true of state legislatures, where an ever-rising number of seats—36 percent in 2014[10]—go uncontested because challengers, and their financial backers, understand that any attempt to unseat the incumbent is futile.

Yes, there can be ground-shifting years, like 1994 and 2010, when the Republicans made significant gains in the House of Representatives, but there can also be years like 2004, the least competitive in U.S. history despite that year's closely fought presidential race, when the number of marginal races plummeted to less than one in twenty. Voter polarization has a lot to do with creeping stagnation—look at a map of Texas, for example, and it's clear that the Democratic vote has increasingly clustered in the big cities and along the Rio Grande valley, to the exclusion of almost everywhere else. But the polarization has also been exacerbated by partisan gerrymandering, the decennial political orgy in which politicians (in most states) get to redraw their own district maps and invariably boost their own party at the expense of their adversaries, to the point where legislative minorities can become majorities without any shift in voting patterns. As a frustrated North Carolina state legislator memorably said in the late 1990s, "We are in the business of rigging elections."[11] In California, the most populous state in the Union, not one of the 153 congressional and legislative seats up for grabs in 2004 changed party hands. "What kind of democracy is that?" California's governor, Arnold Schwarzenegger, asked at the time, making him one of the few elected politicians who seemed to notice, much less care.[12]

It doesn't help that in recent congressional elections this system has given a clear, less than democratic advantage to one party—the Republicans. Not only is the GOP routinely overrepresented relative to the number of votes it receives, there have also been instances since 2000 when it has made gains in both the House and Senate despite winning *fewer* votes than the Democrats. In 2000, Democrats did better overall than Republicans in the 371 House districts where the race was remotely competitive, yet they picked up only 179 of those seats to the Republicans' 191. In 2012, things were even worse: the Democrats won 1.4 million more House votes nationwide, yet ended up with thirty-three fewer seats. Political scientists refer to this politely as an *inefficient distribution of votes.* Democratic support tends to be concentrated in smaller geographical areas with denser populations (in other words, big cities), so their candidates win by bigger margins. In the Senate, where

big states are on par with small states, the unevenness is even more pro-
nounced. California, a solidly Democratic state, has roughly 66 times
the population of Wyoming, a solidly Republican state, yet both get
the same two senators. In 2004, and again in 2010, 2012, and 2014, the
Democrats won more Senate votes than the Republicans nationwide but
lost seats—and, in 2014, their majority.[13]

No wonder many people, especially minority voters who are often
the biggest targets of gerrymandering, feel that their votes don't count.
Some of the imbalances have come about by accident as much as by
design, but the feeling remains: there is something almost Soviet about
these races. Politicians don't have to worry about public accountability
because they know that no matter how poorly they perform (barring a
scandal involving marital infidelity, sexting, or child molestation) they
will almost certainly get reelected. Brecht's once-satirical line about the
government dissolving the people and electing another[14] has in many
ways become an American reality.

It would be a mistake, however, to think of these issues as a recent
phenomenon, or to blame them on one party alone. When the Democrats controlled Congress, as they did without interruption from 1955
to 1995, Republicans frequently complained that the system was rigged
against *them*. Some of the system's structural flaws go back to the country's founding, when the Southern states successfully negotiated for an
outsize say in the affairs of the republic and became the pivot on which
Congress rested—and frequently has since. Other issues can be traced
to the effects of industrialization in the mid-nineteenth century, when
America's attachment to mass political participation collided with the
interests of an emerging capitalist class more interested in subjugating
workers than empowering them. Politicians and the leading thinkers
of the day raised the alarm about what had been a steadily expanding
franchise and made distinctions between those they regarded as "real"
Americans deserving of full voting rights (white Protestant landowners,
mostly) and the rest (industrial workers, agricultural laborers, women,
immigrants, and former slaves), whose legitimacy they deemed more
questionable. They, too, liked to cite ignorance and apathy as excuses to
do their worst.

From the Confederate defeat in 1865 to the end of World War I, the
voting rights of vast numbers of Americans were systematically and

drastically checked—and not just in the South. All aspects of voting, from registration to polling-place access to the intelligibility of the ballot, were made as arduous and obstacle-ridden as possible for those considered undesirable. If would-be voters were not hamstrung by poll taxes or quizzes about their state constitutions, they might find that registration in their county was restricted to an impossibly few hours a month, or that their precinct location had been moved thirty or forty miles away without warning.

These restrictions helped the Republicans and the Democrats establish their duopoly and encouraged both parties to restrict electoral competition to voters they could count on while ignoring everyone else. With the Democrats firmly in control in the South and the Republicans dominant almost everywhere else from the late 1890s until the 1929 Wall Street crash, party competition collapsed, and voter participation shriveled along with it.

Despite the great advances in voting rights since—the advent of women's suffrage in 1920, the end of segregation in the South, and the expansion of the franchise to eighteen- to twenty-one-year-olds—the damage done in that earlier period has never been repaired. Other industrialized countries have experienced problems with voter apathy, but only in the United States has there been an almost exact correlation between participation and socioeconomic status. In other words, it is the bottom half of the electoral heap that fails to show up time after time, and it's worse in the South than in the North. One widely cited study from 1980 found that Southerners with fewer than eight years of schooling voted 16 percent less often than Northerners with the same educational profile.[15]

At least until the 2000s, both parties seemed quite comfortable with this arrangement, preferring to fight over the electorate they knew than to try to grow themselves a new one. In contrast to many more obviously corrupted parts of the world, where democracy has been threatened or subverted by an excess of ideology, America's two major parties may have suffered, curiously, from a lack of it. Until the last decades of the twentieth century, both represented such a grab bag of constituencies and interests it was sometimes hard to say what each of them stood for and where the boundary between them lay. The GOP was the party that ended slavery before it embraced big business, and pushed progressive environmental reforms before sinking into climate change denial.

The Democrats, meanwhile, were forged as an improbable coalition of white Southern racists, Northern industrialists, and immigrant workers. Unlike European political parties, which divided more neatly into business versus labor camps, the Republicans and Democrats sought to make a virtue of their diversity and appealed to voters more on personality and gut allegiance than on any particular set of policy prescriptions. If elections brought out the worst in everyone, it was in large part because, in the absence of a coherent program with which to mobilize support, power for its own sake was often the only tangible thing at stake. And where power led, the money followed. Call it the *American Idol* model of democracy: the voters were told the choice was theirs, but really the key decisions on form and content were made already, mostly at the behest of advertisers; the contest was skewed to favor superficial attention grabbing over substance, and only a wavering, highly confused few had not made up their minds in advance. The whole thing reeked of deception—and still does.

If the calculus has shifted, it is because the electoral map has changed and, with it, the complexion of both major parties. Voters are now polarized along racial as well as geographical lines, and what was once a fuzzy separation between the parties has developed into a chasm. The Democrats, having shed their reactionary Southern wing (by electoral attrition more than active choice), are now much more interested in registering and turning out new voters, as attested to by the remarkable grassroots movement that swept Barack Obama into the White House in 2008. They still struggle to forge a coherent identity out of their disparate and contradictory parts, fail time and again to embrace populist causes because of the need to accumulate vast war chests of corporate campaign money, and have been far from perfect in their advocacy of voting rights. The Democrats should have been much quicker to embrace same-day registration in North Carolina, for example, but they were haunted by the 1998 governor's race in Minnesota, when Jesse Ventura snuck past both major-party candidates with a late insurgent campaign greatly helped by his supporters' ability to register and vote on the same day. Only when party operatives were satisfied that reform served their partisan interest did they change their tune.[16]

The Republicans, meanwhile, have spent the past half century remaking themselves as a more explicitly ideological party serving a narrowing range of interests. The trigger was the remaking of the American South in the wake of the Voting Rights Act, which emboldened the GOP to go after the white Southern vote for the first time in its history. It did so with coded appeals to the racism that had kept segregation alive for so long, and with populist campaigns on wedge issues like abortion and gay rights that resonated most strongly with fundamentalist Christians, a key target constituency. The effort was so successful it ended up defining the modern Republican Party—first, through its association with the Christian Coalition, then through the emergence of a new class of Southern politicians who came to dominate Congress and take over the White House, and latterly through the rise of iconoclastic Tea Party populism.

The party has certainly expanded its class appeal, somehow convincing heartland Americans that the Democrats alone are the party of rich, urban elitists and corporate fat cats. But this success has come at the cost of becoming an almost entirely white party at a time when America's white population is in decline and every minority category except African Americans is growing rapidly. That in itself has fueled insecurities about the party's ability to appeal to a mass electorate and has caused the GOP to develop an unerring instinct for voter suppression—even when it goes against the party's own self-interest. Both in 1993, in the debate over the National Voter Registration Act (better known as the Motor Voter law), and in the 2004 election Republicans assumed that higher registration and higher turnout rates would tip the field to the Democrats. But on both occasions they were wrong. More Republicans than Democrats registered through Motor Voter in the first flush of the law's passage,[17] and Republican turnout in rural Ohio in 2004 did more to give George W. Bush a second term in the White House than any whining about voter ignorance or attempts to suppress Democratic votes in Cleveland, Cincinnati, or Columbus.

A more pragmatic Republican Party might look to the future and seek ways to broaden its support so it doesn't lose the ground it gained so successfully over four decades. Many party stalwarts have proposed exactly that. But there is nothing pragmatic about the present-day GOP, which loves to promote the occasional minority candidate or official to present a veneer of diversity[18] but has overwhelmingly resisted calls from within the party to reach out to minority voters. Instead, it has preferred radical posturing against illegal immigration and barely coded racial invective against welfare recipients and the "inner city." Those old-guard leaders who have advocated immigration reform or minority outreach—including George W. Bush, once just a bogeyman on the left—have been spurned as lacking in ideological purity. The party has sought refuge instead in a panoply of voter-suppression mechanisms and alarmist rhetoric about illegal voting by foreigners and criminals. The quality of American democracy has declined markedly as a result.

In case it wasn't already obvious that the Republicans' Southern strategy was premised on racial discrimination, the party's most prominent campaign operative, Lee Atwater, spelled it out in a devastatingly frank interview in the early 1980s. "You start out in 1954 by saying, 'Nigger, nigger, nigger,'" he told a political scientist from Case Western Reserve University. "By 1968 you can't say 'nigger'—that hurts you, backfires. So you say stuff like forced busing, states' rights, and all that stuff, and you're getting so abstract. Now, you're talking about cutting taxes, and all these things you're talking about are totally economic things, and a byproduct of them is, blacks get hurt worse than whites. . . . Obviously sitting around saying, 'We want to cut this' is much more abstract than even the busing thing, and a hell of a lot more abstract than 'Nigger, nigger.'"[19]

Around the same time, the founder of the Heritage Foundation and the American Legislative Exchange Council, Paul Weyrich, made a similarly revealing admission about the party's overall voter outreach strategy. "Many of our Christians," he said, "want everybody to vote. I don't want everybody to vote. . . . As a matter of fact, our leverage in the elections quite candidly goes up as the voting populace goes down."[20]

These sentiments, shocking as they sound to the uninitiated, were hardly secret within the world of political strategists; in fact, they had informed the thinking of *both* parties for the previous hundred years. Winning, as Weyrich also said, wasn't about attaining a majority; it was about attracting just enough votes to beat the other party and persuading everyone else to stay home.

The most remarkable thing, perhaps, was the Republicans' eagerness to take over the Democratic Party's segregation-era playbook. It's not that the Republicans were now overtly racist—some were and many were not. The point was, they were so focused on winning they didn't particularly care. They were filled with pent-up frustration about being shut out for so long—from the South and from the majority in the House of Representatives—and that guided everything they did.

In many ways, the party's progress down the path of antidemocratic thinking and behavior can be measured by a long series of grievances and resentments. Nixon spent his presidency raging against the Kennedys, against Johnson, against the CIA and the State Department and anyone else who smacked of establishment privilege or was suspected of being out to get him. He was outspoken about Jews in the arts and the media and about blacks in general. ("The whole problem is really the blacks," he told his chief of staff H.R. Haldeman. "The key is to devise a system that recognizes this while appearing not to.")[21] Nixon's resentments and paranoia ended up destroying him, but they would also continue to infect the party as it pursued the Southern strategy he pioneered over the next several decades.[22] In 1984, the Republicans were outraged, and rightly so, when the Democratic leadership in the House voted to reseat an incumbent from Indiana's Eighth District even though he had not actually won reelection. It was true, as the Democrats argued, that Frank McCloskey had come out narrowly ahead on election night, but he'd fallen several hundred votes behind Richard McIntyre, his Republican challenger, after a recount. When the Democrats seated McCloskey anyway, a then-obscure congressman from Wyoming named Dick Cheney said, "We ought to go to war. . . . There's unanimity. We need bold and dramatic action."[23]

Another resentment came in 1992, when Bill Clinton benefited from the third-party candidacy of Ross Perot to deny George H.W. Bush a second term in the White House. Since Clinton won with a plurality but not a majority of the popular vote, many Republicans felt they had a license to act as if he were not president at all—"the enemy of normal Americans," in the infamous words of Newt Gingrich, who became House Speaker following a Republican midterm landslide in 1994.[24] The GOP didn't stop piling on Clinton as long as he was president. They knew the effort to impeach him in 1998 was sure to fail, but they pursued it anyway, because it was good for stirring up their core supporters and turning others away in disgust—the very model for political activism that operatives like Weyrich had long embraced. To the extent that the effort hastened the Republican takeover of Arkansas and Tennessee, the home states of Clinton and his vice president, Al Gore, it was also successful—more successful, arguably, than Clinton's high overall poll numbers at the end of his presidency would suggest.[25]

Such were the raw emotions informing the presidential fight in Florida in 2000, when George W. Bush found himself 537 votes in the lead the day after the election, and the Republican establishment moved heaven and earth to keep it that way. The thirty-six-day battle for the White House was touted by the party's communications team as a victory they always knew was coming, but beneath the surface the closeness of the race, and the embarrassment of having to fight for it so publicly, had a profound effect on Republican thinking. Bush, acting on the advice of his political guru Karl Rove, concluded that being declared winner was mandate enough, and he pushed for every conservative agenda point he could wrest out of Congress—a Congress that, like the White House, was now in Republican hands even though the Democrats had won more votes.

Soon, conservative thinkers began openly questioning the utility of voting at all. Benjamin Ginsberg, who had been one of the Bush campaign's lawyers in Florida, wrote a book in which he wondered whether elections were a better engine of effective government than, say, congressional committees or media investigations. He was clearly nostalgic for the Progressive Era, when government reformed itself largely without the input of the voters. He even declared, "The era of the citizen is now coming to an end."[26] A Cato Institute report published a couple of years later took Ginsberg's argument a step further, envisioning a future in which the citizen's primary tool of political expression would no longer be the ballot box but rather "foot-voting"—that is, staying in a community if its leadership was acceptable and leaving if not. The author, a George Mason University law professor named Ilya Somin, despaired of the ignorance of many voters and proposed a system of radically "decentralized federalism" in which cities and townships would compete in a civic free market for their inhabitants' custom.[27] It's questionable whether there's a difference between privatizing democracy in this way and simply abolishing it.

Similar doubts gnawed at the institutions of government. The Supreme

Court, in its election-ending *Bush v. Gore* decision, threw into doubt the notion that citizens even have a right to vote in presidential elections.[28] One Christian fundamentalist elevated to the job of deputy undersecretary of defense intelligence, General William "Jerry" Boykin, freely acknowledged Bush was not the choice of "the majority of America," but in his view that only proved the forty-third president must have been chosen directly by God.[29] Many influential figures in the defense establishment under Bush—including Paul Wolfowitz, the Pentagon's number two; Boykin's boss, Stephen Cambone; Richard Perle of the National Defense Policy Board; Adam Schulsky, head of the Pentagon disinformation office; and Elliott Abrams, a veteran of the Iran-Contra scandal who sat on the National Security Council—were avowed admirers of Leo Strauss, a University of Chicago philosopher who saw liberal democracy as a recipe for weak, flabby, decadent societies and reserved his greatest admiration for the enlightened tyrants of the Classical era.[30] In many ways, this was analogous to a worldview that Democrats as well as Republicans had perpetuated since the dawn of the Cold War through the national security establishment: tell the people they are a shining city on a hill and let covert operatives and secret government programs do the dirty work of waging clandestine wars, funneling money and weapons to questionable allies, and overthrowing democratic governments deemed hostile to the United States.[31] The Bush administration, though, took this precedent a step or two further and, under the influence of the Straussians, extended it in both the domestic and the foreign policy arenas in ways that had not previously been explored.

Strauss believed power was too important to be entrusted to the vulgar masses, preferring an elite that could be relied upon to invoke religion, nationalism, and a world divided into good and evil to rein in the population's essential wickedness and keep it happy with the opiate of "consoling lies." And so, in many respects, the Bush administration came to govern. They spurned public opinion and the expertise of scientists, scoffing at what one administration member memorably called "the reality-based community."[32] In Iraq, they pressed for regime change—another Straussian term—without worrying unduly whether the pretext, that Saddam Hussein had a dangerous arsenal of weapons of mass destruction, was true or just another consoling lie.

The party cast off any doubts about its mission after the 9/11 attacks, which it saw as a license to push any agenda it wanted, including the aggressive pursuit of Republican seats at the congressional and state legislative levels.[33] Allen Raymond, a party operative who pressed so hard in the 2002 midterms that he ended up serving time for jamming Democratic Party phone banks in New Hampshire, marveled at the turnaround from the Clinton victory of 1992, "a decade . . . in which my party had gone from getting our asses kicked out of Washington to treating all three branches of the federal government like our own personal amusement parks." He seemed genuinely shocked to be caught, much less prosecuted, in a year in which a triple-amputee war veteran, Max Cleland, was drummed out of the Senate in Georgia with an ad campaign insinuating he was on the side of Osama bin Laden and Saddam. "It seemed preposterous that anything you did to win an election could be considered a crime," Raymond wrote in a distinctly Nixonian vein. "Just about every Republican operative was so dizzy with power that if you could find two of us who could still tell the difference between politics and crime, you could probably have rubbed us together for fire as well."[34]

When Democrats started winning again, Republicans responded by banging once more on the drum of resentment and drawing a distinction between the votes of "real" Americans (meaning white Republican voters) and the rest. "Liberals hate real Americans," Congressman Robin Hayes of North Carolina told a campaign rally in 2008. Sarah Palin, picked as John McCain's presidential running mate that year, talked about the "pro-America areas of this great nation" and implied that Barack Obama and his supporters were somehow "anti-America," a line for which she was later forced to apologize.[35] As a growing number of states started adopting voter ID laws as a way of separating out those "real Americans" and keeping the rest away from the polls, some Republicans even revisited the question of whether voting was a right, as enshrined in the Fourteenth and Fifteenth Amendments and upheld by the Voting Rights Act. Michael Bennett, a state legislator from Florida, described voting in 2011 as "a hard-fought privilege" as opposed to a right, and said he wanted people to have to "fight for it" so they could understand its value.[36]

The push for voter ID has seen the Republican resentment machine go into full throttle. Party loyalists see it as payback for Obama's election or, for those who can remember that far back, the bitterly contested

2004 gubernatorial race in Washington State, which the Republican candidate narrowly lost after multiple recounts overshadowed by bureaucratic incompetence and suspected malfeasance. For a party whose supporters often equate democracy with their own election victories, and a lack of it with their defeats (a blind spot shared by many grassroots Democrats), the voter ID issue has acted like crack cocaine—addictive and highly effective in the short term, because it boosts Republican turnout and suppresses the other side, but disastrous in the long term because it defines the party entirely by its radical Tea Party wing while alienating moderates and pushing away the black- and brown-skinned voters it will need to compete nationally in the future.

Many in the party are already worried that the country's shifting demographics will lock them out of the White House for years to come. Others continue with the "real America" mantra and point to the one institution that could help a Republican candidate squeak into the White House even without a popular mandate: the electoral college.

The peculiar arithmetic of the college is what allowed Bush to become president in 2000 even though he lagged more than half a million votes behind Al Gore, and it's entirely possible something similar could happen again—to either party's advantage. In the new Republican mindset, coming in second need not be an obstacle to legitimacy; it's a matter of how the votes are defined. Back in the early 2000s, Gary Gregg of the University of Louisville characterized Gore's supporters as "a narrow band of the electorate"—an interesting way to describe a 48.4 percent plurality—that was "heavily secular, single, and concentrated in cities." The electoral college, by contrast, stood up, like the Republican Party, for "the values of traditional America."[37]

At the time, Gregg's argument was a stretch even for many Republicans, who recognize that the college is a historical relic. They appreciate, as the Democrats do, that its greatest practical benefit is in allowing presidential candidates to concentrate campaigning in a handful of swing states instead of having to travel the length and breadth of the country for months on end. It's still rare to hear anybody actively *defend* an institution that has been a cause of major crisis four times in American history (in 1800, 1824, 1876, and 2000) and created many other near misses (every other election between 1872 and 1892, 1948, 1960, 1968, and 1976).[38] There are signs, however, that the tide turning.

Gregg professed fondness for the college for many of the same reasons that modern-day Republicans like the architecture of the Senate—because it allows smaller red states to punch above their weight and diminishes the voice of big, populous blue states like California and New York. Before the Civil War, Southern plantation owners effectively voted on behalf of their slaves; now, the sparse populations of the Great Plains and the West effectively cast votes on behalf of elk, buffalo, and longhorn sheep.

Whatever this is, it is not an argument for democracy, which explains why many reformers would prefer to do away with the electoral college altogether. Most of the country has no meaningful say in presidential elections, because the results in all but a dozen of the states are a foregone conclusion. The effect on turnout of this startlingly unrepresentative arrangement is unknown and unknowable, although Gregg has said he thinks the Democratic vote count would be higher if candidates spent real energy campaigning in Chicago, Los Angeles, Philadelphia, or New York.[39] Every presidential season, hundreds of political operatives become tourists in other states, where they can work for a candidate but cannot cast a ballot of their own, much as they might volunteer to work on an election in Haiti, Indonesia, or Angola. Wealthier Californians and New Yorkers can, and do, participate in the money election, contributing and helping to raise funds for candidates they want to push toward their party nomination. But it's questionable, even in an age of boundless cynicism about money in politics, whether that's a democratic sort of election either.

2

SLAVERY AND THE SYSTEM

Democracy as we now understand it has been superimposed on an old governmental structure which was inhospitable to the idea.

—*E.E. Schattschneider*[1]

The foundations of the American political system were not laid, as is often supposed, by semi-mystical sages working harmoniously to extend their wisdom across the ages. The framers of the U.S. Constitution were politicians, and as such they bickered, schemed, clashed, cut side deals, broke promises, and walked out on each other before reaching an ineluctably messy compromise. For three months, from May to September 1787, delegates from twelve of the thirteen independent states sat behind closed doors at the Pennsylvania State House (and occasionally in the shade of Benjamin Franklin's mulberry tree) to sweat out the details of their nascent republic. Only thirty-nine of the original fifty-five delegates endorsed the final result; the rest merely agreed not to oppose it. The "miracle" later hailed by Washington, Madison, and others lay not so much in the system of government they devised, remarkable though it was in many ways, as in the fact that they reached agreement at all.[2]

Many of the document's faults were evident from the start. The big states capitulated to the smaller states, and Northern states to the Southern ones. Key issues, including the manner of choosing a president, were ducked, deferred, or otherwise left in a state of confusion. The Bill of Rights was omitted altogether and reintroduced as a list of ten constitutional amendments, to be ratified at the states' own pace. (Georgia and Connecticut did not give final approval until 1939.) Each concession or accommodation took the young country a step or two further away from the Declaration of Independence, which had proclaimed all men to be created equal and vested legitimate political authority in the "consent of the governed."

Then again, the consent of the governed was never envisioned the way we think of the term now. Democracy did not exist in the late eighteenth century, and the very concept scared most of the framers rigid. Edmund Randolph, future attorney general and secretary of state, saw democracy as the province of "turbulence and follies."[3] Alexander Hamilton was careful to point out that the new country was a republic, not a democracy, and warned that excessive popular participation might precipitate a backslide into monarchy and tyranny. Others fretted about the possible erosion of America's spirit of enterprise, or believed that giving the franchise to the poor would induce them to sell their votes to the rich and so create a new class of aristocrats. Elbridge Gerry of Massachusetts, originator of the ingenious manipulation of popular will still known as "the gerrymander," dismissed democracy as "the worst . . . of all political evils."[4]

When the framers talked about liberty, they generally meant the protection of property rights, not democracy. At its origin, the United States was primarily a country of landowners, farmers, and small businessmen who wanted to tend to their interests without interference or challenge—from above or below. They wanted no new nobility to replace the British ruling classes, and intended no concession to the agrarian classes or to Southern slaves. Voting rights, such as they were, were granted on the basis of property owned by male citizens of European ancestry. Blacks, Native Americans, women, and the non-propertied were almost entirely excluded.

For many political leaders of the time, this arrangement was the key to maintaining social and political order. Universal suffrage, according to Chancellor James Kent of New York, could only give power to "the poor and the profligate" in ways everyone would regret. "Universal suffrage, once granted," he said, in terms that would resonate across the Western world for the next century, "is granted forever, and never can be recalled . . . but by the strength of the bayonet."[5] With Britain still recovering from the Gordon Riots of 1780 and France on the verge of overthrowing its ancien régime, such nervousness was perhaps understandable. But it also blunted the revolutionary spirit that had informed the uprising against the British.

The new country did not reinvent government so much as adapt existing structures from the Old World.[6] The framers cannibalized Sir William Blackstone's six-volume *Commentaries on the Laws of England* (1765–69) wherever they felt it applicable and followed the example of Britain's institutions as much as they departed from it. They shared Blackstone's distaste for universal suffrage and the fear that poor people, given votes, "would be tempted to dispose of them under some undue influence or other." In rejecting a parliamentary system, the framers invested the presidency with many of the powers associated with the monarchy they had rebelled against; Thomas Jefferson called it an "elective monarchy." John Adams suggested the president should be commonly addressed as His Highness, and Washington himself initially fancied being known as His High Mightiness.[7]

Nothing, of course, betrayed the ideals of the Declaration of Independence more than the continuing indulgence of slavery. It was the price the Southern states insisted on for their participation in the Union, and it was absorbed into every aspect of the new governing structure. The decision to give each state two Senate seats regardless of size or population shifted the center of political gravity decisively toward the South and gave slaveholders disproportionate representation at the expense not only of the North but also of blacks, Native Americans, and other minorities. This arrangement alone guaranteed the preservation of slavery, turning the Senate into what one historian has described as "the last bastion of white supremacy." Its raison d'être was not, as generations of schoolchildren have been taught, to act as a democratic check on the rest of the government but rather, as another historian, Robert Dahl of Yale, has observed, to be a bulwark against "too much democracy."[8]

Slaveholders also won outsize influence in the apportionment of congressional seats. One of the biggest sticking points during the Philadelphia negotiations was the possibility that slaves, who were of course barred from voting, might not be included in the calculations to determine the size and number of congressional districts. The deal they obtained allowed them to have it both ways: counting each slave as three-fifths of a person for the purposes of population weighting, but zero-fifths of a person in almost every other respect. Plantation owners, among them Washington, Jefferson, and Madison, were thus permitted to cast ballots on behalf of their human chattel as well as themselves, an arrangement euphemistically known as the "federal ratio." The North might not have liked such blatant political knavery, but the Union's economic fortunes depended on the South's ports and sugar and cotton crops, and it acquiesced.

The design of the presidential electoral college, based on the size of each state's congressional delegation, only compounded the outrage. This was the single stickiest issue at the convention and the lone outstanding question forcing delegates into a fourth month of deliberations. They considered everything from direct election of the president to appointment by Congress, going back and forth so often and taking so many votes it later emerged they had in fact rejected the concept of an electoral college before finally embracing it. Like many dissatisfying compromises, Article II of the Constitution was as notable for what it did *not* achieve as for what it did. It did not establish a constitutional right to vote, an omission that has never been fully corrected. It did not establish a single method for selecting presidential electors, throwing that decision back to the state legislatures. And it did not establish clear rules for handling a tied or disputed election, a miscalculation that would expose the country to serious risk of constitutional crisis four times over the next 213 years.

In many instances the convention suffered from indecisiveness as much as wrongheadedness. Delegates couldn't bring themselves to back popular election of the president—Madison, for example, worried that it would give an unfair advantage to candidates from the larger states—but neither could they entirely let go of the idea. Five times delegates voted in favor of appointment by Congress, but by margins too slim to hold. That indecisiveness arguably opened the door to greater democratic accountability in the future. But, in the moment, the electoral college compromise was one more capitulation to the South, which, not coincidentally, would go on to dominate the presidency, the speakership in the House, and the most influential congressional committees for the next half century. Without the federal ratio, Missouri would have become a non-slave state, Andrew Jackson's Indian removal policy would have been voted down, and slavery would have been outlawed in territories won from Mexico. As designed at Philadelphia, the presidency, House, and Senate were all creatures of slavery, not democracy.[9]

The electoral college was not put to the test during George Washington's two terms as president. But as soon as the general retired to Mount Vernon the trouble began. The 1796 presidential election became so complicated, in fact, it was only a technicality that awarded the job to John Adams instead of his rival Thomas Jefferson. Each state had one of three methods of selecting its electoral college members (popular election statewide, popular election by congressional district, and appointment by the state legislature). The candidates for president and vice president ran separately, not in teams. And each elector had two votes instead of one, a wrinkle devised by Alexander Hamilton in a failed attempt to promote his Federalist ally Thomas Pinckney of South Carolina over Adams. The confusion was so great, and the vote so close, that the outcome rested on two electors from Virginia and North Carolina who, with just a slight variation in the rules, would have been obliged to switch their affiliation to another candidate.[10]

The presidential election of 1796 was just a warm-up for the Adams-Jefferson rematch of 1800, at which point the system melted down altogether. Jefferson and the man he intended as his running mate, Aaron Burr of New York, ended up with the same number of electoral votes, a scenario the framers had not properly considered. The election was thrown to the House of Representatives, as the rules dictated, and Jefferson prevailed—in part because of the distorting effect of the federal ratio, which accounted for twelve of his seventy-three electoral votes. Without those extra votes, he would have fallen not only behind Burr, but also behind Adams, who trailed the front-runners by eight. The race came down to furious haggling with individual House members, the last of whom, Representative James Bayard of Delaware, went with Jefferson after six days and thirty-six ballots.

The 1800 election was the undoing of the Federalists and the beginning of a more representative phase in the life of the republic—a new revolution, as Jefferson called it. But the awkward truth was that he didn't really win, not in a meaningful, democratic sense. "The election of Mr. Jefferson to the presidency," John Quincy Adams later commented, "was, upon sectional feelings, the triumph of the South over the North—of the slave representation over the purely free." Timothy Pickering, who had served as secretary of state under Washington and Adams, took to calling him "Negro president" and did not mean it as a compliment.[11]

The structural problem of electing the vice president was fixed easily enough by the Twelfth Amendment, which was passed in time for the 1804 election and formalized the idea of a single presidential ticket. Not everyone was thrilled with the change, though, because it accorded more power to the top of the ticket, and thus tilted the balance even further to the South. Pickering never stopped campaigning to repeal the Twelfth Amendment, arguing that it served only to elevate fools to the second most powerful office in the land, a position historians have generally agreed with. "That office had some stature before 1800," Leonard Richards has written, "but after 1800 the Virginians turned it into a dead-end job, and made sure that it always went to a political has-been."[12]

Outside the confines of university political science departments, it is not usually considered polite to point out the shortcomings of the Constitution, or indeed to engage critically with it at all. In the popular imagination, it has come to be seen as almost divine in inspiration, a document so pure that to question it is to attack the very marrow of the country's being. This mythology is, in some respects, as old as the Constitution itself. In a letter to John Adams, Jefferson described the Philadelphia delegates as "an assembly of demi-gods."[13] What impressed Jefferson, though, was the process more than the result—the fact that states disinclined to find common ground had put in the exhausting work of founding a country. Talking up the framers' achievements had clear political benefits at the time; *The Federalist Papers* were nothing if not an exercise in propaganda to secure ratification of the Constitution by the individual states.

Constitution worship for its own sake did not take full flight until after the Civil War, when the manifest fragility of the Union thrust new significance on its founding document. George Bancroft's six-volume *History of the United States*, published in the mid-1880s, described the wording of the document as "sublime" and "faultless" and the founders themselves as "awestruck" by the nobility of their achievement.[14] Over the next century, as the United States took an ever more commanding role on the world stage, the Constitution acquired what the historian Michael Schudson has described as the "trappings of a religious cult"[15]—no longer just a foundational law but rather a timeless national creed. We hear plenty today about originalism and "strict constructionism," the conservative notion that if we can just divine the intent of the founders we will have all the guideposts we need to sort out telecommunications law, gay marriage, and modern-day health care management. Gore Vidal memorably derided this approach as "deliberation by Ouija board."[16]

Today, few doubt it was the Constitution that raised the United States above the ranks of ordinary nations. But that presents an incomplete picture, at best. After all, if the U.S. system of government was so great from the beginning, how come so few countries have chosen to copy it?

In a fascinating analysis published in his 1968 book *Political Order in Changing Societies*, the conservative historian Samuel P. Huntington argued that the Constitution was in fact a strikingly reactionary document that had more in common with England under the Tudors than the cutting edge of contemporary political thinking. England and France had spent a century and a half centralizing their power structures through parliament and the development of a technocratic civil service, but America refused to believe that robust government intervention was necessary to manage public affairs. "Political modernization in America has thus been strangely attenuated and incomplete," Huntington wrote. "In today's world, America's political institutions are unique, if only because they are so antique."[17]

The constitutional separation of powers, often cited as the cornerstone of the American democratic system, was really an adaptation of a Tudor model establishing some distance between the Crown, the Church, and the aristocracy. It wasn't the power that was separated in the American system so much as the institutions of government, which were made to overlap and compete in ways that have created enduring inefficiencies—one reason why Americans tend to be so suspicious of governmental authority. When in doubt, Americans like to invoke "the people" as the ultimate arbiters of power. But Huntington argued this was wishful thinking, not a true characterization of the institutions the framers created. "The voice of the people," he wrote, "can be about as readily identified as the voice of God."[18]

That nebulousness has certainly had its political uses. Under Andrew Jackson, America's first true politician of the masses, the idea of popular sovereignty became a rallying cry and catchall for every government initiative, and also a cover behind which every abomination could conveniently lurk. Naturally, it came to fruition through another botched election.

By 1824, America had no parties to speak of—everyone was now a Jeffersonian Republican—so the competition for the White House was highly personalized, ruthless, and vicious. John Quincy Adams was the best-qualified contender, having served as minister to the Russian Court and as secretary of state. Henry Clay, the Speaker of the House, was the most ambitious. Jackson, the storied general who had beaten back the British at New Orleans and conquered the Florida swamps, cut the most flamboyant figure. But Jackson was also regarded with alarm in elite circles—brutish, unlearned, singularly unqualified, and barely literate. The elite did not hold quite as much sway as it had before the War of 1812, because the government had extended the franchise to almost all white men in exchange for their military service. Thus the election became, in many ways, a furious struggle between the old notion of patrician stewardship and the untested, emerging power of popular democracy. And democracy lost the first round.

With the military vote largely on his side, Jackson won ninety-nine electoral votes to Adams's eighty-four. This was only a plurality, however, not a majority. William H. Crawford, the secretary of the treasury recently paralyzed by a stroke, gathered forty-one votes, and Clay had thirty-seven. The race was thrown to the House of Representatives, as it had been in 1800, and Clay, acting as kingmaker, decided there and then that Jackson could not be allowed to prevail. After several furious rounds of horse trading and outright bribery, Adams was declared the winner with the support of thirteen state delegations to Jackson's seven.[19]

That, however, was not the end of the story. The country had evolved rapidly since 1800, and public tolerance for such backroom haggling had eroded. Democracy was not only Jackson's rallying cry; it was now part of the air Americans breathed. Only six of the twenty-four states still appointed electoral college members, and that number would soon dwindle to just two. A furious Jackson took swift advantage of the public mood, making one strident speech after another on his way home from Capitol Hill to Tennessee. "The people have been cheated," he thundered in Frankfort, Kentucky. "Corruption and intrigues . . . defeated the will of the people." When Adams appointed Clay his secretary of state, Jackson and his followers cried foul over what was famously called their "corrupt bargain." The line was so powerful that even Adams's vice president, John Calhoun, declared himself incensed. He said the deal with Clay was the most dangerous blow the liberty of the country had yet sustained.

Jackson's anger propelled him to do something entirely new in the annals of politics: he hit the campaign trail for the next election. Until then, presidential aspirants had always remained silent on their own behalf, but Jackson broke that rule with glee, making up his populist campaign more or less as he went along. He didn't like formal debates, but he organized countless barbecues, tree plantings, parades, public rallies, and dinners. He and his supporters encouraged the expansion of the burgeoning newspaper trade, and courted many titles for their endorsement. He lavished funds on flyers and printed advertisements— the 1828 campaign was the first to hit the $1 million spending mark— and put his personality front and center, complete with his own symbol, a sprig of hickory. The Jacksonians founded a new party, the Democrats, and formed an alliance with the Albany Regency, the powerful political machine in New York State, to add to their base in the South and West.

The establishment responded with a vituperative ad hominem campaign, much of it coordinated by Jackson's nemesis Henry Clay. Jackson was denounced in popular pamphlets and newspapers as an adulterer and the offspring of a "common prostitute" and a mulatto—none of it remotely true. His wife, Rachel, was accused of bigamy—also untrue— and went to her grave shortly thereafter. Jackson gave as good as he got, helping to inaugurate the era of negative campaigning by portraying Adams as an oligarch and a snob, full of "kingly pomp and splendor," who had betrayed the popular will and, as minister to Russia, had acted as a pimp for Tsar Alexander I.

The 1828 presidential election didn't just reach a high-water mark of popular participation; it was also the first with known instances of ballot fraud. Wagonloads of Jackson supporters spilled over from Tennessee into Kentucky and Ohio to cast votes in the names of citizens who had died, a technique that would become all too familiar in the decades to come. When the ballots were counted, Jackson had a crushing majority in the electoral college, 178 to Adams's 83. His 56 percent score in the popular vote would remain unbeaten throughout the nineteenth century.

Jackson never veered from the conviction that he was the people's champion, placed in the White House to root out corruption and privilege. Once in office, he continued to encourage political participation at levels that made the United States truly exceptional among nations. Turnout more than doubled, from 27 percent to 56 percent of eligible voters, between his defeat in 1824 and his victory four years later. It continued to climb steeply throughout the 1830s, putting America far ahead of any European country in its embrace of popular democracy—even if the franchise was still limited to white males. Mass political movements in the nineteenth century emerged largely in reaction to industrialization; only in the United States did mass participation largely *precede* it.

Whether Jackson always governed with the popular interest in mind is another matter. Unpropertied voters certainly enjoyed his demonization of Adams as an aristocratic fop, and they responded, too, to his anti-intellectualism and his appeal to Protestant fundamentalism, then gaining its first significant foothold.[20] But he was never much of a champion of the working man, either in rhetoric or in practice. Time and again he defended the rights of property owners against the emerging industrial working class, notably when he sent federal troops to break up a strike on the Chesapeake & Ohio Canal at Williamsport, Maryland, in 1834. His battle to destroy the Second Bank of the United States, which he sold as a grand populist showdown, probably did more harm than good to the average American, since the bank was a guarantor of middle-class economic stability, and its collapse precipitated a sharp recession.

The ideology of Jacksonian democracy was also blatantly racist, exclusionary, and expansionist. It led directly to the Cherokee "Trail of Tears" and other bouts of Native American ethnic cleansing; later, under presidents cast from the Jacksonian mold, the same ideology inspired

Manifest Destiny and war with Mexico. Jackson was both a slaveholder and a supporter of slavery; it was his appointee as chief justice, Roger Taney, who in 1857 would write the notorious *Dred Scott* decision upholding the legality of slavery and denying citizenship rights to African Americans. Jackson's was an ideology that celebrated "toughness, maleness, and whiteness,"[21] as Michael Kazin has written, and did so largely by scapegoating blacks and Indians.

The disconnect between Jackson's campaigning rhetoric and the results he produced in office remains a subject of furious debate among historians. By any measure he was a "strange democrat," as his recent biographer Sean Wilentz termed it, a champion of the common man who nevertheless ushered in an industrial era of mills and factories and railroad companies offering a pittance for wages and few protections. James Parton, Jackson's first biographer, deplored "this most lamentable divorce between the people and those who ought to have been worthy to lead them." Thomas P. Abernethy, in his 1955 biography, dismissed Jackson's democratic rhetoric and appeal to nationalist expansionism as little more than a convenience "to win the favor of the people and thereby accomplish ulterior objectives." Jackson, he wrote, "never really championed the cause of the people; he only invited them to champion his."[22]

In terms of absolute numbers, the Jacksonian era was a high point of participatory democracy in the United States, an outpouring of energy and enthusiasm later emulated but never entirely recaptured. Voters gladly traveled for hours to reach their polling places, glowing with a "feverish excitement," as Alexis de Tocqueville noted.[23] Turnout climbed to a high point of 80 percent of eligible voters in the 1840 presidential election and stayed at much the same level for the next fifty years.[24]

None of that, however, translated into meaningful popular representation in Washington. Jackson and his followers only cheered on the industrial revolution that, in European countries, provoked popular uprisings and calls for radical political reform. The blame for that failure rests largely with the framers and the distortions they foisted onto a young country, even as its idealistic citizens dreamed of leading the world into a new democratic future.

3

PATRONAGE, LIQUOR, AND GRAFT: THE ASCENT OF MACHINE POLITICS

A big city like New York or Philadelphia or Chicago might be compared to a sort of Garden of Eden, from a political point of view. It's an orchard full of beautiful apple trees. One of them has got a big sign on it, marked: "Penal Code Tree—Poison." . . . I never had any temptation to touch the Penal Code Tree. The other apples are good enough for me, and O Lord! How many of them there are in a big city!

—*George Washington Plunkitt,* Plunkitt of Tammany Hall[1]

I don't think there was ever a fair or honest election in the City of New York.

—*William Marcy "Boss" Tweed*[2]

In the early morning of the November 1868 election in New York City, gangs of young men poured out of saloons, flophouses, and gambling dens to do their worst on behalf of the Tammany Hall political machine. Armed with brass knuckles, slingshots, clubs, and the occasional firearm, they chanted war whoops and paraded exuberantly through the streets. Some were under instruction to stuff ballot boxes or falsify the count to conform to a predetermined outcome. Others wanted only to vandalize polling places favored by the Republican opposition and beat up their election officials. Others still were "repeaters" who had each been given five dollars, a list of the recently deceased to impersonate, several changes of clothing, and as much liquor as they could hold. "Vote early and often" was Tammany's much vaunted maxim, and that's what these men did.[3]

Many repeaters were known criminals—"thieves who had several aliases," according to a police patrolman in the Seventh Precinct who knew better than to go up against the power of Tammany and its figurehead, William Marcy Tweed. Their ringleader, an Englishman who went by the street name Nibbs or Nibbsey, was a celebrated pickpocket who "has stolen fortunes, but somehow or other always slips through and is never prosecuted."[4] Often, the repeat voters would start the day with a full beard, cut it down to "side lilacs" and a mustache, and end up clean shaven. As they switched from one precinct to the next, they presented themselves as young men and grandfathers, new immigrants and third-generation New Yorkers, working men and affluent merchants. When one scruffy repeater tried to pass himself off as a well-known Episcopalian clergyman, a poll worker told him, "You ain't Bishop Doane." To which he responded, "The hell I ain't," and threatened to punch his lights out.

This was a crucial election for Boss Tweed and the Tammany machine, then at the apogee of their power. Tweed already had a stranglehold on the Tammany machine itself, with the figurehead title of Grand Sachem. He also had the run of several state committees, including the all-important Finance Committee (of which he was chair), sway over many state and municipal courts, and control of both the New York public schools and the city's Public Works Commission. On this occasion, Tweed's handpicked New York mayor, John Hoffman, was running for governor, and Hoffman's ally "Elegant" Oakey Hall was running to replace him as mayor. The Tweed Ring stood to exert total control at both city and state levels.

The groundwork was laid several months in advance through the fraudulent naturalization of tens of thousands of Irish immigrants who could be counted on to vote for the Democratic Party ticket. New York had been acquiring new citizens at a rate of about nine thousand per year, but in the run-up to the 1868 election Tammany opened a dedicated naturalization office in a saloon bar and sent close to sixty thousand names to the New York Superior Court. In the words of the *New York Tribune*, they were approved "with no more solemnity than the converting of swine into pork in a Cincinnati packing house." One witness supplied by the Tammany machine to attest to the good character of many hundreds of new citizens was caught stealing a gold watch and two diamond rings less than forty-eight hours later.

Boss Tweed won his election, but the triumph soon turned unexpectedly sour. The excess of his henchmen and the greed of the cronies he had catapulted into power became liabilities that led to his betrayal, a vast official investigation, and, ultimately, imprisonment and disgrace. Within three years, Tammany had become a nationally reviled byword for election fraud and strong-arm tactics of all stripes.

It was, in many ways, a richly deserved reputation. Tweed had been stealing votes since the start of his career, on a scale that a State Assembly report issued ten years before the 1868 election described as "extensive and enormous." But his demonization also had a political dimension, propagated and encouraged by Tammany's enemies—Republicans, Protestant nativists, upstate "hayseeds" who resented the power of the city, and antidemocratic reactionaries who trembled at the thought of immigrants and the working class having any say in the electoral process.

Tweed's boys were hardly the only ones who played dirty; they were just better at it than anyone else. New York in the 1850s and 1860s was a furious battleground pitting Tammany politicians against all comers: each other, the state Democratic Party, Whigs, Know-Nothings, and the City Reform movement. All employed street gangs; all resorted to intimidation and violence. The mentality was to steal the other guys' votes before they stole yours. Some repeat voters were not volunteers but kidnap victims, grabbed on Election Day and forced, under the influence of large quantities of alcohol, to keep casting ballots—a practice known as "cooping."[5] Voters coming into New York illegally from other states were nicknamed "pipe-layers," because they were instructed to say they were recently arrived contract workers in town to lay some pipes.[6] Elections were elemental struggles in which the most effective campaigning tool was often a lively criminal imagination.

What set the Tammany machine apart was organization and, strange to say, a genuine commitment to mass political participation. To the extent that Tweed and his boys sought to represent the working class of the city and expand suffrage rights, they were in fact a positive influence on the country's democratic well-being. The deeper problem, one kept well hidden by Tweed's enemies, was that the system as a whole was rotten to the core, and had been for some time.

The voting practices established in colonial America were never designed for a democracy of the masses. Instead of adapting as the requirements evolved, however, election administrators set a pattern that has continued to this day: changing too little too late, and often for the wrong reasons. The gentleman voters of seventeenth-century New England foresaw no need for ballot security and conducted most ballots by an open show of hands, a tradition that persisted in some parts of the South into the 1880s. Massachusetts was the first territory to introduce a rudimentary ballot box—a hat into which voters dropped strips of paper or colored beans—but there was no attempt at secrecy. Indeed, one rule from 1647 insisted on the ballot papers being "not twisted nor rouled up, that they may be the sooner perused." When the United States was founded, most ballots were still being written out by hand; printed ballots did not become common until the Supreme Court authorized them in 1829, the year Andrew Jackson became president. By then, ballot production had fallen into the hands of political parties, which used different paper sizes and colors to distinguish themselves. Secrecy was not only impossible, it was deemed undesirable by party operatives. Even in states with laws insisting on plain paper ballots, parties adopted different shades of white and different paper weights. Theoretically, this was meant to help illiterate voters, but in practice it also allowed party poll watchers to exercise near-total control.[7]

The first formal complaint of vote fraud came in 1789, in a congressional race in Georgia between two Revolutionary War generals. The ostensible loser, James Jackson, discovered that in one county there were more votes than voters, and that in another a crooked judge had suppressed votes. Other "undue and corrupt practices" included recording voters who had not shown up. Congress threw the ostensible winner, Anthony Wayne, out of the House and left the seat vacant until the next election.[8]

After the political parties took over the electoral process, such corruption became rampant. The best that could be hoped for, in the absence of a professional class of public administrators, was that competing parties would police each other, on the principle that it takes a thief to watch a thief. But, as the elections administrator Joseph P. Harris noted a century later, thieves are apt to make bargains. Rival parties quickly staked out swaths of territory in city wards and county precincts, and their operatives came to view vote rigging not as an abomination but as a solemn duty. In certain parts of Philadelphia in the 1830s, election officers were sworn in on a city directory instead of a Bible and vowed to "do justice by their party."[9] In the 1844 presidential election, New York City had a turnout of 55,000, with only 41,000 eligible voters.

The problems were most visible in the cities, especially as industrialization took hold and urban populations began to mushroom.[10] In New York, the opening of the Erie Canal in 1825 transformed what had been a sleepy Dutch village into a hard-living, hard-drinking, faction-ridden metropolis in which slums rubbed up against fine rows of brownstones and rowdy Irish Catholic immigrants overturned the orderly existence of the original Protestant settlers. By the 1840s the city population had quintupled, and both the Whigs and the Democrats were hiring street toughs to press for partisan advantage on Election Day. Convicts who promised loyalty to one party or the other were routinely let out of prison to cast a ballot. Historians puzzling over the mystery of Edgar Allan Poe's death in Baltimore in 1849 have often wondered why the poet was found on the day of a sheriff's election, in a tavern doubling as a polling station, wearing uncharacteristically shabby clothes not his own, and struggling with what his friend Joseph Snodgrass described as "a state of beastly intoxication." Could he have been voted to death, in a cooping scheme pulled off by the toughs of Baltimore's Fourth Ward? His contemporaries certainly thought so. "The general belief here," a Johns Hopkins professor named William Hand Browne wrote to a Poe biographer, "is that Poe was seized . . . stupefied with liquor, dragged out and voted, and then turned adrift to die."[11]

No longer could America live the Jeffersonian dream of a peaceful nation of small freeholders; Jefferson himself had warned, in fact, that "when we get piled upon one another in large cities, as in Europe, we shall become corrupt as in Europe, and go to eating one another as they do there."[12] The challenge was to manage the chaos and maintain the country's economic dynamism, despite the proliferation of poverty, disease, drunkenness, and violence.

That was the problem to which political machines offered an answer: a system for providing jobs, building infrastructure, and offering patronage to the downtrodden. In exchange for the help they offered in cutting through municipal red tape and negotiating the criminal justice system, the machines expected loyalty and votes. And that's what they got. In many ways, the system resembled eighteenth-century Britain with its gin, corruption, and rotten elections. But there was no other way. America in this period did not possess a civil service to take on the cities' social and political problems. It did not have an established social safety net outside the volunteer efforts of private religious charities. The cities operated instead on the spoils system, which had the undeniable virtue of creating political structures capable of perpetuating themselves without recourse to the public purse or the sponsorship of rich men with an agenda. Politics was conducted on an intensely local, personalized level. Yes, public morality and the law were treated with a fluidity we might find shocking today. But the city machines were more efficient and more attentive to personal needs than any bureaucratic system, and participants frequently expressed pride in their ability to get things done—for their constituents as well as for their party.[13]

Nobody has ever explained this more memorably than George Washington Plunkitt, a Tammany Hall stalwart who sketched out his "regular system" in a famous oral history:

> If there's a fire on Ninth, Tenth or Eleventh Avenue, for example, any hour of the day or night, I'm usually there with some of my election district captains as soon as the fire-engines. If a family is burned out I don't ask whether they are Republicans or Democrats, and I don't refer them to the Charity Organization Society, which would investigate their case in a month or two and decide they were worthy of help about the time they are dead from starvation. I just get quarters for them, buy clothes for them if their clothes were burned up, and fix them up till they get things runnin' again. It's philanthropy, but it's politics, too—mighty good politics. Who can tell how many votes one of these fires brings me? The poor are the most grateful people in the world, and, let me tell you, they have more friends in their neighborhoods than the rich have in theirs.[14]

Reformers later expressed shock at the influence peddling, fraud, and embezzlement such a system inevitably spawned. But people were engaged in a daily struggle for survival, and politics was an inescapably vicious business. The rich, who had the most to fear from outright insurrection, understood better than anyone the price to be paid for a modicum of political and social peace. Plunder was something one could accept or deplore, but it was a fact of life, the venal juice that kept the whole system circulating. "A politician in coming forward takes things as they are," Boss Tweed said with characteristic bluntness after his fall from grace. "This population is too hopelessly split up into races and factions to govern it under universal suffrage, except by the bribery of patronage, or corruption."[15]

Historians have not entirely disagreed. D.W. Brogan wrote in 1954 that political machines like Tammany Hall "gave some kind of coherence to a society in perpetual flux."[16] To the poor they gave bread, in the form of favors, and circuses, in the form of parades and stirring rhetoric about the people versus the powerful. Some of this was a sham, but some of it was entirely genuine. The whole delicate art of big-city politics was about finding a balance between demagoguery and delivery, between ripping people off and giving them what they wanted.

It was not venality that put the young Bill Tweed on the map when he first entered New York politics in the early 1850s. It was his organizational skills as a bookkeeper, a skill that would never cease to pay dividends. He was in many ways an outsider, a Scottish Protestant in a city dominated by Irish Catholics. But he also had an instinct for street-level politics. He began his career as a firefighter in the Seventh Ward, leading a company of seventy-five men who became his loyal troupe. Their emblem, a snarling red tiger, was later appropriated by the cartoonist Thomas Nast as an enduring symbol of big-city graft, but the company's principal concern at the outset was to get their chief elected alderman. Tweed stumbled on his first attempt at the alderman's office, in 1850, but learned from the experience and put up a straw-man candidate the following year to split the Whig vote. It worked. Once elected, Tweed joined the Common Council of New York, a group of political opportunists known as the Forty Thieves. They earned thousands in kickbacks from the sale of franchises for the Third Avenue Railroad, the Gansevoort Market, and the Broadway streetcar line. They even made money from Fourth of July fireworks and the flags and bunting ordered for Henry Clay's funeral in 1852.

Legend has it that Boss Tweed took shameless advantage of Democratic Party dominance in New York City to line his pockets and trample on the rights of his adversaries, but it was never as simple as that. Tammany Hall and the Democrats did not assert full control over the city until the Civil War. They faced stiff competition from the Whigs and, after the first big wave of Irish immigration, from the nativist Know-Nothings. The working-class vote was never a foregone conclusion, and splinter groups were forever accusing Tammany of "aristocratic" aloofness and support for the national party's position on slavery. Elections were an orgy of cheating and intimidation, not because Tammany Hall ran a tyrannical one-party system, but because the competition for power was so ferocious. The Tweed Ring's greed was, ultimately, an expression of its insecurity—it didn't know how long the beanfeast could last.

Tweed himself was out of the picture for two years after he was elected to Congress in 1852 and engineered his comeback only by exploiting the many cracks in the city's political factions. He took control of an ostensibly bipartisan Board of Supervisors through the key spending and planning committees, and by bribing members who might otherwise have stood in his way. In 1859, he paid Peter Voorhis, a Republican member, to stay away from a meeting set to appoint the city's six hundred election inspectors. Democrats—including a generous smattering of barkeepers, gamblers, and street thugs—ended up with five hundred and fifty of the open positions.

Next, Tweed outmaneuvered his archrival and fellow Tammany man, Fernando Wood, who served several terms as mayor but could not hold on to power after the draft riots during the Civil War. Tweed didn't just have him thrown out of office. Wood was expelled from Tammany Hall, exposed for fleecing a quarter of a million dollars from city coffers, and kicked upstairs to a congressional seat, effectively exiling him from New York forever.

Tweed was now in full control, but he preferred to pull the strings from behind the scenes. He was not much of a public speaker; his strength was the committee room, where his bulk and outsize personality were suitably intimidating. One contemporary, Francis Fairfield, said he "looked like something that God hacked out with a dull axe" with his large head, scraggly strands of reddish-brown hair, vast nose, broad shoulders, and bony fists. When anyone accused him of dishonesty, he insisted that he was a man of his word. His secretary commented that he was "not an honest politician, but a level one."[17]

While a diamond reliably shone from his lapel pin, it was never primarily about wealth for him. Power was the thing that truly mattered. The bedrock of his organization were the twelve thousand Tammany men appointed to public jobs throughout the city, known as the Shiny Hat Brigade. He sank much of his graft money into the New York Printing Company so he could take over yet another piece of city business and keep the newspapers in his thrall. In so doing, he provided more jobs for his organization and generated fresh opportunities for profit. After 1868, he moved to amend the New York City charter so that department heads could be appointed for fixed terms of four years or longer, a move designed to make it harder for a rival organization to challenge the Tammany machine.

Over the eight years that the Tweed Ring was in charge, from 1863 to 1871, New York developed Central Park, incorporated the Metropolitan Museum of Art, and turned Broadway into a boulevard. The city was asserting itself as a major urban center, and the efficiency of the machine had much to do with it. The weak link, in the end, was Tweed's inability to know when to stop. Before he took over, the standard kickback on city contracts was 10 percent. Once he asserted control, it shot up to 35 percent, with Tweed taking 25 percent for himself. The system simply could not sustain itself when the public purse was being depleted of anywhere from $20 million to $200 million. (Estimates vary because ledger manipulation was one of the Tweed Ring's hallmarks.) Nothing symbolized the greed more than construction of the New York County Courthouse, which had been budgeted at $250,000 but ended up costing more than $6 million, not least because the stone came from a Massachusetts quarry belonging to Tweed himself. The city was gouged all over again with the interior decoration—$2.5 million for plastering, $4.8 million for carpets, and so on. It cost more to furnish the courthouse, the Republican congressman Roscoe Conkling complained, than it did for the Grant administration to run the U.S. mail.

It couldn't last. When the New York County sheriff asked Tweed for a large payoff and was turned down, he took revenge by leaking the city's bookkeeping records to the *New York Times*. The *Times* editor, George Jones, was offered a fabulous $5 million bribe himself to keep the story out of the paper, but he demurred. The state Democratic Party launched an official investigation, and Tweed was indicted on one hundred and twenty counts of forgery, grand larceny, false pretenses, and conspiracy to defraud. He ran away to California, only to be brought back for two separate trials that ended in convictions and long sentences. In 1875, the master of graft paid $60,000 to engineer an escape, but he was tracked down in Spain, rearrested, and sent back home. He died behind bars three years later.

The downfall of the Tweed Ring was not just a scandal; it was a public spectacle from which many individuals and interest groups sought profit. The popular press then coming into its own used it as a launchpad. Indeed, Thomas Nast's satirical anti-Tammany cartoons in *Harper's Weekly* became almost as celebrated as the scandal itself. Samuel Tilden, who spearheaded the investigations, rose swiftly to the New York governor's office and, from there, made an ill-fated run for the presidency in 1876.

Tweed also became a rallying cry for politicians of all stripes who found it expedient to view the organizational power of the urban machines with alarm. They initiated a full-blown campaign to suppress the urban vote under the banner of electoral reform, and did so with gusto, as we shall see in the following chapters. They didn't have to make much of a case, because Boss Tweed all but made the case for them when he appeared before the Board of Aldermen in 1875.

> *Q. Now, Mr. Tweed, with regard to elections—to the management of the elections for the city and county officers—and generally, the elections for the city and county: When you were in office, did the Ring control the elections in this city at that time?*
>
> A. They did, sir; absolutely.
>
> (. . .)
>
> *Q. What were they to do, in case you wanted a particular man elected over another?*

A. Count the ballots in bulk, or without counting them announce the result in bulk, or change from one to the other, as the case may have been.

Q. *Then these elections really were no elections at all? The ballots were made to bring about any result that you determined upon beforehand?*

A. The ballots made no result; the counters made the result . . .

Q. *Mr. Tweed, did you ever give any directions to any persons to falsify or change the result of the actual bona fide ballots cast in any election?*

A. More in the nature of a request than a direction.[18]

Tweed didn't think he was giving away any great secret, because this was how the electoral system worked across the board, in rural areas as well as big cities. The Republicans, much as they might have pretended otherwise, had their own machines, whose wheels were largely greased by the distribution of pensions to Civil War veterans. "From New England to Minnesota," the historian Lawrence Goodwyn wrote, "hundreds of small towns, as well as broad swaths of rural America, became virtual rotten boroughs of Republicanism."[19] Vote buying was rampant everywhere, and the going rate was, if anything, higher in rural areas because it was more difficult for political operatives to make block purchases there. In upcountry Tennessee, it might take no more than a glass of whiskey or a plug of tobacco to win over a voter. But elsewhere the price was steeper. "Men of standing in the community have openly sold their votes at prices ranging from fifteen to thirty dollars," one contemporary, J.L. Gordon, wrote. "For securing the more disreputable elements—the 'floaters', as they are termed—new two-dollar bills have been scattered abroad with a prodigality that would seem incredible but for the magnitude of the object to be obtained."[20]

Vote stuffing, especially the use of tissue-paper ballots that could be folded into each other, would soon become another epidemic. A number of states passed laws stipulating that when the number of votes exceeded the number of eligible voters the excess should be discarded—a process that was prone to manipulation of its own.

Still, the talk in the press and in public debate was all about corruption in the cities—government "of the people, by the rascals, for the rich," as the muckraking journalist Lincoln Steffens would later describe it.[21] There's no doubting that the stories were most colorful there, featuring a rich tapestry of politicians, policemen, whores, gamblers, saloon keepers, and backstreet abortionists. Every city seemingly had its own larger-than-life machine boss, or was poised to acquire one: Blind Boss Buckley in San Francisco, Doc Ames in Minneapolis, Chris Magee in Pittsburgh, and James McManes and the Gas Ring in Philadelphia.

Philly, with its City Hall tower that rose higher than the Great Pyramid of Egypt, was a worthy rival in venality to New York. Even the inimitable Plunkitt of Tammany Hall reeled in horror. "The Philadelphians ain't satisfied with robbin' the bank of all its gold and paper money," he said. "They stay to pick up the nickels and pennies."[22] Everyone in Philadelphia was registered to vote—dead dogs, children, fictional characters, even Founding Fathers. As a Gas Ring notable once said, "These men, these fathers of American liberty, voted down here once. And they vote here yet."[23] Elections were run by division assessors, who were in turn political appointees of the city machine. In one notorious case, it was shown that an assessor was running elections out of his house, which happened to be a brothel and also the address at which two of his election officers were registered. "The major part of more than 200 names on the assessor's list," the complaint filed with the court said, "were registered from brothels, badger houses, gaming houses and other places of revolting wickedness."[24]

It's easy to forget, with so many irresistible stories in circulation, that the urban machines of the nineteenth century produced the highest voter turnout rates in American history. Nothing before or since has touched their efficiency in bringing people, especially the working classes, to the polls. One can, of course, be cynical about numbers when the voter rolls were padded, the ballots were routinely miscounted, and the official tally bore only an incidental relationship to the actual vote totals. But something about this deeply flawed system worked. The impatience of the age—the refusal to distinguish the good from the bad—played directly into the hands of would-be reformers whose true target was not corruption but rather the very notion of popular participation in politics. Thus it was that when reaction against the city machines began in earnest, the effect was precisely the opposite of what many liberals, Mugwumps, and assorted civic-minded reformers had been lobbying for. The corruption, graft, and fraud remained largely intact, while voter participation—the one indicator of democratic robustness worth preserving—plummeted dramatically, never to recover.

4

THE THEFT OF THE CENTURY

No amendment or statute has yet solved the central problems that bedeviled the election of 1876. Irregularities in the selection of electors can still occur in the states. The Negro voter can still be intimidated and defrauded of his right to vote. A "minority President" like Hayes, who receives a majority of the electoral vote but not of the popular vote, can still be elected. These disquieting possibilities, which were at the bottom of the trouble in 1876, could arise to haunt us again.

—*Louis W. Koenig,* The Election That Got Away *(1960)*[1]

On November 7, 1876, Samuel Tilden went to bed convinced he was the first Democrat in twenty years to be elected president. Nationally, he had chalked up a quarter of a million votes more than his Republican challenger, Rutherford B. Hayes. He was leading handily in his home state of New York, had a lock on most of the South, and appeared to be leading even in the three states—Florida, Louisiana, and South Carolina—still controlled by Republican "carpetbag" governments with the support of federal troops. By late evening, Tilden was assured of 184 electoral college votes, just one shy of the magic number needed for victory, with every prospect of pushing the total over 200 by the time the count was complete.[2]

He was not the only one to think the race was in the bag. Almost every major newspaper called it for Tilden in their morning headlines. Zachariah Chandler, the chair of the Republican National Committee, drowned his sorrows in whiskey, and the mood at party offices across the land was glum. Hayes himself spent the evening consoling his wife at their home in Columbus, Ohio. According to his journal, he "soon fell into a refreshing sleep and the affair seemed over."[3]

Not everyone was ready to give up, however. In New York, a one-legged Civil War general and disreputable former diplomat, "Devil Dan" Sickles, stopped by Republican Party headquarters on his way home from the theater and realized, as he checked through the returns, that Hayes could still squeak by in the electoral college if the vote in the three closely contested Southern states went his way. It's not that the Republican numbers looked good in Florida, Louisiana, and South Carolina—they did not—but all three were under Republican control, leaving open the possibility of delaying, massaging, or otherwise manipulating the figures to the party's advantage. After trying in vain to rouse Zachariah Chandler, General Sickles fired off telegrams in the chairman's name telling party operatives in the key Southern constituencies to "hold your state." South Carolina's Republican governor, Daniel Chamberlain, replied, "All right. South Carolina is for Hayes. Need more troops."[4]

The ardently pro-Republican editor of the *New York Times*, John C. Reid, was having similar thoughts. He'd received repeated inquiries from the Democratic Party on election night asking him for the *Times'* latest vote estimates, which made him suspect the party was not as confident about Tilden as it seemed in its public statements. For his first edition, he ordered the headline "Results Still Uncertain," and he sent his own volley of telegrams to Republican friends in the South: "Can you hold your state? Answer immediately." By the time the *Times'* second edition went out, Reid had put Louisiana and South Carolina in the Hayes column, leaving only Florida's four electoral votes in doubt. The provisional tally, according to the *Times*: 184 for Tilden, 181 for Hayes.

At 6 a.m., Reid and Senator William Chandler of New Hampshire hastened to Republican Party headquarters, where they shook Zachariah Chandler awake and agreed that, from now on, the party would base its estimates not on field reports but on the figures put out by the *New York Times*. "Hayes has 185 votes and is elected," they proclaimed in a public statement. The plot to steal the presidency was in full swing.

This was an election destined to stir unusually strong passions. A de-

cade of postwar reconstruction in the South was on the verge of collapse. As federal garrisons withdrew from one state after another, black
emancipation ran into a wall of white supremacist bigotry, and carpetbagger state governments imposed by the North were "redeemed" by
the indigenous plantation-owning class. The Republicans, who had held
the presidency since before the Civil War, saw the election as a last-ditch
effort to hold the fractious Union together. Much of their campaign
involved waving the "bloody shirt"—invoking the personal wartime
sacrifices made by soldiers like Devil Dan Sickles, who lost a leg at Get-
tysburg. Many genuinely feared that a Democratic victory would bring
back slavery and create a new wedge between North and South, perhaps
even a second Civil War.

The Democrats, for their part, seethed with bitterness, especially in
the South, where the sting of defeat was still vividly felt. They resented
the presence of federal troops and believed Negro rights were being promoted ahead of the interests of poor whites. Even moderate Democrats
believed the Republican experiment had failed and saw their unortho-
dox coalition of liberal Northerners, Southern whites, and the industrial
working class as the best hope for holding the country together. They
campaigned enthusiastically against the corruption that had emptied
out a good portion of President Grant's cabinet over the previous four
years and blamed the Republicans for the Wall Street panic of 1873. In
that sense, Tilden was their ideal candidate. Who better to close down
the "carnival of thieves" than the man who bagged Boss Tweed?

Unfortunately for the Democrats, Tilden didn't have a lot else to
go on. He was bookish, pedantic, uncharismatic both in private and
at the speaking podium, devoid of outward signs of passion, secretive,
and indecisive. He had the ear of Wall Street, a notable asset against
an increasingly business-minded Republican Party, but he could count
on the sympathy of almost nobody. His nickname, from his time as a
corporate lawyer restructuring bankrupt railroad companies, was the
Great Forecloser.

Hayes was scarcely more attractive. The Ohio governor was a "third-
rate nonentity,"[5] in the words of Henry Adams, and his chief attraction
to the party factions who nominated him was that they didn't know
enough about him to hate him. He was also untainted by corruption,
unlike James G. Blaine, the more obviously attractive Maine senator

and former house Speaker, whose candidacy was blown up by a railroad financing scandal.

Odd as it might seem, the colorlessness of the candidates was one of the main reasons why the country did not lapse into widespread violence. Tilden accepted defeat gracefully, and Hayes agreed to govern as the compromise victor that he was. But their pusillanimity also revealed how broken both major parties were—and, with them, the entire machinery of American democracy. The manipulations visited upon the presidential electoral system were shocking in themselves, but they were also manifestations of a much deeper malaise.

The dirtiness of the race was hardly confined to the Republican side. In all three contested Southern states, black voters had suffered repeated intimidation and violence at the hands of Democratic Party supporters. In Louisiana, armed gangs of party faithful burst in on Republican meetings and murdered several elected officials, a rampage so brutal it "would have disgraced Turks in Bulgaria," according to an account in *Harper's Weekly*.[6] In Lake City, Florida, a group of black men endured a mock hanging and had to promise not to vote Republican before they were let go. Elsewhere in Florida, black sharecroppers were warned that if they were even suspected of voting for Hayes they would face a 25 percent surtax from local shopkeepers, landlords, doctors, and lawyers.

In South Carolina, the campaign was overshadowed by a July Fourth massacre in Hamburg, a black-majority town on the Georgia state line, in which six people including the town marshal were killed by white farmers during a celebration to mark the country's hundredth birthday. The violence had a chilling effect on black voters throughout the western part of the state, and also mobilized white South Carolinians in force against Governor Chamberlain after he condemned the killings. Tit-for-tat reprisals persisted until Election Day, including a campaign by the former Confederate general Martin Gary to drive freed slaves from their homes, whip them, and, in some cases, kill them. "A dead Radical [Republican] is very harmless," Gary remarked.[7]

Election Day itself saw Democratic repeaters and ballot-box stuffers out in strength, especially in the western counties of Edgefield and Laurens, where the party racked up large enough majorities to offset a record Republican showing elsewhere in the state. Not only did the vote count put Tilden narrowly ahead; it also spelled defeat for Governor Chamberlain, who was so outraged by the way the race had been fought he refused to concede for five months.

President Grant attempted to intervene in the late stages, but his dispatch of troop reinforcements in October looked like too little, too late and opened him to the accusation that he was seeking to politicize the army. Already a new calculus was taking hold in the Republican Party, that the cause of black emancipation was too much trouble for too little reward. Northern Republicans were more interested now in cultivating the support of business owners and capitalist entrepreneurs, whose interest was in exploiting the labor of the working poor, black or white, not empowering them. Party elders like Senator Roscoe Conkling of New York bristled at the fact that the end of slavery had expanded the South's voting population and given the region extra weight in Congress and in the electoral college. He did not think blacks had the intelligence or the independence to vote for themselves, and assumed they would continue to do the bidding of their former white owners. "Shall one white man have as much share in the Government as three other white men merely because he lives where blacks outnumber whites two to one?" he thundered. "No sir; not if I can help it."[8]

In short, both major parties were losing interest in democratic integrity. The Tweed scandal became an excuse to limit suffrage rights in the cities, and the end of Reconstruction became an excuse to do the same in the South. The 1876 election was the moment when all their worst instincts came together in one putrid package. Neither party had the remotest faith in the system's fairness, so both relied on the tactic they knew best: brute partisan strength. The Republicans controlled the election canvassing boards in the three contested states, so they threw out Democratic votes for one flimsy reason or another until Tilden's initial advantage had been erased and reversed. In Louisiana, they rejected 13,000 Democratic ballots and only 2,500 Republican ones. In Jackson County, Florida, they used a technicality to disqualify the large Democratic majority entirely.

Corruption flourished at every stage. Senator Chandler of New Hampshire showed up in Florida in mid-November with $10,000 in cash stuffed into a carpet bag, and the lone Democrat on the state's three-man canvassing board, Samuel B. McLin, was subsequently induced to side with the majority with assurances that he would be "taken care of" in a Hayes administration. (He died before he could take up the opportunity.) In Louisiana, the Republican canvassing board chairman, Madison Wells, tried to squeeze his own party for $200,000 in exchange for the two white votes on the board and "a smaller amount for the niggers."[9] When that gambit failed—the House Speaker and future president James Garfield described Wells and his cronies as "a graceless set of scamps"[10]—Wells approached the Democrats with an offer to throw all four votes to Tilden for a million dollars. He was turned down a second time, although it later transpired that Tilden's nephew continued to conduct secret negotiations by way of coded telegrams. Even after the election was settled and Louisiana sent its Republican electors to Washington, two of the eight signatures approved by Wells were shown to be forgeries—a fraud that came to light only as a result of a congressional investigation two years later, by which time it was too late to remedy.

Despite everything, it was evident to any reasonable person that Tilden had carried Louisiana, almost certainly carried Florida, and with them the presidency. Only South Carolina could be described as too close—or too dirty—to call. That was what Hayes himself wrote in his diary on November 12, five days after the election. It was also the view privately taken by President Grant and a number of senior Republicans, including Senators Blaine and Conkling. None of them felt that a Tilden administration would spell the end of civilization as they knew it. On the contrary, Grant sent a telegram to General Sherman three days after the election stating unequivocally, "Either party can afford to be disappointed in the result, but the country can not afford to have the result tainted by the suspicion of illegal or false returns."[11]

None, however, dared express such sentiments in public, and it soon became plain the situation was anything but reasonable. Rank-and-file Republicans cried foul about fraud, even as they stole votes of their own, while the Democrats set up their own rival slate of electors and refused to back down. Everyone looked to Congress to decide which slate to accept, but it was uncertain whether this duty should fall to the president of the Senate, whose constitutional task was to open the returns from the states, or to the House of Representatives, designated under the Constitution as the ultimate arbiter of presidential elections. Since the president of the Senate was a Republican, and the Speaker of the House was a Democrat, there was no prospect of reaching bipartisan consensus to resolve the question. As had happened in 1800, when Thomas Jefferson and Aaron Burr finished with the exact same number of electoral college votes, a presidential election had sprung a surprise outcome for which there was no precedent.

The Democrats looked to Tilden for vigorous leadership, but he refused to lobby publicly for his own cause and eventually withdrew to his private study in Albany to write, incredibly, a book-length study of the previous twenty-two presidential elections. His purpose, to determine whether the head of the Senate had any discretionary power over the outcome of a disputed race, may have been pleasing to certain constitutional scholars, but it drove Abram Hewitt, his party boss and campaign manager, to distraction. "It was absurd for the head of the party to labor on it to the neglect of more vital tasks," Hewitt complained. In the popular press and in the streets, Democratic partisans were beginning to rally under the slogan "Tilden or War!" But Tilden himself was about as belligerent as a feather bedspread.

With their candidate out of commission, the Democrats cast around for any glimmer of a possibility of an extra electoral college vote. To their delight, they found one in Oregon, a state carried handily by Hayes, after they discovered that one of the Republican electors was a federally appointed official—a conflict of interest explicitly barred by the Constitution. The fact that the elector, one John W. Watts, had never been more than a fourth-class postmaster, drawing the less than princely salary of $268 a year, did not deter them. Nor did the fact that he had resigned his commission on receiving his appointment. Oregon's Democratic governor, L.F. Grover, removed him from the electoral college, even though he had no authority to do so under state law, and replaced him with a loyal Democrat, E.A. Cronin, who received the considerably more princely sum of $3,000 from the Democratic National Committee to cover the "expenses" of a $200 trip to Washington.[12] Naturally, the Republicans objected. And so Oregon became the fourth state to offer up rival slates of electors.

For more than two months, the impasse showed little sign of a solution. At length, a compromise between the two chambers of Congress was reached with the creation of an extraordinary Electoral Commission—made up of five House members, five senators, and five justices from the Supreme Court—that was to decide the election on Congress's behalf. The party split offered seven Republicans, seven Democrats, and one Independent—understood at the time the deal was struck to be David Davis, a Supreme Court justice who had started his political career as Abraham Lincoln's presidential campaign manager and was trusted to act *super partes*. At the moment of the commission's formation, however, the Illinois legislature, dominated by a Democrat-Greenback coalition, elected Davis to the Senate, and Davis proved his unimpeachable probity by resigning from the commission. His replacement, Justice Joseph P. Bradley of New Jersey, was a Grant Republican much more likely to side with Hayes.

Bradley essentially had three choices: award all the contested states to Hayes, award one or more to Tilden, or throw out the contested electoral votes and give the election to Tilden by default. The night before the commission was to render its decision, Abram Hewitt sent a surrogate to Bradley's house to see which way he was leaning. According to Hewitt, Bradley read his decision aloud and made clear he was siding with the Democrats. Shortly after, however, he received a visit from Senator Fred Frelinghuysen of New Jersey who, together with Bradley's outspoken wife, spent half the night talking him into changing his opinion. By morning, the election belonged to Hayes, the Republicans were jubilant, and the Democrats erupted in indignation at what they called the bullying of "seven patriots" by "eight villains."

They had every right to be furious. As Jeremiah Black of Pennsylvania, a former secretary of state, put it, "If this thing stands accepted and the law you have made for this occasion shall be the law for all occasions, we can never expect such a thing as an honest election again. If you want to know who will be president . . . you need only to know what kind of scoundrels constitute the returning boards, and how much it will take to buy them."[13]

A handful of Democrats threatened to filibuster the final vote on the House floor and so postpone the election past the expiry of President Grant's term on March 4. That would have created a whole new constitutional headache, but they abandoned the plan under a compromise hashed out between four Southern Democrats and five Republicans at the Wormley House Hotel in Washington in late February. Under this final deal, Hayes would assume the presidency, but he would also withdraw all remaining federal troops from statehouses in the South and allow the contested Democratic gubernatorial candidates in the region to take office.

This was the Compromise of 1877, which formally ended Reconstruction on the understanding that it would also avert a second civil war. Congress ratified the election with less than forty-eight hours of Grant's term still to run. Hayes was secretly sworn in as soon as the vote was completed, just to make sure nothing else could go wrong. Two days later, at his public inauguration, he took the oath of office all over again. As the historian Roy Morris Jr. noted, "It was all a sham—he was already President."

The compromise was seen at the time as the final resolution of a long and anxious drama, but in many ways it was a recognition of what was already an emerging reality. The Democrats' big concession, letting Hayes enter the White House, had already been decided by the Electoral Commission. And the Republicans' big concession, withdrawing federal troops from the South, was already looking well-nigh inevitable. The only thing the agreement determined, in the end, was the timing.

It was not a remotely honorable outcome. True, war was averted, but not the violence, bloodshed, and misery that Southern blacks faced now that their political protectors were abandoning them. The Lincolnian ideal of democratic fairness was giving way to an altogether more hard-nosed politics of economic opportunity. Zebulon Vance, a moderate Democrat who ran and ultimately won his race for governor in North Carolina, remarked glumly in a private letter that the South was powerless to stop the destruction of constitutional government and the North was "too busy making money" to care. James Garfield, writing to Hayes at the same time, concurred: "The Democratic businessmen of the country are more anxious for quiet than for Tilden."[14]

At the Wormley House negotiations, the question of a land grant for the Texas Pacific Railroad, one of the bargaining chips the Republicans conceded in exchange for acceptance of a Hayes presidency, occupied more of the delegates' energy than the integrity of the electoral process. The will of the people was no longer a priority. This was America's Gilded Age, and the rights of both the majority and the country's vulnerable minorities only stood in the way of the true national mission, to let capitalist entrepreneurs accumulate as much wealth as possible.

One hundred and twenty-eight years later, an eccentric book sought to argue that the 1876 election was not in fact the low point of American presidential democracy, but its finest hour.[15] By far the most significant thing about *Centennial Crisis: The Disputed Election of 1876* was that it was written by William Rehnquist, the chief justice responsible for putting George W. Bush in the White House in similarly controversial circumstances in 2000. In seeking to rehabilitate one of the darkest episodes of U.S. history, Rehnquist apparently hoped to go some way toward rehabilitating himself. Thus, he found genuine inspiration in the Electoral Commission's decision to put Hayes in the White House, because it allowed America to go on "about its business." "This outcome," he wrote, "was a testament to the ability of the American system of government to improvise solutions to even the most difficult and important problems." That's a bit like asserting that a group of penniless men who rob a bank are to be commended for their initiative. Are chief justices supposed to say things like that?

Rehnquist's hero was Justice Joseph P. Bradley, a man "placed in an almost impossible position" because he knew he would be criticized no matter how he ruled. Rehnquist thought Bradley made the right decision, not because his choice reflected the will of the voters—he more or less admitted it did not—but because it was the speediest, most effective way to shut down debate and prevent overeager advocates of democracy from getting in the way of the continuity of government. "Perhaps a truly independent commission could, in due time, have produced satisfactory proof that, at least in Louisiana, Tilden had received a majority of the vote," he acknowledged. "But at what cost in terms of future challenges in close presidential elections?"

This is a mind-boggling argument—that democracy, in a pinch, is just too darn messy to be convenient. Given Rehnquist's long personal history of skepticism about the usefulness of voting rights, going back to his documented efforts to challenge and deter minority voters in Phoenix in 1962,[16] his position was not entirely surprising. He was the kind of conservative who always gets nervous when the machinery of state breaks down and previously well-hidden flaws start to surface. Hence his impulse to lock society's demons back in the cupboard as quickly as possible. In the end, his book only reinforced what could already be gleaned from the majority ruling in *Bush v. Gore*—that sometimes the people have to be saved from themselves.

Rehnquist's defense of the Bradley decision bears many similarities to the contorted reasoning of *Bush v. Gore*. Since it was the Republicans who were in control of the three disputed Southern states in 1876, he argues, it was their slate of electors that had the greater stamp of authenticity, and it was not up to the federal government or the courts to "go behind" the certifications they provided. Not only was Justice Bradley correct in upholding a Hayes victory, but he also demonstrated an admirable impartiality. "One need not choose between the Democratic and Republican arguments to say that the position accepted by Bradley was a reasonable one," Rehnquist concluded. In other words: better to validate fraud, so long as it is officially sanctioned, than to denounce it.

Rehnquist chose not to point out that the Republican governments in Florida, South Carolina, and Louisiana were installed by force at the end of the Civil War. He said nothing about the mounting opposition to Northern carpetbaggers, nothing about the incendiary issue of race, and nothing even about Tilden's quarter-million margin in the popular vote. His argument only made sense, in fact, in the light of the 2000 election, when the Supreme Court majority he led accepted the returns provided by a blatantly partisan Republican state government in Florida instead of insisting that the votes be counted properly and in full.

Why worry about the suppression of black votes in 1876 when his own court made so light of the problem in 2000? Why would Tilden's lead in the popular vote seem relevant when Al Gore's substantial edge over Bush was so roundly ignored? At the head of this chapter, I quote Louis Koenig's warning that the bedevilments of the Tilden-Hayes race risk recurring at any time because they have never been fully confronted and resolved. The events of 2000, and the Rehnquist court's reaction to them, demonstrate exactly what he was warning against.

5

THE 1896 WATERSHED AND THE PARADOX OF REFORM

We are all pots, and our bottoms are all sooty.

—*Mark Hanna*[1]

In 1878, Francis Parkman published an influential essay lamenting the corruption of American democracy and the takeover of the country's largest cities by "blackguards . . . abject flatterers, vicious counselors and greedy plunderers." The blame for this lamentable state of affairs, Parkman wrote, lay not with the city machine bosses, or in the venality of the emerging capitalist system. The problem was the voters, who had become too numerous, too disparate, too unreliable, and too ignorant to be trusted. Parkman's essay was called "The Failure of Universal Suffrage," and in it he unleashed a torrent of grandiloquent invective against a system that, he said, allowed "the weakest and most worthless" to be counted as equals with "the wisest and best":

> It is in the cities that the diseases of the body politic are gathered to a head, and it is here that the need of attacking them is most urgent. Here the dangerous classes are most numerous and strong, and the effects of flinging the suffrage to the mob are most disastrous. Here the barbarism that we have armed and organized stands ready to overwhelm us. Our cities have become a prey. Where the carcass is, the vultures gather together. The industrious are taxed to feed the idle, and offices are distributed to perpetuate abuses and keep knaves in power.

This was red-meat rhetoric in the wake of the Tweed scandals, but it resonated widely in a country preoccupied with the challenges of industrialization, mass immigration, the legacy of the Civil War, the Negro question, and graft on an epidemic scale at every level of public office. Not so long before, Jefferson and his heirs had imagined good government as a consensus of property-owning country gentlemen, and America itself as a land of limitless space, opportunity, and plenty untouched by the corruption of European cities. Now, New York and Philadelphia had taken on the same sprawling, overcrowded, violent, liquor-soaked aspect as eighteenth-century London—the epitome of everything the heroes of the American Revolution had fought against. Parkman's essay is infused with nostalgia for the "wholesome traditions" of an idyllic Jeffersonian past:

> A New England village of the olden time—that is to say, of some forty years ago—would have been safely and well governed by the votes of every man in it; but now that the village has grown into a populous city, with its factories and workshops, its acres of tenement houses, and thousands and ten thousands of restless workmen, foreigners for the most part, to whom liberty means license and politics means plunder . . .

Parkman wasn't merely nostalgic. He was filled with exclusionary disdain for foreigners, blacks, and "the masses," which is to say the entire industrial working class. He denounced the "monstrosities of Negro rule in South Carolina" as vehemently as the corruptions of New York, and returned again and again to bestial imagery when talking about the lower orders. Democracy, he said, was the new despotism, worse even than the old tyranny of kings and aristocrats. "If we are to be oppressed," he declared, "we would rather the oppressor were clean, and if we are to be robbed, we like to be robbed with civility."[2]

Parkman was, in many ways, a white Anglo-Saxon Protestant out of central casting, taking for granted his own place in America's natural ruling order and looking down on everyone else as another species entirely. His essay bore many similarities to one by a University of Michigan geologist named Alexander Winchell that appeared a few years later. Nothing was more natural, Winchell wrote, than to "seek to lodge political influence in the wisest and safest hands," much as a passenger on an ocean liner "gladly relegates command to the best captain and the best engineer."[3]

This anti-suffrage argument appealed to something base and enduringly elemental in American politics: the sense first cultivated by the Jacksonians that the white religious rural heartland was the *real* America and that everything else—cities, foreigners, Catholics, intellectual ideas, black emancipation, Native American rights, secularism, and multiculturalism—was a dangerous aberration to be resisted as a matter of national pride, even of national security. This has been a powerful, insidious idea throughout American history, justifying, among other things, Jim Crow, the anticommunist witch hunts of the 1950s, and the evangelical nationalism of the Tea Party wing of the modern Republican Party. What Parkman and Winchell were offering was a catch-all explanation for corruption, vote fraud, industrial-era alienation, the collapse of Reconstruction, the cowboy justice of the West, and Custer's last stand at Little Bighorn. Why not blame everything on universal suffrage, especially when so many unlearned, unwanted voters were clogging up their definition of what it meant to be a proper American?

It wasn't exactly rational to heap the shortcomings of American democracy at the feet of the people the system was designed to serve. But rationality was not nearly as persuasive a motivator as fear and confusion, both of which abounded in the America of the time. As governor of New York, Samuel Tilden responded to the Tweed scandals he helped expose with a proposal to allow only taxpayers and rent payers to vote in municipal elections. His measure failed, but the issue remained insistent enough for the *New York Times* to write a couple of years later, "It would be a great gain if people could be made to understand distinctly that the right to life, liberty and the pursuit of happiness involves, to be sure, the right to good government, but not the right to take part, either immediately or indirectly, in the management of the state."[4]

John Davenport, who conducted a major investigation of Boss Tweed's fraudulent naturalization drives, concurred that democracy could be successful only when its participants were "free, unprejudiced, sober and educated."[5] In 1883, Justice Joseph P. Bradley, the man who denied Tilden the presidency, wrote a Supreme Court opinion invalidating the 1875 Civil Rights Act (granting equal access to hotels and public transportation) on the grounds that blacks—then facing a torrent of discriminatory laws, an attempt by plantation owners to yoke them to a neo-feudal agricultural labor system, and the wrath of the Ku Klux Klan—must cease "to be the special favorite of the laws."[6]

Much of the opposition to universal suffrage was fueled by industrialists, who saw the will of the people as a dangerously unpredictable obstacle to their business ambitions and became ever more cynical about manipulating it to suit their needs. A Senate report from the 1880s showed that workers at New England textile mills were routinely marched to the polls or transported in their employers' carriages. They were given ballots in advance and instructed to hold them up in full view at all times. Workers who went against the mill owner's political wishes risked losing their jobs and their company housing. The *Boston Herald* commented, "It is very improper to intimidate voters, but there is a way of giving advice that is most convincing."[7] In Augusta, Georgia, newspapers reported that a "job-lash" was used to force mill employees, both white and black, to vote "regular."[8]

In the West, where new communities were sprouting and foreigners were hired en masse to pick fruit and work on the railroads, voters were bought off more than they were coerced. In Los Angeles, for example, the city fathers overcame popular opposition to an 1872 bond issue and land grant needed to lure the Southern Pacific Railroad line into their city by buying up the votes of hundreds of Mexican Americans. As Henry O'Melveny, founder of one of L.A.'s most powerful law firms, wrote: "[They] not only did not understand the questions submitted at the election, but they did not care. It was just the common, ordinary practice to buy their votes." The anti-bond forces also offered money in exchange for the Latinos' support, but they were outbid.[9]

Politicians and business leaders got away with these practices in part because of the abiding belief, going back to the Jacksonian era, that the interests of democracy and the interests of capitalism were one and the same. That theory had been challenged, if not wholly undone, by the popular revolutions that had punctured European political life for almost half a century, as workers clamored for the right to challenge their capitalist masters in the workplace and at the ballot box. But America persisted in the belief that it was immune from such pressures. As late as the 1950s, the political theorist Louis Hartz insisted that "the mass of the people . . . are bound to be capitalistic, and capitalism, with its spirit disseminated widely, is bound to be democratic." Hartz admitted that nineteenth-century America offered plentiful examples to the contrary, but these he described as "ironic," not indications that his fundamental faith was misplaced.[10]

The truth, poorly understood at the time, was that American democracy was at its most dynamic when the capitalist system was in competition with the political parties, and the accumulation of wealth was tempered by keen solicitation of the popular vote. City machines worked best when their power was an even match for the industrial interests anxious to do business with them. And they were at their least corrupt when forced to fight for survival in the court of public opinion. As Frances Fox Piven and Richard A. Cloward have written, "So long as machine control was contested, turnout of working-class voters remained crucial to machine success, and the machines exerted themselves to enlist voters and help them hurdle whatever barriers they confronted."[11] It was when the machines became too comfortably entrenched that corruption ran rampant, at the expense of both the public and their business clients.

The reform movement, such as it was, believed fervently that a prosperous, capitalistic society run in the public interest was both desirable and possible. Such was the agenda of the liberal Republicans known as Mugwumps who clamored for wide-ranging public sector reorganization in the wake of President Garfield's assassination by a disgruntled office seeker in 1881.[12] Some believed progress was possible only if the uneducated classes were kicked out of the electoral process. Others were at least willing to accept their exclusion as the price for moving society forward. In 1883, the laissez-faire guru and prominent Mugwump William Graham Sumner wrote a book pondering *What Social Classes Owe to Each Other*. His answer: precisely nothing.[13]

To the reformers' credit, they managed to create a professional civil service in place of the old spoils system and, later, inspired some of the more heartening changes of the Progressive Era. When it came to the management of elections, however, they failed to learn a lesson that has been shunned or forgotten by every generation since: changing the mechanics of voting does nothing, on its own, to clean up the system, and often it makes things worse. Yes, they took elections out of the parties' direct control and introduced the secret ballot. But it's also doubtful whether any period has been more disastrous for American democracy.

The secret ballot was, on the face of it, an unimpeachable harbinger of progress, because the old party-printed ballots, with their identifying shapes and colors, were an invitation to coercion, bribery, and theft. They also made it hard for voters to pick members of different parties for different offices. Australia became the first country to switch to a uniform ballot, printed at public expense, listing all candidates and all parties together. It also introduced curtained voting booths and sealed ballot boxes to maximize secrecy. The so-called Australian ballot made its first appearance in 1856. It was adopted in Britain in 1872 and in Canada two years later. In the United States, it was first proposed by the Philadelphia Civil Service Reform League in 1882, and was introduced on an experimental basis in Kentucky in 1888. Within a year it had been adopted in seven states, and by the time of the 1896 presidential election it was being used in thirty-nine. By 1916, only two states, Georgia and South Carolina, had not adopted it—largely because they were under de facto one-party rule and saw no point.[14]

The Australian ballot was greeted with suspicion at first and was derided in the popular press as a "penal-colony reform" that promised "kangaroo voting." Then its more underhanded possibilities began to be appreciated, and the complexion of the debate changed entirely. The key realization was that access to voting was in fact *easier* to manage when the process was under unified city or county control, because interparty competition was taken out of the equation. It was not long before literacy tests, education tests, good character requirements, and similar restrictions were written into state laws. Many observers thought suffrage restriction was the point of the Australian ballot. "So obvious is the evil of ignorant voting that more stringent naturalization laws are being demanded, because too many of our foreign-born citizens vote ignorantly," the labor reformer George Gunton reported in 1893. "It is to remedy this that the Australian ballot system has been adopted in so many states."[15]

The reform did not go through without a fight. Gunton also argued vigorously against the notion of compulsory voting, popular with some reformers, saying the franchise should rather be withdrawn from anyone who chose not to use it. "Political power should never be forced on any class," he said imperiously.[16] On the other side of the argument, the *New York Sun* sprang to the defense of voters likely to be disenfranchised in the way Gunton envisaged. "Whatever tends to increase the number of legal voters and to make citizens more active participants in the affairs of government is wise and salutary," the paper wrote in 1889. "Whatever tends to impair or restrict the rights of franchise, to limit the number of voters, or to vex and harass them in the exercise of this most important duty is pernicious and dangerous."[17]

That viewpoint reflected, among other things, the enduring tension between New York and Albany. The *Sun* recognized, correctly, that the state legislature wanted to curb the power and influence of Tammany Hall, just as other state legislatures approving the Australian ballot sought to rein in their own urban populations.[18]

Even without qualifying tests, the Australian ballot made voting significantly more difficult for the illiterate, still a significant proportion of the adult population, especially in the rural South. The old party voting papers had been coded by size or color and required no word-recognition skills, but the new ballots offered no such assistance, except in cases where the local authorities were conscientious enough to place party symbols next to the candidates' names. That, though, was a rarity. Florida abandoned party designations, either symbols or words, as a matter of state law, and made sure the Democratic Party candidates were always listed first. Anyone wishing to vote Populist or Republican had to count down five, ten, or even fifteen names, and had to be familiar with the names to avoid mistakes.[19] Even when the ballot layout was not deliberately confusing, the multiplicity of candidate names and races often made it inadvertently so, prompting an Ohio court to issue a nonbinding dictum in 1909 questioning whether the state's ballot laws were not in themselves tantamount to an unconstitutional, back-door education test.[20]

Many political leaders loved the Australian ballot for its chilling effect on voter turnout, especially when it could be engineered to affect one party more than the other. When the head of Alabama's state constitutional convention was asked if Jesus Christ would qualify under a particularly stringent good character clause, he replied, "That would depend entirely on which way he was going to vote." In Louisiana, the introduction of the Australian ballot was timed deliberately to affect the outcome of the 1896 presidential election. The Republicans later estimated that passage of the new law cut the black vote it had relied on by half. [21]

One attraction of the Australian ballot—much like the photo ID laws popular with Republican state legislatures today—was that it kept the unfairness it propagated largely hidden from view. Indeed, it purged polling stations of many of the outward signs of corruption and chaos. Drunkenness, violence, and direct intimidation diminished markedly, to the point where Big Dick Butler, a New York bruiser who had worked to undermine the Tammany Hall machine, complained, "Elections nowadays are sissy affairs."[22] Ballot stuffing became more difficult, as did the use of tissue ballots.

Overt corruption was hardly eliminated, however. Repeat voting remained a durable feature, for example in St Louis, where the Democratic Party boss, Colonel Ed Butler, was notorious for calling out across police lines on Election Day, "Are there any repeaters out here that want to vote again?"[23] In other jurisdictions, party precinct captains found it simpler to infiltrate local election boards and get them, as insiders, to write down the names of bogus voters in the register and fill out ballots on their behalf. Not for the last time, true reformers would understand that you can change the mechanics of voting more easily than you can ever hope to change the people running the show. Atlantic City boss Louis Kuehnle would hand out carbon paper so he could later verify how his cohorts had voted and decide if they deserved payment or not.[24] In Arkansas, the carbon paper was part of official electoral procedure.[25]

In many cities, chain voting—also known as the "Tasmanian dodge"—became common. Someone would obtain a blank ballot, usually from a corrupt poll worker; a local boss would fill it out and hand it to a voter; the voter would drop the completed ballot in the box and bring the one he was given inside the polling station back out, untouched; the boss would then fill it out for the next voter, and so on. All these transactions involved payment of one kind or another.[26] One independent study from 1892 estimated that about one in six Connecticut votes were purchasable. A decade later, a judge in Ohio found that more than a quarter of Adams County residents had been selling their votes as a matter of routine, and as many as 85 percent had done so on a more occasional basis. One woman who pleaded guilty of vote fraud on behalf of herself, her husband, and son explained, "We thought it was the law to pay us for our votes."[27]

Why was the Australian ballot such a disaster for the United States when its introduction was resoundingly successful just about every-where else? Part of the reason was the intensely local nature of party politics in the United States, and the emphasis Republicans and Dem-ocrats both placed on winning over adhering to any rigid ideological position. And part of it arose from structural flaws introduced in the wake of the Civil War with the passage of the Fourteenth and Fifteenth Amendments—two more attempts at reform that ended up hurting the citizens they were designed to help.

Ostensibly, both amendments had much to recommend them. They introduced the concept of a right to vote for the first time and made it impossible for former slave states to deny blacks the vote outright, or to use racial discrimination as an explicit instrument of public policy. But this was not enough. As Henry Adams said, the Fifteenth Amendment was "more remarkable for what it does not than for what it does con-tain."[28] A stronger amendment, proposed by Senator Henry Wilson of Massachusetts, would have abolished all discrimination on the grounds of "race, color, nativity, property, education or religious belief"[29] and eliminated even the possibility of restrictions or qualifications for vot-ers or aspirants to public office. But Wilson's proposal fell short by just a handful of votes, and the version that passed was more limited. It said "the right of citizens of the United States to vote shall not be denied or abridged . . . by reason of race, color, previous condition of servi-tude." That left plenty of room to introduce restrictions on the grounds of something other than race and still penalize blacks and other unfa-vored social groups through more circuitous means.

It is striking that, even in the first flush of victory for the Union, Northern politicians could not muster sufficient enthusiasm for Negro voting rights. Instead of slamming the door on slavery and discrimi-nation, the two amendments left it maddeningly ajar. The Fourteenth Amendment gave Southern states the option of continuing to disenfran-chise former slaves as long as they were willing to have their congressio-nal districts and their weight in the presidential electoral college shrunk accordingly, while the Fifteenth, in continuing to allow discrimination as long as it was not explicitly racial, paved the way for the essential architecture of Jim Crow and the suppression of voting rights across large swaths of the country.

The Fifteenth Amendment might have made less progress still if the Republican Party hadn't almost lost the 1868 presidential election and understood that its future viability as a governing party would depend on the Negro vote. Its passage, paradoxically, was much smoother in the South, where white elites regarded black suffrage as regrettable but inevitable, than in the North. Thomas Carlyle, the great British historian, summarized the divergent attitudes admirably. The message Negroes received from the South, he said, was "God bless you! and be a slave," while the message from the North was "God damn you! and be free."[30] The Civil War had propelled the country into ending slavery and expanding voting rights more quickly than it could tolerate, and the result was an ugly backlash.[31]

One reason why the United States felt so insecure about suffrage rights was that it had started out far ahead of the rest of the industrialized world. In Europe, voting rights were granted incrementally to an industrial working class that threatened to overturn the ruling order altogether if its demands were not met. In the United States, the advent of Jacksonian democracy largely preceded industrialization, so the working class was empowered in advance, and the political and business elites were spurred into throwing the expansion of suffrage rights in reverse. While the European trend was toward the formation of broad-based union movements and the establishment of full-fledged parties of labor, those aspirations were squashed in the United States. In Europe, the secret ballot was a boon because it sealed the gains made by the movement for popular democracy. In the United States, its introduction was an opportunity to pay lip service to democratic integrity while ensuring that such a thing became impossible.

Thus, the thirty years after the Civil War saw a confrontation between capitalism and popular democracy unlike any on the old continent. The battle lines were blurred and often incoherent. Anti-suffragists and laissez-faire capitalists were challenged by a surging Populist movement, which seethed at the abandonment of rural America in favor of the industrial cities and believed bedrock America was being betrayed by the coastal elites. The America most commonly idealized by foreigners in this period—the America of Emma Lazarus, Ellis Island, and penniless immigrants dreaming big in the land of opportunity—ran headlong into the moral opprobrium of Nativists and rural Puritans.

Reformers straddled all sides of these fences, taking either the Mugwump position that politics needed to be orderly to be effective or the Populist view that only an urban-rural alliance of working people could rein in the capitalists—or, as a third variant, believing that industry and the labor movement should make common cause in the service of wealth creation and protecting the common man. The country wavered between razor-thin pluralities for Republican presidents and razor-thin pluralities for Democrats. In 1888, Benjamin Harrison captured the White House for the Republicans without winning the popular vote—the last time that would happen until 2000. Even in Congress, which was then more powerful than at any time before or since, the parties yo-yoed between progressive and reactionary prescriptions.

The contradictions finally came to a head in the 1896 presidential election, when the Populists and Democrats joined forces behind William Jennings Bryan, the golden-tongued Boy Orator from Nebraska, and the Republicans went all in behind William McKinley, an amiable but taciturn figurehead backed by the first significant outpouring of corporate money in the country's history. It was as important a presidential contest as any the United States has held. McKinley's victory ushered in an era of Republican rule that lasted almost without interruption until the Great Depression. The collapse of the Populist movement in the wake of Bryan's defeat asserted the primacy of the capitalist ethic—flawed and overreaching though many, including McKinley, thought it was. It also scuttled any hope of a European-style social democracy.

The election marked the Republican Party's final abandonment of Southern blacks and removed the last obstacles to segregation and Jim Crow, to which the Populists had been the last significant line of resistance. At almost every level, from the White House to Congress to state government, meaningful two-party competition collapsed, as the Democrats consolidated their grip on the South and—with the notable exception of the four-way presidential election won by Woodrow Wilson in 1912—more or less abandoned their leadership ambitions everywhere else. The country was reduced to a patchwork of uncontested political fiefdoms in which rival factions within the dominant party argued furiously about policy and reform with strikingly little input from the voters. While the Populist impulse did not die so much as migrate into the progressive wings of both major parties, it was still a disastrous period for the cause of representative democracy.[32]

The standard textbooks on the era don't generally paint things so starkly. They like to point out that the Progressive Era ushered in by McKinley was a time of rapid modernization in which the robber barons were reined in by a raft of regulations governing the railroads, the food industry, sweatshops, and child labor; by the Sherman Anti-Trust Act; by the advent of the income tax (initially levied only on the richest 10 percent), and by the explosive growth of public education.

It was in many ways a remarkable period, but one of its paradoxes— and perhaps its greatest puzzle—is that almost none of the important reforms came about as a result of popular participation in elections. Progressives across party lines recognized a need to act on behalf of the public good, because popular sovereignty itself had been eroded to the point of meaninglessness; they disagreed only on whether this was a good or a bad thing. By 1904, just one in seven American voters lived in a state where presidential elections were still competitive. By 1920, when women were granted the vote for the first time, that proportion had dropped to one in nine. Voter participation collapsed from 79 percent in the 1896 election to just 49 percent in 1920. Turnout in the Southern states tumbled from 57 percent in the McKinley-Bryan election to less than 20 percent in the 1920s.[33] Evisceration of black voting rights was responsible for a large part of that, but not all. The decline correlated closely to socioeconomic status for blacks and whites, in the North and the South. The bottom half of the population simply fell out of the process.[34]

One part of the Progressive movement mourned the loss of participatory democracy, but another part was happy to live the Mugwump dream of good works and wise government without the chaos of mass popular participation. As the Yale historians Charles Seymour and Donald Paige Frary wrote in 1918, "The theory that every man has a natural right to vote no longer commands the support of students of political science."[35]

The movement's dynamism grew chiefly out of factional struggles within the major parties (especially the Republicans) and from civic activism, including muckraking journalism, that stayed strictly within the confines of the educated classes. Some reforms impinged directly on the electoral process, including the Seventeenth Amendment mandating the direct election of senators; the advent of party primaries, ballot initiatives, and the recall of underperforming officeholders; and, in 1920, the culmination of the seventy-year struggle for women's suffrage. All but the last of these was conceived not so much to empower the electorate as to circumscribe the power of corporations and their lobbyists. And party primaries, as we shall see in the next chapter, were used to disenfranchise certain voters even further. Even the advent of women voters did not shift the overall shape of American politics much. The suffragist movement was a rare and remarkable instance of pressure from outside the established political system leading to meaningful and lasting change. But the women who started voting in 1920 entered a broken system and would not be taken seriously as an independent force for decades to come.[36]

The Republican Party in power underwent a generational shift from the Civil War–era invocations of the "bloody shirt" to a broader program reflecting America's growing economic power and its first major forays into military adventurism, starting with the Spanish-American War and the occupation of the Philippines. During the 1896 campaign, McKinley successfully painted himself as the face of America's future—urban, industrial, modern, diverse, and committed to the fast-track prosperity of hard money. His support base was truly impressive, reaching as far left as socially conscious reformers like Robert La Follette and Lincoln Steffens, by way of Samuel Gompers, the influential leader of the American Federation of Labor. McKinley was soon torn, however, between his own instinct for reform and the unapologetic business-first agenda of his campaign manager, Mark Hanna.[37]

Hanna, like McKinley, was an Ohioan, a successful magnate from Cleveland who applied the ethos of the marketplace to the political world in ways that had never been attempted but would become an enduring model for the future. (One of his biggest modern-day fans is George W. Bush's political consigliere turned Republican mega fundraiser Karl Rove.) During the campaign, Hanna kept McKinley largely on his front porch in Canton, where he received business leaders and assorted influence seekers by the thousands. Hanna, meanwhile, solicited hefty corporate campaign contributions, including a quarter of a million dollars each from Standard Oil and J.P. Morgan. "All questions of government in a democracy are questions of money," Hanna once said, directly contradicting Thomas Jefferson's warnings about the dangers of creating an "aristocracy of our monied corporations."[38]

Hanna used his money and the influence it bought him to reel every major newspaper into the McKinley camp. He also pioneered a new, aggressive approach to campaigning by mail, spending $60,000 a week on postage and sending out at least 300 million pieces of literature. He hammered home the message that McKinley was the "advance agent of prosperity" who would keep America's economic engines running smoothly. It was, as Lawrence Goodwyn has described it, the "first concentrated mass advertising campaign aimed at organizing the minds of the American people on the subject of political power, who should have it, and why."[39]

The Bryan campaign was knocked flat. Its biggest vulnerability was its rejection of hard money, the subject of Bryan's rousingly memorable "Cross of Gold" speech at the Democratic convention. But the Democrat-Populist alliance was also torn apart by its own contradictions. It was deeply split on the question of race. The Farmers' Alliance felt not the slightest commonality with the urban industrialists, or even industrial workers in the Democratic Party. There was a rural versus urban divide, a Protestant versus Catholic divide, an evangelical versus liberal-intellectual divide. Many Populists understood that their differences were being exploited by their opponents—and perhaps also by their allies—but felt powerless to do anything about it. The Populist leader Tom Watson of Georgia (later to become a startlingly caustic racist) valiantly told one audience of blacks and poor whites during the 1896 campaign, "You are made to hate each other because upon that hatred is rested the keystone of the arch of financial despotism which enslaves you both."[40]

In the end, McKinley and the Republicans projected coherence, the Democrat-Populist alliance only incoherence. It's not that the better man lost, or that McKinley was a bad president—he was not. But the consequences of the structural shift in American politics that 1896 represented were profound and long lasting. Popular democracy sustained a hit from which it has never fully recovered. America became a country of enormous wealth but also of vast neglect of its neediest people. The cause of reform, while worthy, relied on the honesty of those in power and soon ran into the deregulatory orgy of the go-go 1920s. And the South was condemned to darkest night for two generations.

6

THE LONG AGONY OF THE
DISENFRANCHISED SOUTH

The slave went free; stood a brief moment in the sun; then moved back again toward slavery.

—*W.E.B. Du Bois*[1]

We have done our level best. We have scratched our heads how we could eliminate every last one of them. We stuffed ballot boxes. We shot them. We are not ashamed of it.

—*Senator "Pitchfork Ben" Tillman*[2]

On the morning of November 10, 1898, two thousand well-organized white vigilantes gathered in Wilmington, North Carolina, to murder as many Negroes as they could find and seize control of the city. They were not ordinary hooligans, not "plug uglies," as one of them later explained, but rather "men of property . . . clergymen, lawyers, bankers merchants . . . asserting a sacred privilege and a right."[3]

Two days earlier, through ballot-box fraud and a well-orchestrated campaign of terror, they helped engineer a resounding statewide electoral victory for the Democratic Party over the mixed-race Fusionist coalition that had run North Carolina for the previous four years. In Wilmington they were frustrated, since municipal elections were not due until 1900 and a Fusionist mayor, council of aldermen, and chief of police all remained in office. After a stop at the city armory for repeating rifles, the mob marched on the printing press of the city's only black-owned newspaper and smashed every window, fixture, and kerosene-powered lamp before setting the wreckage alight.[4]

In Brooklyn, a black-majority neighborhood, they opened fire on all they encountered, leaving a trail of at least fourteen dead and dying. When they came across Daniel Wright, a local black politician, they threatened to string him to a lamppost, then turned him loose and, with cries of "Run, nigger, run!" cut him down in a hail of at least forty rounds. Wright lay bleeding for ninety minutes, "like a pigeon thrown from a trap," according to one account, and died in the hospital the next day.

A handful of the vigilantes stormed City Hall and forced Mayor Silas Wright to resign at gunpoint along with his board of aldermen and the entire police department. Every last black officeholder was run out of town, along with the cream of the city's black professional class. Most fled of their own accord, but some were frog-marched to the railroad station and loaded on a special car where they were held under armed guard until the train had crossed the state line into Virginia. The women and children they left behind were expelled from their homes and forced to huddle in swamps on the city's edge before they, too, made their exodus. Within a month almost 15 percent of the black population had abandoned the city. Colonel Alfred Moore Waddell, a former Democratic congressman who led the armed uprising, became the new mayor and distributed the other prize city positions among his cohorts. "We have taken a city," Reverend Peyton H. Hoge of the First Presbyterian Church said from the pulpit the following Sunday. "To God be the praise."

Historians have referred to the events of November 1898 as a race riot, an uprising, a rebellion, a pogrom, or a coup, but none of these words alone carries the full weight of the subversion that took place. The killings and the subsequent white takeover signaled not just the end of biracial government in the American South, but also a period of one-party rule so absolute it amounted to white supremacist dictatorship across the eleven states that had seceded from the Union at the start of the Civil War. North Carolina had been the only state where the Fusionists controlled both the governor's office and the legislature. By their mere existence they posed a threat both to the white plantation-owning class and to industrialists alarmed by populist talk of reining in the excesses of monopoly capitalism.

Wilmington, an attractive city thirty miles up the Cape Fear River from the coast, had made itself a target in the months leading up to the election by playing host to a vituperative debate about interracial sex. When the city's white newspaper, the *Messenger*, reproduced a speech by the Georgia feminist Rebecca Felton, in which she advocated lynching "a thousand negroes a week" to protect the honor of white women, the publisher of the black-run *Daily Record*, Alex Manly, felt compelled to point out that most reports of rape by black men were untrue; often, he wrote, the couplings were consensual and were only called rape once the woman's family found out about them.[5] That was enough to make Manly, who was biracial, a lightning rod of white fury from one end of the state to the other. "The impudent nigger ought to be horsewhipped and run out of town," one prominent Wilmingtonian told his friends. Serious thought was given to organizing a lynching, but Senator "Pitchfork Ben" Tillman of South Carolina urged patience. Better, he said, to wait until after the election. It was Manly's printing press that was torched at the start of the uprising, by which point he had already fled to Washington.

The Manly controversy fed into the Democrats' near-messianic campaign to wrest control of the state back from "race traitors." In several cities, including Wilmington, a Democratic Party militia called the Red Shirts broke up political meetings and issued warnings to blacks who dared show up at the polls. Colonel Waddell was part of a committee called the Secret Nine, which made meticulous preparations to ensure a Democratic victory, including circulation of a document repudiating the constitutional rights of "an ignorant population of African origin." "We will never surrender to a ragged raffle of Negroes," Waddell told one cheering crowd, "even if we have to choke the current of the Cape Fear with carcasses." The night before the election, he told his followers, "If you find the Negro out voting, tell him to leave the polls, and if he refuses, kill him, shoot him down in his tracks."

In the end, intimidation and a little judicious ballot stuffing were enough to transform Wilmington's five-thousand-vote margin for the Republicans into a six-thousand-vote margin for the Democrats—in a city of just twenty thousand. On Election Day, the *Messenger* published one last provocation urging the "sons of Carolina, proud Caucasians, one and all" to rise up and protect the "spotless virtue" of their women with "strong and manly arms." The Red Shirts stood guard with Winchester rifles at polling stations all over the city; the police were nowhere to be seen. When North Carolina's Fusionist governor, Daniel L. Russell, arrived in Wilmington to vote, he was intercepted by a raging mob that vowed to lynch him on the spot. He barely escaped in one piece and never made it to the polls.

Throughout the violence that followed, no authority at the state or national level thought to intervene. One anonymous Wilmingtonian wrote to President McKinley to ask why he hadn't sent federal troops to prevent black citizens dying "like rats in a trap," but he received no good answer. McKinley's administration was afraid of being dragged into a new, most likely futile Reconstruction effort. The Justice Department considered pressing criminal charges, but concluded that any trial before a Southern jury would most likely end in acquittal and backed off. Thus, the abandonment of the South reached its shockingly heartless climax.

The Wilmington events were exceptional, even set against the beatings, whippings, and lynchings that regularly punctuated life in the South in the last decade of the nineteenth century. Since the end of the Civil War, violence on such a scale had generally been deemed unnecessary to achieve the twin goals of suppressing black votes and stifling the Populist movement; much better to get there through discriminatory suffrage laws and control of the electoral process. "It penetrated gradually to the consciousness of the most brutal white politicians that the whipping or murder of a Negro, no matter for what cause, was likely to become at once the occasion of a great outcry in the North," the journalist and historian W.A. Dunning wrote in the *Atlantic Monthly*, "while by an unobtrusive manipulation of the balloting or the count very encouraging results could be obtained with little or no commotion."[6]

The governments of the old confederacy had to tread carefully, even after the threat of federal troop garrisons faded to nothing, because the Fifteenth Amendment outlawed overt forms of discrimination, and they did not want Washington interfering in what amounted to home rule. Violence was thus meted out sparingly but effectively, first by regional militias like the Ku Klux Klan and then by the Democratic Party's own marauding gangs—the Red Shirts in North Carolina, the Mason Guards in Tennessee, and so on. The political leadership initiated its legal onslaught with voting bans on felons and ex-felons, a category the police was happy to widen to include as many former slaves as possible. Since the whole country was undergoing a period of doubt about the wisdom of universal suffrage, the Southern states got away with more than they otherwise might have. To that extent, the advent of Jim Crow had the tacit blessing of the entire political system.

Much of the repression was motivated by revenge against the North. The perception was that, during Reconstruction, carpetbagger governments had granted ex-slaves more civil rights than poor whites, and now it was time for payback. "Give us a convention," Bob Toombs of Georgia said in 1876, "and I will fix it so that the people shall rule and the Negro shall never be heard from."[7] A few years later, the chair of Tennessee's senate redistricting committee put it even more bluntly, "The Radicals disfranchised us, and now we intend to disfranchise them."[8]

Georgia introduced an unusually onerous poll tax, which came due not just in election years, but every year. This remained, for many decades, the single most effective vote suppression mechanism in the American South. Elsewhere, the emphasis was on gerrymandering—especially "packing" black voters into the fewest possible number of legislative districts—and administrative control of voting. Black voters typically had to travel farther, sometimes as far as forty miles outside a densely populated urban area, and wait longer to cast a ballot. Locations would change at the last minute without warning; river ferries and other transportation services would be disrupted on Election Day; and even voters who arrived in time risked being denied entry as they endured challenges to their eligibility. The Democratic Party made sure county officials toed the party line; if they did not, they risked being dismissed. Sometimes, the state government would then withdraw the counties' power to make their own appointments.

As the Farmers' Alliance and Populist movements took off in the 1880s, state governments opened a second front of vote suppression via the registration process. Alabama chose to register voters in May, one of the year's busiest farming months. In North Carolina, voters were required to prove "as near as may be"[9] their age, place of birth, and place of residency—requirements all but guaranteed to suppress the turnout of former slaves, many of whom did not have accurate birth records. These restrictions were applied unevenly, depending on race and income level. In Louisiana, already known for its sharp political practices, the number of registered white males rose above 100 percent of the eligible population, even as overall participation slumped by a third from 1876 to 1884. Louisiana senator Samuel McEnery said bluntly the intention was "to treat the law as a formality and count in the Democrats."[10]

South Carolina, which felt especially vulnerable to the risks of universal suffrage because it was the only Southern state with a black-majority population, pioneered the so-called eight-box law, a rule that called for a separate ballot box for each race being contested. The best hope for illiterate voters was to memorize the position of the boxes in advance, but poll workers regularly rearranged them into new configurations.[11] Once party workers established which voters were unlikely to come to the polls because of these obstacles, they took to casting fraudulent ballots on their behalf.

By the time the Populist revolt reached its zenith, some combination of these restrictions—poll taxes, gerrymandering, eight-box laws—was in place in every Southern state. Voter participation plummeted, and by 1890 the Republican Party was all but annihilated in Florida and Tennessee. Still, this was not enough for states pushing back where the Populist movement was strongest. Mississippi, a bastion of the Farmers' Alliance, became the first to rewrite its state constitution so it could achieve what its governor Robert Lowry called "the quiet . . . so desirable and important for the public welfare."[12] The new constitution, enacted in 1890, was a blueprint for circumventing the Fifteenth Amendment; a later governor, James Kimble Vardaman, admitted it had "no other purpose than to eliminate the nigger from politics."[13] Among its provisions were residency requirements of two years in the state, and one year in the district (a safeguard against "vagrancy"—also known as being poor, dark-skinned, and on the move in search of work); proof of poll tax payment over two consecutive years; an "understanding" clause requiring voters to be able to read and give a "reasonable interpretation" of the state constitution; and a long list of disqualifications for crimes as nebulous as bribery, forgery, embezzlement, and bigamy. The framers were even emboldened to add this:

> Every provision in the Mississippi Constitution applies equally, and without discrimination whatever, to both the white and Negro races. Any assumption, therefore, that the purpose of the framers of the Constitution was ulterior, and dishonest, is gratuitous and cannot be sustained.[14]

Within a few years, other states were following Mississippi's example and adding their own wrinkles and innovations. South Carolina's constitution, passed in 1895, exempted voters from taking a literacy test or understanding test if they could show they owned and had paid taxes on property assessed at $300 or more. Louisiana (1898) instituted a "grandfather clause" which said that any son or grandson of a voter deemed eligible before 1867 had an automatic right to the franchise. Since blacks were all slaves before 1867, this was a backdoor way of readmitting illiterate or semi-literate whites to a process that otherwise risked excluding them.

With every new constitutional convention, the white supremacists became more confident and more brazen. Senator Tillman said of South Carolina's understanding clause, "Some poisons in small doses are very salutary and valuable medicines." When the Virginia state senator Carter Glass was asked about discrimination in his state's 1901 constitution, he replied: "Discrimination! Why, that is precisely what we propose; that exactly is what this convention was elected for."[15]

However ambiguous their wording, there was no doubting the racial abuses that went on in the new constitutions' name. Some years after the rules kicked in, a teacher in Birmingham, Alabama, took the trouble to memorize the preamble to the state constitution but failed the qualifying test because she skipped a single word. A more cynical voter who was asked for the meaning of the term *habeas corpus* famously responded, "Habeas corpus—that means this black man ain't gonna register today."[16]

Over time, the process did not even get as far as testing. Once Democratic Party domination over the region was established, a new form of exclusion was cooked up—the all-white primary. The Fifteenth

Amendment had prohibited the systematic exclusion of blacks from general elections, but it did not apply to primaries, which were strictly intra-party affairs. Since the South was now a one-party fiefdom, however, the primary was the only election that counted, and restricting it to whites restricted overall participation to a small club of good ol' boys.

It's worth emphasizing that many lower-income whites were victims of this system as well as blacks. As the Democrats grew more powerful, they also became more conservative and more inclined to bow to corporate interests at the expense of the broader public, independent of skin color. In many states, taxes on the rich were cut and incentives lavished on developers and corporations, while employment opportunities for the poor were sharply restricted. Some Democrats, like William A. Handley of Alabama, saw a distinct economic interest in suppressing votes rather than stealing or buying them. "We want to be relieved of purchasing the Negroes to carry elections," he said.[17]

All this was cheered on by the pro-Democratic press. In 1898, the New Orleans *Daily Picayune* denounced universal suffrage as the "most unwise, unreasonable and illogical notion that was ever connected with any system of government" and said it was as important to exclude "every unworthy white man" from the electoral process as it was "every unworthy Negro."[18] The *Houston Telegraph* in Texas made a similar comparison between "low, groveling" black voters and "the miserable apologies for men with white skins, who exercise the right to vote only because it furnishes them with whiskey."[19] Even with the introduction of the grandfather clause, Louisiana's white voter registration figures fell from 164,000 in 1897 to fewer than 92,000 in 1904. Black registration shrank from 130,000 to just over 1,000 in the same period.[20]

The federal government's response was nothing short of disgraceful. Congress, which had vigorously upheld the rights of black voters during Reconstruction, simply gave up on federal supervision of state and local elections. The Supreme Court, which had a lousy record of defending civil rights, kept repeating—accurately but undemocratically—that the Constitution conferred the right of suffrage on no one. *Plessy v. Ferguson* (1896) endorsed the notion of "separate but equal" status for the races and became the template for more than half a century of segregation. *Williams v. Mississippi* (1898) refused to recognize that Mississippi's new constitution was discriminatory to black voters. In

Giles v. Harris (1903), concerning the voting rights of thousands of Alabamans, the court effectively removed itself from any role in policing elections.[21]

Soon it was open season for demagogues, oligarchs, and dictators, who became so entrenched they barely bothered to campaign for office, because they knew they didn't have to. Paradoxically, the governor most commonly *called* dictator in this period, Huey Long of Louisiana, deserved it the least. Yes, Long resorted to strong-arm tactics and the power of patronage. Yes, he was corrupt and self-serving. But he also smashed the cozy, bigoted network of parish sheriffs who had previously held sway in his state, abolished the poll tax, greatly expanded voter participation among poorer Louisianans, and held the segregationists and Klansmen in deep contempt. Of one Klan leader, he said, "When I call him a son of a bitch I am not using profanity, but am referring to the circumstances of his birth." What made Long threatening was not his authoritarianism (his detractors called him a "tinpot Napoleon") but rather his fearless populism. He gave white Louisianans something the rest of the South scarcely knew during this dark period: a real choice at the ballot box, which they embraced gratefully, his defects be damned.[22]

In 1946, the Evers brothers, Charles and Medgar, rolled up at the courthouse in Decatur, Mississippi, figuring that after seeing combat in World War II they deserved a chance to register to vote. It escaped nobody's attention that the U.S. Army had gone to Europe to oppose a racial ideology dividing the world into natural-born masters and slaves. If it was right to fight the Nazis, why should racial discrimination be allowed to persist at home? The state of Mississippi did not entirely disagree. The state legislature allowed its ingrained loathing of the black man to be tempered by the swell of patriotism and exempted returning soldiers, black and white, from paying the poll tax for two years. And so the Evers brothers tested the waters.

Their white neighbors followed them incredulously to the courthouse, where at length one of them snarled, "Who you niggers think you are?"

Charles Evers responded: "We've grown up here. We've fought for this country, and we should register."[23]

Their applications were received in stunned silence. Later, when Charles tried to vote, he was turned away by a gang of white men brandishing guns. Still, some kind of point had been made, and the campaign to restore black voting rights was under way.

The shift in attitudes after the war turned entrenched segregationists like Eugene Talmadge in Georgia and Senator Theodore G. Bilbo in Mississippi into dinosaurs more or less overnight, and they found themselves fighting last-ditch battles for things they had long taken for granted. As he ran for reelection as Georgia governor in 1946, Talmadge issued a warning that "wise Negroes will stay away from the white man's ballot boxes." Bilbo railed furiously against Mississippi's poll tax repealers, calling them "Negro lovers" who would go straight to hell. "You know and I know what's the best way to keep the nigger from voting," he told one rally. "You do it the night before the election. I don't have to tell you any more than that."[24]

It proved to be the final campaign for both men. Talmadge died before Election Day and was replaced on the ballot by his son, whose narrow victory relied on a purge of thousands of hostile voters from the rolls to counter a surge in black turnout. Bilbo faced a revolt by Senate Republicans who threatened not to seat him because of his openly racist views. Before the matter could come to a head, however, he fell ill and spent the next several months dying of cancer of the jaw.

Nationally, the tide had been changing for some time. Franklin Roosevelt never quite dared challenge the hegemony of the Southern wing of his party because he needed their votes, but he made sure government aid reached the black population during the Great Depression, and he instituted a system of annual crop-restriction referenda that he opened to cotton operators, tenants, and sharecroppers irrespective of race. His Fair Employment Practices Committee insisted that wartime armaments factories hire all races on an equal basis, causing disquiet in white supremacist strongholds from South Carolina to Long Beach, California. Roosevelt also backed moves to abolish the poll tax, which disappeared in Florida in 1937 and in Georgia in 1945, having previously been scrapped in Louisiana and North Carolina. The biggest reform of his tenure, however, came from the Supreme Court, which woke up from its century-long slumber on racial issues and, in a landmark 1944 ruling, declared the white primary to be unconstitutional. In response, the most conservative states threatened to do away with primaries altogether, but their efforts bogged down in legal complications, and the threat went away.

Harry Truman was considerably bolder than his predecessor, integrating the navy in 1946 and the rest of the armed forces two years later. His 1946 Commission on Higher Education recommended repealing segregation altogether, as did the U.S. Commission on Civil Rights, which Truman founded, in a landmark report entitled *To Secure These Rights*. Truman consciously broke a Democratic taboo on challenging the Solid South, watched the Dixiecrats wave good-bye to the rest of the party, and almost lost the 1948 election as a result. He did reap some political dividends; black voter registration quadrupled over his eight years as president. But the numbers remained disappointingly low—more than three-quarters of Southern blacks remained unregistered—because of continuing intimidation and violence, and the legacy of decades of systematic repression.[25]

The rapidly changing postwar world made some sort of break with the past almost inevitable. If black veterans felt empowered after World War II, they felt doubly so after Korea, the first conflict with a fully integrated military. The establishment of United Nations headquarters on American soil in 1946 and the publication of a Universal Declaration of Human Rights two years later shone an international spotlight on the South like never before. As a subsequent brief on segregation in public schools filed by the attorney general's office explained, it was now a matter of national security: "Racial discrimination furnishes grist for the Communist propaganda mills, and it raises doubt even among friendly nations as to the intensity of our devotion to the democratic faith."[26]

It was not just liberals who felt this way. One of the more outspoken advocates of reform, at least at that time, was a certain anticommunist Republican congressman from California named Richard Nixon.[27] When, in 1957, the school district in Little Rock, Arkansas, refused to abide by the Supreme Court's *Brown v. Board of Education* desegregation ruling and blocked nine black students from entering Central High School, President Eisenhower and Nixon, now his vice president, sent federal troops south of the Mason-Dixon line for the first time in eighty years to enforce the law. Thereafter, the Eisenhower administration and the Democratic Senate, led by Lyndon Johnson, fell over each other to enact one piece of civil rights legislation after another. The Republicans wanted to win back the black vote it once claimed as its own, and the Democrats—especially white Southerners like Johnson—wanted to demonstrate they were now Roosevelt's party of the working man, not a cabal of racist bigots.

The civil rights movement led by Martin Luther King Jr. fed off this political energy and brought it into sharp focus. King's civil disobedience campaigns, the Birmingham church bombings, the March on Washington, and the Selma protest gave the Johnson administration the moral imperative it needed to sweep away the legal apparatus of segregation and grant full electoral rights to all eligible adults regardless of race, education, or literacy—thus closing the loophole that the Fifteenth Amendment had left so gapingly open. Even before passage of the Voting Rights Act (VRA) in 1965, the march toward progress had spurred an increase in black voter registration from 20 percent in 1952 to 35 percent.[28] In response, it also spurred attempts by the Republican Party to mount mass challenges to black voter eligibility, including a notorious nationwide effort known as Operation Eagle Eye.[29] President Johnson knew his party would end up losing much of the old white South but, like Truman before him, hoped he could make up the numbers with a groundswell of new black voters. The VRA did not lack in audaciousness; it lowered a remarkably effective beam on almost a century of ingrained racial discrimination and gave the Justice Department extraordinary enforcement tools rarely granted by Congress before or since.[30] Initially, Johnson's calculations paid off as registration continued to soar[31] and turnout, encouraged by the dispatch of federal election monitors and Washington's new powers of scrutiny over electoral laws in states with the worst voting rights records, hit its highest point in decades.

Any hopes of a quick end to America's tortured racial history were quickly dashed, however. Five days after Johnson signed the Voting Rights Act, riots broke out in the black Los Angeles suburb of Watts and soon spread to major cities across the country—Baltimore, Washington, and Detroit. The message was plain: voting rights were a good start, but nowhere near enough. The legal segregation that had existed in the South was mirrored by a de facto segregation in housing and schools across the country, especially in big cities where a swelling black population scared many white residents into fleeing for the suburbs. Voting, on its own, did nothing to change that, and neither did Justice Department oversight of new election laws in the South. In many jurisdictions, North and South, the Democratic Party fought as hard against its own black candidates as the Republicans did—as exemplified by the monumental struggle Richard Hatcher waged in Gary, Indiana, in 1967 to become the country's first black mayor in the face of death threats, financial pressures, attempts by both parties to curb black voter registration, officially sanctioned absentee vote fraud, and ballot stuffing.[32] The political fortunes of African Americans undoubtedly improved, and improved dramatically, but it was far from the end of the story.

Conservative ideologues made sporadic attempts to weaken or overturn some of the key provisions of the VRA during the Nixon and Reagan presidencies, but a bipartisan consensus in Congress reliably stepped in to defend the act and, if anything, expand its scope when it came up for periodic renewal.[33] It was hardly a golden age for black voters, however. The primary electoral weapon wielded against them, much as it had been after the Civil War, was the redrawing of electoral districts at state and local levels. Since African Americans tended to live in the same neighborhoods, it was relatively easy to "pack" them into small numbers of homogenous districts, thus minimizing their influence, or else "crack" their neighborhoods—that is, split them apart—so they would be attached to different white-majority districts and fail to have their voices heard at all.[34] Section 5 of the VRA gave the Justice Department veto power over any new electoral arrangement proposed in the old Confederate states, but packing and cracking were practiced in the North as well as the South, so the tolerance level was relatively high. That helps explain how Arkansas, a state where blacks made up just under half the population, managed to avoid sending an African American to Congress for several decades.

Too often, the Democratic Party took black votes for granted, knowing that the Republican Party was even less appealing, and approved policies damaging to minorities and the poor—such as NAFTA or Bill Clinton's bills on crime and welfare reform—in the face of heated opposition from its own Black Caucus.[35]

At the state and county levels, single-member district systems were replaced in many states with at-large elections, making it much harder for black-majority wards or counties to win black representation. Offices that looked likely to fall into the hands of African Americans were sometimes abolished or turned into appointed posts instead of elected ones. A handful of states saw a revival of runoff elections, a tactic first employed after Reconstruction to block the path of black or progressive candidates who came out ahead on the first round. Since runoffs usually saw a precipitous decline in turnout, they were also an effective vote-suppression mechanism.

A flurry of lawsuits filed in the early 1990s challenged the legality of packing and cracking, denouncing them as a form of "racial gerrymandering." Mostly these were brought by Republicans using arguments of convenience to challenge Democrat-organized redistricting maps, and they generated mixed feelings among African American politicians and activists. A majority on the Rehnquist Supreme Court handed down two rulings, *Shaw v. Reno* (1993) and *Shaw v. Hunt* (1996), that gave voters the right to challenge any redistricting plan they could show to have been decided "predominantly" on racial grounds. Justice Sandra Day O'Connor, writing for the majority, expressed alarm at a North Carolina district drawn so tightly to create an African American majority that it even split a freeway down the middle; she found that such redistricting plans bore "an uncomfortable resemblance to political apartheid."[36] A number of voting rights activists welcomed these findings, even if they had misgivings about the ideology motivating the conservative majority and the court's seeming lack of concern about gerrymandering when it did *not* involve the creation of majority-minority districts. Democratic Party stalwarts saw the issue in more partisan terms. They worried about the threat the rulings posed to existing safe black districts and the creation of new ones in historically underrepresented areas, in much the same way that the court's subsequent rulings striking down affirmative action in universities made them worry about continuing African American access to higher education.

Such ideological battle lines might be with us still, were it not for a far bigger threat to black suffrage that has dwarfed all else: the dramatic rise in the prison population, which has not only had a disproportionate effect on African Americans but also deprived them of their voting rights in staggering numbers. As of 2015, almost six million Americans were disqualified from participating in elections because of a felony conviction—including one in thirteen otherwise eligible black voters.[37] Those figures are roughly six times higher than they were in 1980—a startlingly rapid trend. In Florida, which has by far the worst record of any state, 23.3 percent of black voters are disqualified, including almost one-third of black men.[38]

There's no pretty way to look at these figures, which have drawn criticism from the United Nations Human Rights Committee and a chorus of international observers even as they have been underplayed in the mainstream U.S. media. If just *former* felons had been allowed to vote in 2000, Al Gore would have most likely carried Florida by about sixty thousand votes. Conversely, if today's incarceration rates had existed in 1960, Richard Nixon would have won the popular vote against John F. Kennedy and possibly the electoral college, too.[39] More African Americans are in the prison system today than were enslaved in 1850.[40] All but fifteen of the states impose voting restrictions on convicts after they complete their sentences. Just two, Maine and Vermont, follow international practice and allow convicted criminals to keep their right to vote even while incarcerated.

The imprisonment of African Americans even affects district boundaries, because the U.S. Census counts prisoners as residents of where they are being held—often rural white communities—not the places they come from. Much as slaves did under the federal ratio, African American convicts thus bolster the political representation of white conservatives while being denied any political voice of their own.[41]

The Ohio State law professor Michelle Alexander has memorably dubbed this state of affairs a "new Jim Crow" because of the justice system's vastly disproportionate impact on African Americans, something that even the election of the country's first black president has been unable to stop. "In an era of colorblindness," Alexander has written, "it is no longer socially permissible to use race, explicitly, as a justification for discrimination, exclusion, and social contempt. So we don't. Rather than rely on race, we use our criminal justice system to label people of color 'criminals' and then engage in all the practices we supposedly left behind."[42]

Ever since the dismantling of the old Jim Crow, black voters have suffered a variety of indignities in the voting arena—in the big Northern cities as much as in the former Confederate states. They have been deterred in numerous ways from registering to vote, misled by flyers and phone calls about where and when to cast a ballot, warned that they risk arrest at the polling station if they have outstanding warrants, even for minor offenses like a parking ticket, forced to travel unusually far to polling stations with too many voters and too few voting machines, and improperly deprived of their right to a provisional ballot after their eligibility was challenged. In Southern states like Florida and Texas, they have often been scared off by the mere sight of police officers outside their precincts, or by poll watchers dressed up as law enforcement officials.[43]

Until recently, the Justice Department's civil rights division was able to keep a close eye on the worst of these abuses, either by stepping in to prevent discriminatory state laws being enacted in the first place or by suing to have them overturned. Then, in 2013, the Supreme Court invalidated parts of the VRA in *Shelby County v. Holder*, lifting the requirement that nine Southern states and a number of counties elsewhere seek Justice Department "preclearance" for new electoral laws that risk penalizing minority voters. Chief Justice John Roberts, who had worked on and off to neuter the VRA since the early 1980s, pointed to the African American in the White House and other officeholders around the country, and to relatively healthy minority voter registration and turnout rates, and argued that the time for extraordinary intervention by the federal government had passed.

Ruth Bader Ginsburg, leading the dissenters, noted that as recently as 2006 Congress had found plentiful "second generation barriers constructed to prevent minority voters from fully participating in the electoral process" and that the number of discriminatory laws modified or dropped under Justice Department pressure had grown, not lessened, over time. Scrapping preclearance, she concluded, was like "throwing away your umbrella in a rainstorm because you are not getting wet."[44] *Shelby* led, predictably, to a flurry of questionable new election laws designed to suppress minority voting, none more insidious or incendiary than the introduction of voter ID requirements, examined in detail in chapters 12 and 13.

As Michelle Alexander has noted, American politicians no longer talk in openly racist terms. If anything, they move swiftly to distance themselves from anyone caught doing so—either because of genuine outrage or because they fear the legal consequences. And so the new tools of voter suppression have been justified, despite ample evidence to the contrary, as righteous, race-neutral weapons against voter fraud. The historical echoes are disturbing. During the first Jim Crow, Southern politicians concluded that invoking fraud and using it as a pretext to suppress the vote was a lot neater, and likely to attract a lot less attention, than lynching and ballot stuffing. Under the new Jim Crow, that mind-set is undergoing a disturbing revival.

7

CHICAGO: THE *OTHER* KIND OF MOB RULE

There was no doubt in the minds of any of us, after the sort of testimony we heard in Chicago, that organized crime and political corruption go hand in hand, and that in fact there could be no big-time organized crime without a firm and profitable alliance between those who run the rackets and those in political control.

—Senator Estes Kefauver[1]

Mr. President, with a little bit of luck and the help of a few close friends, you're going to carry Illinois.

—Chicago's Mayor Daley to John F. Kennedy
on election night, 1960[2]

On the night of September 28, 1920, Alderman Johnny Powers of Chicago's Nineteenth Ward was shaken out of bed by a bomb blast on his front porch. Someone wanted him to know that, after forty-two years as the undisputed boss of the Nineteenth, it might be time to move on. That someone was almost certainly Tony D'Andrea, the Sicilian sewer diggers' union leader, macaroni manufacturers' agent, and president of the secretive Unione Siciliana, also known as the Black Hand, who planned to unseat "Johnny Da Pow" at an upcoming election. The Nineteenth had once been all Irish, but now it was 80 percent Italian. With Prohibition just under way, there was money to be made from bootlegging and gambling if the Italians could just muscle in on Powers's turf. But Powers had no plans to go quietly, or at all.[3]

Eleven days before the election another bomb exploded, this time at a crowded D'Andrea rally, punching a three-foot hole in an auditorium wall and injuring seventeen people. D'Andrea's campaign headquarters blew up soon after, along with the home of one of his lieutenants. It wasn't long before gunmen and heavies were roving the streets, beating people up and standing guard outside candidates' homes. The Powers campaign accused D'Andrea of bombing his own side to bring out the sympathy vote, but produced no supporting evidence. D'Andrea appealed to the Cook County state's attorney, Robert Crowe, who proposed tougher sentencing guidelines for acts of political violence, but otherwise sat on his hands.

On Election Day, three of Powers's campaign workers, including an election judge and a precinct captain, were kidnapped and held until the vote was over. The police arrested fifty people before lunchtime—though not the kidnappers—and found two hundred pounds of dynamite in an abandoned building. When the counting was done, Powers was declared the winner by a wafer-thin margin of 435 votes—not that anybody believed the figures, or showed any inclination to give up the fight. A month after the election, two of Powers's precinct captains were gunned down. Two months after that, D'Andrea was hit by thirteen shotgun blasts as he arrived home from dinner with his friend and fellow politician Diamond Joe Esposito. The police later recovered a freshly sawed off shotgun from the apartment across the hall, along with a hat and a $20 bill stuffed into the band. "For flowers," said a hastily scribbled note.

So began an extraordinary decade of political violence in Chicago. D'Andrea died with vengeance on his lips, although the hit man he urged to kill Powers, Two-Gun Johnny Guardino, was felled himself before he could carry out the deed. The machine guns hardly stopped rattling, in the Nineteenth Ward or anywhere else. Chicago's political leadership thought at first it could do business with the bootleggers and racketeers. Then, in 1923, Chicago's larger-than-life mayor Big Bill Thompson was unseated, and his Democratic successor, William Dever, went into full crackdown mode, shuttering four thousand saloons and revoking sixteen thousand business licenses in his first year alone.

That only pushed the bootleggers further underground and made their syndicate so powerful nobody could touch it. As James Merriner wrote in his history of corruption in Chicago,[4] the Mob graduated from City Hall's joint venture to its parent company.

Electoral corruption also reached new heights. It's not as though Chicagoans were unused to vote buying and ballot stuffing. On the contrary, they'd been pioneers in the field, ever since John "Bathhouse" Coughlin and Michael "Hinky Dink" Kenna, the colorful aldermen of the First Ward, perfected the art of rounding up vagrants on Election Day and offering them limitless food and booze for a day of intensive repeat voting. Chicago had even developed its own vocabulary—"stingers" (the local term for repeaters), "ghost voters" (those casting ballots in the name of the dead), and "four-legged voting" (when a party heavy came into the booth to offer some helpful pointers).[5]

Prohibition, though, was something else entirely. The roles of ward boss and crime boss merged, which meant the furious political struggles of the period were also an expression of gang warfare. The Republicans were split between Big Bill Thompson's faithful and protégés of the reformist senator Charles Deneen, a feckless but essentially honest former prosecutor and Illinois governor. The Democrats, reflecting broader national trends, were split between a populist wing, which embraced Chicago's thick goulash of immigrant constituencies, and a reactionary rump, which considered blacks and foreigners to be corrosive to the moral good. Both parties contained supporters and opponents of Prohibition, and supporters and opponents of good-government reform.

The violence shaking the Nineteenth spread citywide by the time of the 1926 Republican primary, a contest so tarnished by violence and fraud it forced an official response. Armed gangs traveled from precinct to precinct, slugging poll workers who got in their way and bundling rivals into the backseats of limousines for safekeeping until the vote was over. An audit of the Twentieth Ward, which was rapidly eclipsing the Nineteenth as the city's most troublesome, revealed close to three thousand votes cast in the names of nonresidents, nonvoters, children, the dead, or repeaters. In the sixteenth precinct of the Forty-Second Ward, notorious for its crooked election workers, the Citizens' Association demanded a partial recount and soon discovered rampant ballot stuffing organized by the local ward heeler.

The reformist judge Edmund Jarecki heard dozens of electoral fraud cases, at one point canceling his summer vacation so he could get through the caseload. By September 1927, he had presided over 169 trials, in which twenty-three defendants—many of them election workers—were found guilty and fifteen were sentenced to prison terms. When a legal technicality threatened to invalidate eleven of the sentences, Jarecki appealed to Robert Crowe, the state's attorney, to iron out the glitch with a simple rewrite. Crowe, rapidly developing a reputation as the gangsters' gutless stooge, declined.

Bill Thompson returned to the mayor's office in 1927 and formed a secret alliance with Al Capone's outfit. The police were all paid off, as were the politicians. Chicagoans called it the Big Fix, but it did nothing to temper the violence. The city's murder rate averaged one a day. More than sixty bombs exploded in the run-up to the so-called Pineapple Primary in 1928, a contest whose biggest fight pitted Crowe[6] against a reformist judge for state's attorney. The homes of two Thompson loyalists were attacked first. Then Senator Deneen and Crowe's primary opponent, John Swanson, had their houses bombed. Tony D'Andrea's former lieutenant Diamond Joe Esposito was pumped full of holes in front of his bodyguards on a Nineteenth Ward sidewalk. The motivation for these attacks was murky at best, but the gangsters appeared to be turning on each other as much as on their political enemies.

With every new explosion, Crowe lost ground with the voters and with the criminal justice lobbying groups that had initially endorsed him. Election Day was as bloody as expected—a parade of "names to be reckoned with in games where pistols are trumps," as the *Chicago Daily News* described it.[7] Poll workers and precinct captains were threatened with shotguns, kidnapped, and, in a handful of cases, shot and killed. An enraged electorate refused to stay away from the polls, however—they had reached their breaking point and threw out Crowe along with every other candidate riding Big Bill Thompson's coattails.

The head of the Chicago Crime Commission launched an investigation into the Pineapple Primary, indicting twenty people on charges of assault, kidnapping, conspiracy to commit murder, and voter fraud. Seventeen went to trial, and sixteen were convicted, including a state senator and assorted saloon owners and brothel keepers. The Thompson administration struggled on for three more years, but its authority was largely gone, and reformers were now in the ascendant. In 1930, citizens' groups petitioned for the removal of the chair of the Board of Election Commissioners after an investigation of fifteen city wards revealed that more than three hundred precinct officers had police records for crimes ranging from murder, assault and battery, armed robbery, and bombing to burglary, rape, gambling, prostitution, and embezzlement. "For Chicago Thompson has meant filth, corruption, idiocy and bankruptcy," the *Chicago Tribune* commented as he bowed out at last. "He has given our city an international reputation for moronic buffoonery, barbaric crime, triumphant hoodlumism, unchecked graft and a dejected citizenship. . . . He made Chicago a byword for the collapse of American civilization."[8]

The corruption did not end with Thompson's removal, however. His replacement, Tony Cermak, was not interested in indulging the reformers, only in replacing the worn-out Republican machine with an equally ruthless but more effective Democratic one. "Tough Tony" pieced together a winning coalition by uniting Chicago's disparate immigrant communities and labor unions, and campaigned to end Prohibition so that the wealth generated by the rackets could start flowing back in the city's direction.

The violence ebbed, but corruption did not. A 1934 report by the Women's Civic Council complained that large numbers of convicted criminals were being hired to serve as election judges and clerks, and votes were being sold for fifty cents each, just as they had been in the days of Hinky Dink Kenna. A follow-up criminal investigation found that Democratic Party operatives were copying the signatures of drunks and vagrants off flophouse registration books, casting ballots on behalf of noncitizens and the dead, and either "running up the count" on Election Day by adding to their side's tally or "leveling the count" by removing votes from the other side. Ninety-nine people were convicted and thirty-seven sent to prison.

Cermak himself did not live to see the trials, because he ended up on the wrong end of two bullets in Miami, where he had gone to recuperate from dysentery. There, he ran into a newly elected President Roosevelt, who many assumed to have been the intended target of the gunman, Giuseppe Zangara. In Chicago, though, plenty of people were convinced Zangara had hit exactly who he was gunning for. Why else would Cermak have two holes so perfectly inscribed on his chest? One widely circulated story had a ward boss back in Chicago asking an aide whether Cermak had died yet. When the aide said he didn't know, the boss retorted, "Well, put a hunnert under his nose, and if he doesn't twitch, then you know he's gone."[9]

Chicago was far from the only city where a corrupt political machine survived the misguided late-nineteenth-century efforts at reform. Prohibition was a boon for bosses everywhere from Jersey to San Francisco; even after Prohibition, many of them benefited from the distribution of federal aid during the Great Depression. Kansas City was, in many ways, a miniature Chicago, with its own bootleggers, gun-toting gangsters, and freewheeling underground jazz clubs. Its police force was so corrupt it was eventually taken over by the state. The city payroll was stuffed with three thousand people who didn't have municipal jobs, and there was enough electoral fraud in the wake of the 1936 general election to generate 278 criminal cases and 259 convictions.[10] In 1946, a notorious Kansas City gangster and election fixer, Morris "Snag" Klein, raided the county courthouse under cover of darkness, blew open a safe, and removed evidence supporting the fraud indictments of sixty-one people, himself included, relating to a dirty congressional primary.[11]

In many ways, the voting restrictions and charter reforms pushed by the Mugwumps made the city machines stronger, because it became easier for them to control the electorate and hold on to power. In many big cities, one party enjoyed uncontested dominance over the other, making the job easier still. Old Baltimore hands recall how voting machines would be induced to "break down" during the hours most voters were at work and then magically right themselves when the union boys showed up in force. Election officials who threatened to do their jobs instead of waving in the machine candidates would have Ex-Lax slipped into their coffee so they would have to leave the counting room.[12]

Chicago was an anomaly, one of the few places in the country where Republicans and Democrats were evenly pitted against each other. Likewise, Illinois as a whole was one of the few genuinely competitive states in presidential elections. That heightened the stakes for politicians of all stripes, not least because Chicago was one of the most enduringly corrupt cities in the country—a result, perhaps, of the dizzying speed with which it developed from a glorified village to a city of four million people in less than a century. The electoral bureaucracy alone was estimated to be worth fifty thousand to one hundred thousand votes per election.[13] In the 1890s, the visiting British clergyman William Stead had viewed Chicago's rapidly multiplying corruptions as positively satanic and said it would take nothing short of a new Jesus Christ to clean them up. When Big Bill Thompson first became mayor in 1915, the spoils system "swept over the city like a noxious blight," according to the reformist and onetime mayoral candidate Charles Edward Merriam, and Chicago became perhaps the "only completely corrupt city in America."[14] Even the World Series was not sacred, as the 1919 "Black Sox" scandal proved.

The bloody battles of the 1920s were, in part, a fight to establish a workable political machine that could perpetuate itself indefinitely. After the excesses of Big Bill Thompson, Tony Cermak and the Democrats created just such a machine, and it remained in place, with only the briefest of interruptions, until the tail end of the Daley era almost half a century later. The good-government types never stood a chance.

The machine had more in common with Boss Tweed's New York than any more contemporary form of government. Like Plunkitt of Tammany Hall, ward bosses took professional satisfaction in performing small acts of personal consideration to help constituents, figuring they'd get their payback come election time. The patronage system was estimated to be worth three hundred thousand votes in all, so competition was fierce. The machine would typically spend a further $20,000 per ward, either in the form of straight bribery to individual voters or, more commonly, in payoffs to poll workers. One precinct captain named Sidney "Short Pencil" Lewis was notorious for filling in blank ballots and spoiling unfavorable ones with a piece of lead wedged into a fingernail.[15]

Bosses like Vito Marzullo of the Twenty-Fifth Ward couldn't imagine playing it any other way. "While reformers want to build a new city, a new church and a new country," Marzullo said, "if you give them ten dollars they could not get a dog out of the pound."[16]

Things were as corrupted as ever when Tennessee senator Estes Kefauver's committee on organized crime visited in 1950. "Every example of rottenness which we found anywhere in the United States was duplicated, in some form or another, in the capital of the Capone mob," Kefauver concluded. Daniel Gilbert, an improbably affluent police captain, told the committee he had taken bets on every city election since 1921 and never lost. In some races, his winnings were as high as $10,000.

"Is that legal?" Kefauver asked him.

"Well, I would say it was legal if a fellow wants to make a bet on an election," came the disingenuous reply.[17]

Five years later, Richard Daley, chair of the Cook County Democratic Party, became mayor despite being denounced by his reformist challenger, Robert Merriam, as "the front man for a pack of jackals who have been feeding off the city for the past twenty-four years." Daley wasn't bothered. He won easily and celebrated by turning his election-night vote tally, 708,222, into his vanity license plate.[18]

Outside Chicago, Mayor Daley is known for two things: unleashing his notoriously brutal police force on antiwar demonstrators outside the Democratic National Convention in 1968, and stealing the 1960 presidential election for John F. Kennedy. Whether he actually *did* steal the election, or how he did it, are not questions that were investigated too closely at the time. The popularity of JFK's presidency and the shock of his assassination made such matters distasteful for the better part of a generation, not least because his challenger, Richard Nixon, was reckoned to have got his due—perhaps more than his due, in the light of subsequent events—when he ran again for the White House in 1968 and won.

Still, the election stank from top to bottom. Kennedy calculated that he needed Illinois because without it he would have been dangerously dependent on the Deep South, where twenty-six segregationist electors were threatening to bolt the party ticket if they did not receive significant concessions on federal civil rights policy. (Fourteen of them ended up choosing Harry Byrd, the veteran Dixiecrat from Virginia, instead of Kennedy.) It was a startlingly close election, a near toss-up in a dozen states or more, with just 118,000 votes finally separating the candidates in the national popular vote. Without Illinois or Texas, which Kennedy also clung to by his fingernails, there was a risk that a presidential election would be thrown into the House of Representatives for the first time in 136 years.

Statewide, Illinois proved agonizingly close, with Kennedy edging ahead by just 9,400 votes. That seemed lucky. In Chicago, his margin was 456,000, on a reported turnout of 89.3 percent. That wasn't luck; those were near-mythical figures, even by the standards of a city with notoriously broad shoulders. True, Daley's margin the year before had been almost 470,000, but that was against a token opponent in a race nobody seriously expected him to lose. Four years before that, against Merriam, Daley's edge had been just 120,000. Was it credible that Chicago voters—who included plenty of Republicans and swing voters— were so single-mindedly in the Kennedy camp, when they knew their state was the pivot on which the presidential race would rest?[19]

Many didn't think so. Even before the election, the *Daily News* had reported on thousands of invalid names showing up on registration lists. The paper also discovered that 177 of the 180 appointees to the city's Board of Election Commissioners were Democrats. In response to these stories, an outfit called the Committee for Honest Elections put in a request to send observers into polling stations. Mayor Daley accused the committee chairman, David Brill, of partisan Republican bias and turned him down.

After the election, it was another journalist, Earl Mazo of the *New York Herald Tribune,* who made the most noise alleging vote fraud in Kennedy's favor. One Chicago precinct, he wrote, had returned 397 votes from just 376 voters. Other precincts had recorded the votes of the dead, or allowed people to cast more than one ballot, or allowed their own poll workers to stuff ballots. Mazo did not limit his ambitions to Chicago. In Texas, where he suspected Kennedy's running mate, Lyndon Johnson, of resorting to some of the same dirty tricks that had got him elected to the Senate in 1948, he alleged that Democratic Party operatives had paid off the poll tax of poor Mexican Americans and dragged them less than willingly to the polls.[20]

All these stories were most likely true, but Mazo had two significant strikes against him. The first was that he had a personal relationship with Richard Nixon and called him his friend, so his impartiality was questionable at best. The second was that his evidence was strictly anecdotal, adding up to no more than a few dozen votes, nowhere near enough to overturn the result.

More evidence surfaced after the election was settled. A special prosecutor dug up enough dirt to indict 677 Chicagoans on vote fraud charges—although he never got the chance to present his evidence because the cases were moved out of the city to the court of a Daley crony in East Saint Louis, who squashed the lot. Many years later, a Pulitzer Prize–winning series in the *Chicago Tribune* uncovered hard evidence that the Daley machine habitually registered vagrants for the purposes of stealing their votes. The paper unearthed stories of uncooperative Republican election judges being locked in police custody on Election Day and ward bosses threatened with expulsion from office if they couldn't come up with the vote totals expected of them.[21]

Perhaps, if these stories had come out in the days and weeks after the election instead of months or years later, they might have triggered a Florida-style post-election showdown. But Nixon was savvy enough to understand he was fighting an unwinnable battle against a political machine dedicated to his defeat. He also understood that even the Chicago machine was not capable of manufacturing nonexistent votes by the tens of thousands. Something else was going on, something he had no leverage over and no realistic opportunity to expose. He could have called for a recount, but most likely it would have been futile. The one recount that did take place, in the race for Cook County state's attorney, shifted only a few hundred votes.[22]

Most likely, the votes for Kennedy *were* there; the question is, how were they generated? Even at a distance of more than half a century we still don't have a precise answer, but we have a pretty good idea. Robert J. McDonnell, a leading Chicago defense attorney specializing in organized crime cases, told the investigative reporter Seymour Hersh that he helped set up a meeting between Joseph Kennedy, the future president's father, and the Mob leader Sam "Mooney" Giancana. McDonnell's understanding was that Giancana mobilized the Mob, and the Mob, by hook or crook, dragged out the required numbers of Chicagoans to deliver Illinois to Kennedy. "They just worked—totally went all out," McDonnell said. "[Kennedy] won it squarely, but he got the vote because of what Mooney had done."[23]

He was not the only one to think so. Frank Sinatra also met Giancana, according to Sinatra's daughter Tina, and talked him into backing Kennedy. It was not an easy sell, because of Bobby Kennedy's tough stance on organized crime. But Giancana was heard on a wiretap offering his support to Kennedy in return for a commitment "to back off from the FBI investigation."[24] Some people believe JFK himself met Giancana over golf. Judith Campbell Exner, who shared a bed with Kennedy and Giancana at different points, wrote in her memoirs that the Mob leader had told her, "Listen, honey, if it wasn't for me your boyfriend wouldn't even be in the White House."[25]

It's hard to say to what extent Mayor Daley was personally involved in any election rigging. It would be naïve to suppose he was unaware of it. The quote at the head of this chapter (which was handed down via Kennedy to the legendary *Washington Post* executive editor Benjamin Bradlee) indicates that Daley knew about the "few close friends" even if he wasn't privy to the details. Certainly, Daley would have been happy to receive a boost to the Democratic Party ticket, because the Republican who posed the greatest threat to him, Benjamin Adamowski, was running for state's attorney, and Daley was anxious to see him defeated— which he was. Adamowski couldn't believe he'd lost, but he, like Nixon, couldn't do a thing about it. As the *Chicago Tribune* put it at the time, once an election in Cook County has been stolen, it stays stolen.

Nixon had another compelling reason not to contest the election: he knew the downstate Republicans were just as capable of shifting vote totals as the Chicago machine, and he didn't want to draw attention to any dishonesty committed on his own behalf. Across Illinois, election night was one big game of chicken, not unlike the big Senate races in Texas in the 1940s, in which one side dared the other to release more results so it could adjust its own figures accordingly. "We're trying to hold back our returns," Mayor Daley told one Kennedy campaign staffer. "Every time we announce two hundred more votes for Kennedy in Chicago, they come up out of nowhere downstate with another three hundred votes for Nixon."[26] If Nixon had kicked up too much of a stink, chances were the Daley machine had enough on him to ruin his reputation and scuttle any chance of a future political career.

Some Republican loyalists refused to forgive or forget the transgressions of 1960. Forty years later, when Mayor Daley's son Bill flew to Florida to head Al Gore's post-election committee, Pennsylvania congressman Curt Weldon vowed he would "use every ounce of energy I have to deny the electors being seated if I believe the political will of the people was thwarted by the son of Mayor Daley of Chicago."[27]

The Nixon loyalists took their cue from the man himself, who nursed a grudge against the Kennedys for the rest of his career. At a Christmas party a few weeks after the election, he was overheard telling several people, "We won, but they stole it from us." In 1968, he set up a fraud squad in Illinois in advance. And when Illinois, once again, failed to report its results the morning after the election, he tried to pressure his opponent, Hubert Humphrey, into conceding anyway.[28] Nixon eventually took the state 43.4 percent to 42.72.

The memory of being cheated in Chicago in 1960 can only have played into the free-for-all illegality that Nixon and his staff orchestrated in the run-up to the 1972 presidential election. Nixon himself admitted, many years later, that payback had been uppermost in his mind. "In this campaign we were finally in a position to have someone doing to the opposition what they had done to us," he wrote in his memoirs, echoing his overall defense that whatever he had done in office, others had done before with impunity. "I told my staff that we should come up with the kind of imaginative dirty tricks that our Democratic opponents used against us and others so effectively in previous campaigns."[29]

These days, most people think of Watergate as a scandal about the abuse of executive power, but the break-in at the Democratic National Committee headquarters that triggered it was all about the election and nailing down Nixon's second term in the White House at any cost. The upshot, in the words of the Senate Watergate Committee chair Sam Ervin, was "to destroy . . . the integrity of the process by which the President of the United States is nominated and elected."[30] If any sitting president has played dirtier in securing reelection, there is no record of it. It has never been clear whether Nixon had direct advance knowledge of the infamous "third-rate burglary"[31] and bugging operation at the Watergate building in downtown Washington. But there's no doubt he planned his reelection campaign with a ruthlessness that promised to overstep the bounds of legality even before he handed matters over to others. "When I am the candidate, I run the campaign," Nixon had said in 1971, words that would come back to haunt him.[32] The election itself proved to be a cakewalk over the antiwar liberal George McGovern, but the fact that McGovern ended up as his opponent at all had much to do with the intrigues Nixon had cooked up with his closest White House associates.

As early as May 1971, according to his chief of staff Bob Haldeman, Nixon thought "we should put permanent tails and coverage on Teddy [Kennedy] and [Maine senator Edmund] Muskie and Hubert [Humphrey] on all the personal stuff, to cover the kinds of things they hit us on in '62: personal finances, family and so forth."[33] These were the Democratic candidates he was most afraid of. Through a reelection committee established outside the White House, the Nixon team funneled hundreds of thousands of dollars in secret funds into an extensive spying, sabotage, and misinformation campaign directed at the Democrats. The Nixon team sent an undercover agent posing as a newspaper reporter to Kennedy's summer retreat in Chappaquiddick with instructions to "catch him in the sack with one of his babes."[34] (It didn't work.) They spread smear stories about Muskie's wife and sent out bogus Muskie campaign literature accusing Humphrey and Henry "Scoop" Jackson of sexual indiscretions. When Muskie, seen as Nixon's strongest challenger, broke down in public and was forced to withdraw from the race, some CIA operatives came to suspect that Nixon's people had also fed a sophisticated form of LSD to the candidate to make him paranoid and unstable.[35]

The operation went far beyond the candidates themselves; it included following their families, disrupting campaign events, seizing confidential campaign files, and investigating the lives of dozens of campaign workers. Messing with the candidates' campaigns from the inside—sending out bogus letters, rearranging schedules, promoting new primary candidates, and generally sowing discord among the Democrats—was infamously dubbed "ratfucking" by the Nixon operative Donald Segretti, a form of foul play that official Washington found profoundly shocking at the time. "I couldn't believe it," one Justice Department attorney told Carl Bernstein of the *Washington Post*. "These are public servants? God. It's nauseating. You're talking about fellows who come from the best schools in the country."[36]

Aside from the Watergate burglary, White House dirty tricksters planned break-ins at the Brookings Institution, the National Archives, and as many as one hundred other locations out of a generalized paranoia about the intentions of those identified as Nixon's enemies. That paranoia, rooted in the ever-deteriorating Vietnam War and the social and political upheavals the war had unleashed, went far beyond concerns about the election, of course. But it infected the electoral process as it did almost everything else. When George Wallace, Alabama's segregationist governor, threatened to split the conservative vote in the South with an independent run at the presidency, Nixon's operatives prevailed on the Internal Revenue Service to audit his state administration and leaked a preliminary document indicating widespread corruption. The institutional pressure eased after Wallace agreed to run on the Democratic Party ticket, not as an independent.[37] Later, after Wallace was shot and almost killed on the campaign trail, Nixon's Plumbers (so called because their primary job was to plug leaks deemed damaging to the administration) made plans, never carried out, to place McGovern campaign literature in an apartment belonging to Wallace's assailant, Arthur Bremer.[38] Likewise, they considered—but never went through with—mugging antiwar demonstrators heading to the 1972 Republican convention in Miami and abducting their leaders to Mexico.

Nixon appeared to believe that as president he could get away with anything, and he bet on an overly trusting public to reject wide-scale presidential malfeasance as inherently preposterous. Back in December 1960, he had told Earl Mazo, "Earl, those are interesting articles you are writing, but no-one steals the presidency of the United States."[39]

On that, he and Mayor Daley could have found a rare point of agreement.

8

THE FALLACY OF THE
TECHNOLOGICAL FIX

The perpetual rush to novelty that characterizes the modern marketplace, with its escalating promise of technological transcendence, is matched by the persistence of pre-formed patterns of life which promise merely more of the same.

—*David F. Noble,* America by Design *(1977)*[1]

Technology alone does not eliminate the possibility of corruption and incompetence in elections; it merely changes the platform on which they may occur.

—*Rebecca Mercuri*[2]

In the early 1970s, the chair of the elections board in Tampa, Florida, found an unusual use for one of the county's hefty lever-operated voting machines. He kept it in his backyard to smoke fish.

Theoretically, Ron Budd's job was to keep an eye on the county elections supervisor, a straggly-bearded eccentric named Jim Fair who ran a thrift store in his spare time, but Budd had been too distracted to notice the "students and hippies with educated minds" that Fair had been taking on as election volunteers. The volunteers drank on the job, left wine bottles lying around the office, and stole loose change from the permanent staff. When the staff complained, Fair had them fired.[3]

Budd's chief distraction, as it turned out, was an overly cozy relationship with the Shoup Voting Machine Co. of upstate New York, which had been providing Hillsborough County with the latest in voting technology—great gear-toothed behemoths with user-friendly levers that were said to be both fraud- and foolproof. In reality, they were all running a scam.

Shortly after Fair started his job in the late 1960s, Shoup informed him that 180 of its machines were obsolete and needed to be replaced, at an extra cost to the county of more than half a million dollars. Fair agreed without a murmur, even though the machines were only a few years old. Shoup took them back for $30 a pop, went through the motions of refurbishing them, and sold them on to Harris County, Texas, for $1,500 each, a markup of 5,000 percent.

A grand jury was convened but found nobody to indict. Then Nixon's attorney general John Mitchell—not a man known for rigorous probity in defense of the public good—stepped in to take personal charge of the investigation. Fair was alarmed enough to go on the run, taking only his pet Weimaraner for company. Later, he claimed he wasn't afraid of prosecution, only of being locked in a mental asylum (which, eventually, he was).

Then the machines stopped working.

They broke down so spectacularly in the 1971 Tampa city elections that the outcome of one council race could not be determined at all. In time, all the dirty secrets spilled out: how Shoup had been writing checks for tens of thousands of dollars to a fictional Tampa city official named Arturo Garcia; how an obliging bank had agreed to cash the checks anyway; how the money had been distributed to several public employees who either were in on the racket or agreed to keep quiet about it.

Ron Budd was the linchpin. Aside from his fiduciary duties with the elections board, he also worked as a private agent who negotiated the deals with Shoup and profited personally from every transaction. He spent the next ten years behind bars. Half a dozen others—county officials and Shoup company employees—were also convicted on charges of bribery and election fraud.

It was far from the only case of its type. The 1970s were to the voting machine business what the Lincoln County wars had once been to the Wild West. Shoup and AVM, the Automatic Voting Machine Co. of Jamestown, New York, were locked in a furious competition for clients, especially since they were feeling the extra pressure of a new, lighter technology, the Votomatic punchcard machine, which threatened to edge both of them out of business. When they couldn't argue the merits of the product they were pushing, they resorted to influence peddling and bribery. "The further east you went, the more corrupt it was," Bob Varni, the founding chairman of the Votomatic company, Computer Election Systems, recalled in 2005.[4]

AVM almost went belly-up in 1973. The chairman of the board, Lloyd Dixon Sr., dropped dead a month after signing the biggest contract in the company's history, a $19 million deal to deliver ten thousand machines to Venezuela. Then the Venezuelans reneged on the contract, lumbering AVM with $13 million in out-of-pocket expenses. Lloyd Dixon Jr., the new chief executive, was soon indicted for bribing election officials in Buffalo, New York, and was forced to resign in disgrace. He was acquitted, but the company's reputation was shot, not least because of lesser bribery scandals in Arkansas and Texas, where the charges stuck. The company's voting machine assets were spun off and left to fend for themselves, eventually reemerging as a major force in the late 1990s under the new name of Sequoia Pacific.[5]

Shoup skirted close to the edge of disaster itself in the wake of the Tampa debacle. The company didn't just have a habit of getting into bed with corrupt elections officials; that was for all intents and purposes its business model, going back to its first big success in Louisiana in the 1950s, when it took advantage of a power struggle between Governor Earl Long and his would-be rival Secretary of State Wade O. Martin to corner the state's voting machine market. By the early 1970s, Shoup and its clients had racked up bribery convictions in Texas, Kentucky, and Illinois. In Philadelphia, one Shoup-associated voting official skipped town rather than face trial, while another, city commissioner Maurice Osser, was acquitted of soliciting bribes from Shoup only to be convicted of accepting $100,000 in a brown envelope from a ballot-printing company.[6]

Bob Varni remembered how, at one point, Shoup lost almost its entire customer service department to the criminal justice system. So he suggested, with some chutzpah, that his company do the job for them. "At first we were rejected," Varni said. "But three or four months later, we got the phone call."[7]

The more the feds cracked down on the older voting machine

companies, the greater the opportunities it opened for Varni and CES. As soon as their customer service team set up shop at Shoup's offices in New Jersey, the first call they made was to the FBI, with an invitation to investigate whatever it wanted. "We all came out of IBM, and nobody at IBM would have thought of passing money over. It didn't enter our minds," Varni said. "We got solicited for 'campaign contributions' from time to time by county supervisors. They wouldn't ask blatantly, but we knew what they were saying. And we just laughed them off. We became the boy scouts of the industry. . . . When the Shoup people started going to jail, everyone loved us."

The Shoups didn't take this challenge lying down. Ransom Shoup Sr. and his son, Ransom II, ran around the country demonstrating how easy it was to rig a punchcard ballot and even earned themselves an invitation to explain it to Congress. They showed how a master punchcard could adjust the vote totals in any given race to a pre-adjusted outcome. They pulled thumbtacks out of their shirt cuffs to punch extra holes to invalidate ballots, a variant on the old short-pencil trick, and described how prepunched ballots could be distributed outside polling stations, a modern version of chain voting.

Their criticisms of the Votomatic were entirely accurate, but at the time most observers saw their posturing as no more than canny business showmanship and couldn't help weighing the evidence they presented against Shoup's growing pile of criminal indictments. Years later, Ransom Shoup II argued that the scandals of the 1970s were the fault of rogue salesmen and shareholders who took advantage of the company's precarious financial position to dictate management practices of their choosing. "It was those kinds of shenanigans that led my father and me to break off and start our own company, and sue to get the family name back," Ransom told *Philadelphia* magazine in 2001. Sure enough, he and his father left the Shoup Voting Machine Co. behind and founded the R.F. Shoup Co. But the trouble didn't stop there.

In 1978, Shoup lever machines in Philadelphia experienced a breakdown during a contentious special election to determine whether Mayor Frank Rizzo should be allowed to break the usual term-limit rules and run for a third term. Federal prosecutors were suspicious because more than three-quarters of the machine failures occurred in predominantly black districts, whose residents were known to be vehemently against extending Rizzo's tenure. (He lost anyway.) An overly trusting U.S. attorney's office asked Ransom Shoup II to come in and investigate. And Shoup reported back that the machines had not been tampered with, just that the models in poorer black neighborhoods were old and poorly maintained.

There the matter might have rested but for a deal Shoup couldn't resist offering to Marge Tartaglione, the formidable city commissioner responsible for administering elections. If she offered Shoup the maintenance contract on Philadelphia's voting machines, Ransom II told her, he would rewrite the report he'd prepared for the U.S. attorney's office to "soften it up some" where she was concerned. His bad luck was that Tartaglione was already in trouble with the law—she'd been arrested on Election Day for making a suspect last-minute change in the location of a sensitive city polling station—and was wearing a wire to their lunch meeting. He ended up with a $10,000 fine and a three-year suspended prison sentence.[8]

In the 1980s, Shoup became one of the early pioneers of direct recording electronic, or DRE, machines, which the company hoped would leapfrog the Votomatics to become the new standard technology. According to Roy Lawyer, Shoup's overseas marketing director, these were immediately popular with foreign dictators and autocrats who invariably asked, "Can the things be rigged?" In Nigeria, President Alhaji Shehu Shagari told Lawyer he had four specifications. The machines had to be able to travel by canoe, to be strapped on a camel, to be nailed to a tree, and, finally, to be foolproof and tamperproof. The fourth specification, however, was not to be fulfilled until *after* Shagari had won the next election. As things turned out, Shagari was overthrown before an election could take place.[9]

In 1957, AVM put out a delightfully cheesy film, *Behind the Freedom Curtain*, which promoted lever machines as a technological wonder that would help America defeat communism, corruption, and every other evil under the sun. Paper ballots, the film insisted, were as antiquated as the horse and buggy, prone to clerical error and mischief of all kinds, whereas machines came with a built-in guarantee that the vote cast would be the vote ultimately counted. "Mechanical counters cannot get tired, cannot get cranky, cannot forget," the earnest narrator explains, over images of oversized paper ballots being ripped, filled incorrectly, and stamped VOID by indifferent clerks lost in a fog of coffee and cigarette smoke.[10]

Ostensibly, the film addresses the voter as the end user and ultimate consumer of AVM's products. But the filmmakers knew exactly who made the decision to buy voting equipment, and it wasn't the people pulling the levers on polling day. They made sure their message would resonate with elections board members and precinct workers, telling them how much money was to be saved after the initial capital outlay, how easily the results could be generated, and how definitive they were. Recounts were not just unnecessary but logistically impossible.

Back in the real world, lever machines were never particularly user-friendly, for voters or administrators. They were bulky and intricate, with thousands of cogs and counters inside each one. They were also irritatingly hard to store, transport, and maintain. In the Louisiana bayous they had to be dragged by barge from the warehouse to the polling stations.[11] Worst of all, they were not remotely immune to mistakes, or to mischief. Earl Long, Louisiana's governor in the 1950s, boasted that with the right election commissioners he could get the machines to sing "Home Sweet Home." Any time voters around the country were given a choice between paper and a lever machine, they chose paper.[12]

The first switch-and-lever machine had been pioneered by Thomas Edison shortly after the end of the Civil War, but at that time ballots were still issued by political parties and nobody was interested. Once the Australian ballot was introduced, lever machines became a Mugwump's dream: shiny, new, and giving all outward appearance of tidiness and efficiency. A safe maker named Jacob Myers came up with the first commercially viable model in 1892 in Lockport, New York, and they were an immediate success.

Appearance, though, was not the same thing as reality, and authorities who spent tens of thousands of dollars on the machines soon came to regret it. Officials found them too unwieldy to transport and operate, too complicated for voters to understand, too expensive to buy in large quantities, and too difficult to maintain. By 1929, lever machines had been purchased in twenty-four states, only to be discarded again in fifteen of them. As Lewis Mumford was to write a few years later, modern societies have "the careless habit of attributing to mechanical improvements a direct role as instruments of culture and civilization."[13] It's a lesson we're still struggling to learn almost a century later, as the widespread buyer's remorse over touchscreen computer voting attests.

The Shoups were in the voting machine game almost from the start. Samuel Shoup, the family patriarch whose inventions included the paper napkin dispenser, studied Myers's invention and wheeled out a prototype of his own in 1895. Even then, the family had a knack for salesmanship, telling clients the machines were indestructible. As the decades went by, they said Shoup machines had been shot at in Kentucky and dynamited in Tennessee and still survived. Card sharks and FBI agents had tried to find a way to rig them, they said, but had never succeeded.

None of that was true. Lever machines were filled with moving parts, and mechanical failures became a problem everywhere they were used. "We had one once that fell onto the hood of a Buick," a New York technician told the *Los Angeles Times* in 2000. "A car has 5,000 parts; a voting machine has 27,000 parts. If a guy drops it from a moving truck, it goes out of alignment. If it's put out of alignment enough, it won't work."[14] What worked to Shoup's advantage, though, was the fact that lever machines, like DREs, generally hid their flaws from their users. The internal counters could malfunction and voters and administrators would never know, because there was no backup verification system. They could be flawless, just as long as people were induced to believe they were.

Corrupt election judges and poll workers, however, saw them differently. Lever machines proved to be very good for casting fraudulent votes in other people's names. In Louisiana this version of ballot stuffing became known as "ringing the bell," because the Shoup machines would jingle every time someone pulled the final lever.[15] They could also be preprogrammed or otherwise tampered with. Michael Ian Shamos, a voting equipment inspector in Pennsylvania, wrote in 1993 that lever machines "can be subtly altered so that a fraction of votes for a particular candidate will not register."[16] In Tampa, the man sent in to clean up after Jim Fair and Ron Budd, an insurance salesman named Jim Sebesta, discovered a way to switch totals between rival candidates with little more than a paper clip. "In a very short period of time—maybe ten seconds—in a particular race in a particular precinct, you could rig it," Sebesta recalled. "When we confronted Shoup with that, they went ballistic."[17]

In 1979, a candidate for governor of Louisiana, Louis Lambert, qualified for the runoff only because of fourteen Shoup machines whose vote totals magically shifted in his favor well after the polls closed. There was widespread speculation that the machines had been tampered with, but nobody could figure out how it had been done until Peppi Bruneau, a young state representative, hauled a Shoup 1023 machine into a public hearing and gave a demonstration. He needed just two tools, a screwdriver and a cuticle stick, to pull off a strip of Plexiglas, prod in the right place, and reverse the totals of two candidates of his choosing. "It was incredibly simple to do," Bruneau said.[18]

Lambert had been the Democratic Party's anointed candidate, so the pressure to keep the fraud quiet was intense. The technician who taught Bruneau how the fix worked, Jerome Sauer, had tried to bring it to the attention of Louisiana's commissioner of elections only to be threatened with arrest if he so much as touched a Shoup machine again. Bruneau issued a subpoena to have the Shoup machine delivered to the state legislature, over the commissioner's vigorous objections, and conducted the demonstration himself so Sauer would stay out of trouble. Afterward, it was agreed that Shoup would fit its machines with thicker, wider Plexiglas. There were no hard feelings toward the company, which was not suspected of involvement in the scam. Even Bruneau said, "I have no problem with the Shoup machine per se if it's engineered right."

Later that same year, the commissioner of elections, Douglas Fowler, was succeeded by his son, Jerry Fowler, who ended up pleading guilty in 1999 to participating in a kickback scam involving AVM's successor company, Sequoia, a voting machine salesman from New Jersey, and cash stuffed into unmarked envelopes. As with the Shoups, certain colorful aspects of the elections business run in family dynasties.[19]

When Votomatic punchcard machines made their debut in DeKalb County, Georgia, in 1964, one official reported that using them was "as simple as stirring coffee with a spoon."[20] The machines were a thirty-year dream come true for Joseph P. Harris, the preeminent chronicler of America's dysfunctional elections in the early twentieth century and a part-time inventor who had come up with the idea in 1962 while lying immobilized in the wake of a cataract operation. Harris studied at the University of Chicago under Charles Edward Merriam, the ultimate well-intentioned good government "goo-goo," and he spent the bulk of his career as a political science professor arguing for greater professionalism and civil service accountability. Harris's one failing in an otherwise glittering career was to believe that technology, on its own, held the answer.

Already in the 1930s, Harris had tinkered with the idea of a miracle machine to end fraud and error once and for all. He didn't give much consideration to the computer, then in its infancy, but imagined a giant sorting machine like a player piano. Then the war intervened, and he shuttled from job to job before settling at the University of California's Berkeley campus. Around 1960, a student asked if he'd ever considered adapting an IBM PortaPunch machine, a delightfully cheap device anyone could buy for $7. Harris approached a mechanical engineering professor named Bill Rouverol, and together they came up with a prototype. The basic idea was simple: place a punchcard beneath a standard paper ballot and use a metal stylus to push out perforated paper squares to indicate the voter's choices. At first, Harris imagined putting the stylus on a long rod that could reach all the way across a full-sized ballot. Then came the cataract operation, and he hit on the better idea of chopping the ballot into pages and placing them on a displaced axis so voters could index their way across the card as they flipped from one race to the next.[21]

Once his head was no longer wedged between sandbags, Harris called Bob Varni, then a West Coast IBM executive, and proposed going into business with him. Varni tried and failed to sell the idea directly to IBM, but gave Harris $5,000 in seed money and persuaded several colleagues to do the same. A prototype was tested, successfully, in five California counties. Two years later, in 1964, IBM took a look through its pile of rejected business ideas and decided the Votomatic was worth investing in after all. The Harris Votomatic Company became Computer Election Services, manufacturing forty thousand machines on IBM's behalf for a cool $16 million. Varni took responsibility for selling the new machine in the western United States, and business boomed.[22]

Unlike lever machines, whose cumulative vote totals still needed to be totaled up by hand, the punchcard system did all the tabulation work itself, spitting out tallies as soon as ballots from the Votomatic terminals were fed into the high-speed card reader. As with lever machines, though, the convenience favored county officials more than individual voters, who had to align the punchcard correctly, make sure it was pushed all the way in, and then punch it cleanly enough to detach the cardboard square, or chad, from the rest. The four corner points of the chad were known in technical jargon as "frangible connections," a description more apt than anyone realized at the time. [23]

Punchcards suffered their first setback in the 1968 California primary, when by sheer bad luck CES placed one of its Los Angeles County tabulation centers next to the Ambassador Hotel, where Bobby Kennedy was shot shortly after midnight. The police swarmed the area and cordoned off ten square blocks, making it impossible for election officials to bring ballots in from their precincts. The delay was hardly disastrous—the count was completed by 6 a.m.—and should have been understandable. But Jack Anderson and a handful of other media pundits couldn't resist having a go at almighty IBM and suggested Votomatics were not all they were cracked up to be.[24] Some even pointed a finger at IBM's chief executive, Thomas Watson, who was believed to harbor presidential ambitions.[25] Had he bought himself a voting machine company to count himself into high office? IBM's response was swift—instead of answering the charges, it pulled out of the elections business altogether.

Other corporations have since come to a similar conclusion, that the elections business carries too many risks for too little reward. Hewlett Packard developed an optical-scan system in the early 1970s, only to drop the project.[26] Dell did much the same with electronic voting after the 2000 election.[27] Diebold, a much smaller corporation specializing in ATM machines, in 2001 went all in, only to regret it bitterly and limp out again eight years later. Its chief executive, like Watson, was accused of political meddling, and the company name became a byword for electoral slipperiness from one end of the country to the other.

Even under the best of circumstances, elections are a tough way to make a living. "It's a big country, but counties don't tend to upgrade their equipment very often," Ransom Shoup's daughter, Kimberlee, said in a 2005 interview. "Mostly, you only get sales here and there, which all the other companies are trying to grab as much as you. Frankly, some of the smaller counties aren't even worth our while. You have to de-velop and manufacture the equipment up front and then spend another $100,000 just to get it through the federal testing process. Then you have to get certified in each state . . . before you can even make your first sale."

IBM got out of CES just in time, because the machines suffered an-other meltdown, a major one this time, in a 1970 primary election in Los Angeles. Ballot cards jammed, candidates' names were either mis-aligned or missing, and computer malfunctions prevented any vote count at all in more than five hundred precincts.[28] Even before this, computer scientists and public officials had been expressing qualms about the integrity of the Votomatic's tabulation software. A study com-missioned by the city of St. Louis earlier that year found punchcards were *more* prone to abuse than lever machines because there was no way of making sure the counters had been set to read the cards correctly. "It is possible to write a program in such a way that no test can be made to assure that the program works the way it is supposed to work," said the report by the accounting firm Price Waterhouse. "It is possible to have instructions in computer memory . . . to create results other than those anticipated."[29]

Breakdowns big and small were reported throughout the 1970s—in Detroit, Houston, and, in almost every election, Los Angeles. In San Antonio, the official canvass of a 1980 election reported that sixteen-hundredths of a percent fewer votes had been cast than was reported on election night, leading the *San Antonio Express* to suggest the slo-gan "One man, 0.9984 vote."[30] That same year, Pennsylvania's vot-ing equipment examiner Michael Shamos ripped the entire system to shreds without even mentioning the problem of improperly detached or "hanging" chad, which had first surfaced four years earlier. Not only were punchcards laughably passé in the computer industry, Shamos wrote, but the machinery was also a security nightmare. A voter, us-ing just his bare hands, could disassemble the ballot-page mechanism and rearrange or substitute pages in less than a minute. Arbitrary num-bers could be entered into the counters and, if that weren't enough, an election fixer could use a rogue programming card to change the vote totals—the same issue the Shoups had raised before Congress.[31]

Shamos pointed to another problem that is still with us: the fact that systems get certified without public authorities having access to the programming software. "It is a complete mystery to me how a program can be 'submitted' for certification unless the examiners are permitted to inspect it," Shamos wrote. In the 1980s, there was no requirement even to submit the software to a private testing lab, much less make it available to county and state authorities. Deborah Seiler, the head of California's elections division who would later become a sales rep for Diebold, told the *New York Times* in 1985 that she had certified a number of systems without inspecting anything. "At this point," she said, "we don't have the capability or the standards to certify software, and I am not aware of any state that does."[32]

Already, then, voting rights campaigners understood that election officials were signing away an alarming degree of control to vendor companies. Often, the companies—which had no fiduciary duties to uphold public integrity—were invited to help run elections because technophobic administrators liked having them around. "The proprietary interests of voting system vendors have been allowed to drive the standards drafting procedure," Mae Churchill of the Urban Policy Research Institute complained to the Federal Election Commission at the time. "The privatizing of elections is taking place without the consent or knowledge of the governed."[33] The FEC published some minimal standards for electronic voting in 1990, but did not even address these potential conflicts of interest.[34]

Three times during the 1980s, the volatilities and quirks of punch-card voting combined with incendiary local politics to create at least the suspicion of a stolen election. The first case was a 1980 congressional race in Kanawha County, West Virginia. The Democratic incumbent, John Hutchinson, was expected to trounce his Republican opponent, Mick Staton, by a double-digit margin, but Staton was oddly confident the polls were wrong and that he would finish ahead by five points. On election night, an impressionable young Republican state legislator saw Peggy Miller, the county clerk, get down on her knees, turn a key on the master computer, flip some switches, and turn the key back again. The legislator also saw Miller's husband—who happened to be Staton's largest campaign contributor—enter the computer "cage" with a sheaf of punchcards, which he handed to his wife so she could run them through a card reader.

When Staton was declared the winner by a five-point margin, exactly as he had predicted, the state legislator, Walter Price, decided to accuse him publicly of vote fraud. The Millers denied everything and, despite the legal challenge, arranged for materials relating to the election to be destroyed as soon as West Virginia's statutes allowed. The case dragged on for years, leading to some modest changes in the state's election laws. But without access to the crucial evidence the prosecution had nothing concrete to work with, and the charges were eventually thrown out.[35]

Next up was the 1985 mayoral election in Dallas. Initial returns showed the incumbent, Starke Taylor, trailing one of his opponents, Max Goldblatt. Then a power failure knocked out the central computer and their positions mysteriously switched. Through the night, odd things happened to the vote counts: 425 Goldblatt votes vanished in one precinct, while Taylor's total unaccountably jumped from 295 to 547 in another. Over the following days, the overall ballot count kept changing, from 80,208 on election night to 79,398 and back up to 80,149 after a recount.

Goldblatt's campaign manager, Terry Elkins, spent the next eighteen months trying to figure out what had happened and persuaded the Texas attorney general to open an investigation. Elkins was sure Goldblatt had been denied a place in a runoff and might have had the election stolen from him altogether. As in West Virginia, though, there was no easy way to prove anything because vital auditing documents either did not exist or were destroyed shortly after the election. The Dallas County elections administrator, Conny McCormack, said the overall ballot count had been inconsistent because certain precincts were split between voters who lived within the Dallas city limits and were eligible to vote for mayor, and those who did not. It had taken some time to sort that out. As for the changing figures at the precinct level, they had been due to ballot-reader malfunctions that were subsequently corrected.[36]

The state attorney general delegated the investigation to the Dallas County district attorney's office, and the DA accepted McCormack's assurances that no fraud or manipulation had taken place, an outcome that made nobody happy. "The electronic voting system in use lacks adequate security features to provide any assurances of the absence of fraud," assistant attorney general Robert L. Lemens wrote to the state director of elections in 1986. "As a result, this office has found that it will be difficult to demonstrate to the complainants that Texas elections are free from fraud and, thereby, free local election officials from suspicion."[37]

In 1987, Texas passed a new election law requiring an audit trail, a compulsory manual recount of one percent of the vote in at least three precincts, and a requirement that computer program codes be deposited with the secretary of state. Other states came to understand the importance of such action. California conducted a study of the Votomatic and concluded that all electronic vote tallying systems should have "reliable tamper-proof audit trails."[38] Getting politicians to act on these recommendations was far from easy, however. "One of the key problems," a *New York Times* reporter, David Burnham, wrote in a letter to a computer science professor at George Washington University, "is that the people who have been elected, who have been placed in power by a possibly shaky system, are understandably, and perhaps unconsciously, reluctant to look at the process that put them there."[39]

The decade's third dubious election was a 1988 Senate race in Florida. Buddy MacKay, the Democrat, was projected to be the winner on election night but ended up trailing Connie Mack, his Republican rival, by 34,500 votes out of more than 4 million cast. The odd thing here was that in four of the state's most heavily populated, Democrat-leaning counties—covering Miami, Tampa, West Palm Beach, and Sarasota—the drop-off between those recording a vote for president and those voting for Senate was a startling and utterly anomalous 20 percent. That meant as many as 200,000 votes had vanished into the ether, votes that most likely would have broken heavily in MacKay's favor.[40]

Some election officials argued that voters had accidentally overlooked the Senate race because it was squeezed onto the bottom of the ballot's first page, right below the candidates for president. That explanation did not hold, however, because a number of other counties had the same ballot design but not the same problem. While Tampa had a drop-off rate of 25 percent, next-door St. Petersburg's was just 1 percent.

MacKay became convinced the election was stolen. "What could have happened," he said years later, "was that the machines could have been programmed so that in my big precincts, every tenth vote got counted wrong."[41] One leading computer scientist, Peter Neumann of SRI International, found that explanation plausible. "Remembering that these computer systems reportedly permit operators to turn off the audit trails and to change arbitrary memory locations on the fly," Neumann wrote, "it seems natural to wonder whether anything fishy went on."[42] MacKay pressed to have the ballots examined and recounted, but under Florida law at the time recounts were at the discretion of county canvassing boards, and they all turned him down, saying he had no concrete evidence to establish a pattern of foul play. "It's a real Catch-22 situation," MacKay complained. "You've got to show fraud to get a manual recount, but without a manual recount you can't prove fraud."[43]

Florida's experience in 1988 was, in many ways, a dress rehearsal for the 2000 meltdown. Both controversies led to calls for the abolition of "old" technologies—paper and lever machines and punchcards—and their replacement with DRE systems. A report by the private technical evaluation group ECRI in the wake of the Mack-MacKay race argued that while paper was *inherently* unreliable, computer voting was only unreliable if it was poorly managed[44]—an argument that overlooked the fact that, in elections, management is everything.

Picking up on this theme, the ever-canny Shoup company wrote to the FEC's Voting Equipment Standards Advisory Committee in response to Mack-MacKay and offered its source code for outside review. "The public interest served by securing public confidence in direct electronic voting systems takes precedence over the remote possibility that some competitor might gain access to our source code and thereby enhance their product's marketability," Shoup's chief engineer, Robert Boram, wrote with uncommon grace. "We would hope all vendors of all election systems using any form of computers would now open their source codes to outside review. Let's put to rest the concerns raised as to the degree of reliability and integrity of computerized voting systems."[45]

It's a pity Boram's sentiments weren't echoed a decade later, when the DRE craze really took off and such scrutiny was sorely needed. In the late 1980s, the technology was still too new, and the motivation to switch systems too lackluster, for his idea to take hold. It's a pity, too, that Boram himself was not heard from more often. He told *New York Newsday* in 1992 exactly why it was a mistake to rely on the internal audit mechanism of a DRE. "I could write a routine inside the system that not only changes the election outcome," he said, "but also changes the images to conform to it."[46]

The Shouptronic computerized voting machine was not without its own problems. In 1988, it was deployed in New Hampshire when George Bush Sr. trounced Bob Dole in the Republican presidential primary by fifteen points, having trailed in the opinion polls by eight or nine points. At the time, political commentators attributed the dramatic swing to a series of last-minute Bush ads dreamed up by Roger Ailes (later the head of Fox News) accusing Dole of "straddling" the issue of raising taxes.[47] Bush also had the crucial support of the New Hampshire governor, John Sununu, later White House chief of staff, and with him the state's Republican establishment.[48] Did they do more than just get out the vote for their man? Conspiracy theorists have hovered over this one for years,[49] but Dole never issued a formal challenge, and there is simply no evidence to substantiate the suspicion of miscounted votes. The most one can say is that the machines made foul play possible. The computer scientist Ken Thompson delivered a famous lecture a few years before the Dole-Bush primary in which he showed how a bug could be introduced into computer software independent of the source code. "The moral is obvious," he concluded. "You can't trust code that you did not totally create yourself. . . . No amount of source-level verification or scrutiny will protect you from using untrusted code. . . . A well installed microcode bug will be almost impossible to detect."[50]

By the late 1990s, it wasn't just the Votomatic technology that was getting old. The machines themselves were wearing out and becoming more susceptible to the problem of imperfectly punched-out chad as styluses grew blunter, the plastic template guiding the stylus eroded, and the runners holding everything in place frayed. Roy Saltman noted these issues in a 1988 report for the National Bureau of Standards and suggested a spring-loaded puncher—an idea that proved unworkable in practice.[51] After 2000, Bob Varni was sure Florida's chad problem had been caused by poor maintenance. "We're talking about a three-dollar part," he said of the plastic template. "We used to recommend counties buy new ones every six to eight years. If they'd done that in Florida, it would never have got to hanging chads. For lack of a three-dollar part, they blew this whole thing."[52]

Not everyone thought the problem was that simple. When Rebecca Mercuri, a computer scientist specializing in voting systems, was presented with Varni's thesis, she reeled off a long list of other reasons why the Votomatics had malfunctioned. The stylus was poorly designed, neither big enough nor square enough, she said. The paper used to make the punchcards was of variable quality. The knives used to score the punchcards in advance tended to dull over the course of a factory pressing, so not all chad detached with equal ease. "The bottom line is, the Votomatic is just a badly designed piece of equipment," she said. "I bought one on eBay after the 2000 election, and the first thing that happened after I opened it up was that years' worth of chad flew out all over the place."[53]

Bill Rouverol, the Berkeley engineer who had partnered with Joe Harris on the original design of the Votomatic, felt personally wounded by the Florida disaster. He spent part of his eighty-third birthday on a plane from San Francisco to West Palm Beach so he could give election officials his own explanation of what had gone wrong. Essentially, the machine needed more light. Already in 1962, Rouverol had thought a backlight would help let voters know they had successfully detached the chad. Joe Harris scotched the idea at the time, thinking it too fiddly, but now Rouverol felt he had been right all along. As soon as he was home from Florida, he set about redesigning the Votomatic from top to bottom.

It was a labor of pure, unadulterated love. Rouverol didn't want the late-night comics, with their endless stream of chad jokes, to have the last word on his career and legacy. He installed a light and enlarged the size of the hole so the beam shooting out at the voter would be unmistakable, like something from *Close Encounters of the Third Kind*. He made the card itself the light-switch mechanism, so voters would know they had inserted the card correctly. And he designed a new puncher in the shape of a helical scissor that was both durable and user-friendly. It took Rouverol four years to develop his new invention—the perfect punchcard machine at last. When he showed it to me in the living room of his one-bedroom apartment in Berkeley in 2004, he hoped it might still find favor somewhere. "My machine would cost around $400 retail, which is a lot less than the $4,000 it costs to buy a DRE with a printer attached," he said. "Could that be attractive to the poorer counties?"[54] Alas, it was not to be.

9

DEMOCRACY'S FRANGIBLE CONNECTIONS: FLORIDA 2000

There is probably a Chernobyl or a [Three Mile Island] waiting to happen in some election, just as a Richter-8 earthquake is waiting to happen in California.

—*Willis H. Ware of the Rand Corporation, 1987*[1]

You know why we never paid attention to this until now? I'll tell you: because we don't want to know that our democracy isn't so sacred.

—*Indiana Elections Division co-director Candy Marendt, December 2000*[2]

On the morning of November 8, 2000, two candidates locked in a tight contest for a vital national office woke up after too little sleep to discover, like Al Gore and George W. Bush, that their race was too close to call.

Slade Gorton, a Washington State Republican running for a fourth term in the Senate, was less than two-tenths of a percentage point ahead of his Democratic challenger, Maria Cantwell, with hundreds of thousands of absentee ballots still to be counted. Already, it was clear this would be a pivotal race. If Gorton prevailed, the Republicans would have a 51–49 majority in the Senate. If Cantwell won, the chamber would be divided 50–50, leaving the deciding vote in the hands of the new vice president—whoever that might be. Yet the candidates resisted any temptation to make high drama of their agonizingly close contest, agreeing to sit back until all the votes had been counted as accurately as possible and one of them was declared the winner.

Gorton remained ahead until the last day of counting, at which point his paper-thin 3,000-vote margin turned into a 1,953-vote deficit because of an unexpectedly high volume of absentee ballots from Seattle. He said only that he had shifted from a position of cautious optimism to one of cautious pessimism. When an automatic machine recount mandated by state law increased Cantwell's margin to 2,426 (out of 2.5 million votes cast), Gorton gracefully conceded. There were no lawsuits, no objections to the state's punchcard voting machines, or anything else.[3]

It would be reassuring to think the candidates' calm adherence to the principle of counting every vote held some sway over the brutal presidential contest being waged at the opposite end of the country. But of course it didn't work out that way.

The thirty-six-day fight for the presidency in Florida was as queasy an episode as any in modern American politics. For those with no personal memory of previous presidential election controversies—and that was most people, since there had been none for forty years—the night of November 7, 2000, was like a long wait for an express train that kept promising to arrive but never quite did. The topsy-turvy numbers and competing claims of victory seemed like an accident at first, a simple accounting glitch that would be put right in due course. But there *was* no putting it right. Anyone who imagined this was a fair fight was laboring under a delusion.

The media portrayed the 2000 election as a low-stakes contest in a country enjoying unparalleled peace and prosperity—"a hotbed of rest," in Jeff Greenfield's witty formulation.[4] But that was not how it felt in Austin, the headquarters of the George W. Bush campaign, where the Republican faithful from across Texas flocked to the Driskill Hotel bar in anticipation of taking back the country after eight years of usurpation and moral turpitude under the Clinton administration. As the key dominoes fell one by one to Al Gore—Michigan, Pennsylvania, and, it seemed, Florida—there was rank disbelief, even talk of insurrection. "If Gore and Hillary both win, I'm leaving the country!" one man shouted.

Minutes later, news of Hillary Clinton clinching her New York Senate seat was met with boos and shouts of "We hate her!"[5]

Across the street at the Four Seasons, the Bush family slipped away from the gala dinner thrown in their honor, food untouched, and retreated to the governor's mansion, where they were later filmed sitting grim-faced in armchairs. "We haven't been up this late in years," said an appalled Barbara Bush, the candidate's mother.[6]

Around nine p.m., the networks took Florida out of the Gore column, saying it was now too close to call. The drink orders picked up at the Driskill. Then, for four hours, nothing. A Houston socialite passed out from the shock and the booze and had to be carried outside to await the paramedics. Those Republican faithful still standing made their way to an outdoor party on Congress Avenue, where they and hundreds of others were doused by a sudden rainstorm. Someone showed up with an industrial batch of yellow ponchos and the waiting continued. Then, at 1:15 a.m., Fox News called Florida for Bush, and the crowd went wild—jumping, hugging their neighbors, raising three fingers in a "W" salute. A montage of images from the campaign flashed up on a giant video screen to the accompaniment of "Signed, Sealed, Delivered"—a premature but carefully calculated declaration of victory.

In Nashville, Gore made a congratulatory call to Bush and was seconds away from stepping onto the podium in Legislative Plaza to make his concession speech when he was intercepted and told the vote totals in Florida were narrowing dramatically. Gore called Bush back to un-concede, and the country was thrown into a suspense that, many times over the next several weeks, felt like it would never end.

Throughout the campaign, Bush had made jabs at his Democratic opponent's "fuzzy math," but the shortcomings of Gore's federal budget figures were nothing compared with the electoral numbers getting crunched, spun, revised, and retracted in the Sunshine State. The networks' original call for Gore was based on an exit poll from the Voter News Service, a media consortium that gave the vice president a seemingly unassailable 7.3-point advantage. The networks were so sure they didn't even wait for voting to end in the Florida Panhandle, which is one hour behind the rest of the state. The effect on voters in those conservative northwestern counties will never be known.[7]

The initial determination in Bush's favor was made, extraordinarily, by John Ellis, the candidate's cousin, who was monitoring returns for Fox News while simultaneously maintaining close personal contact with both George W. and his brother Jeb, the Florida governor.[8] The other networks, naively mistaking Fox's naked partisanship for an old-fashioned journalistic scoop, followed Ellis's call—a misjudgment that was to give the Bush campaign a key psychological advantage.

Within hours, complaints poured in about irregularities, obstruction, and foul play. Black voters were furious with Governor Bush for dismantling Florida's affirmative action policies and came out in force to show their displeasure at "Jeb Crow," only to encounter police roadblocks, long lines, unhelpful or overtly intimidating poll workers, voter rolls that omitted their names, confusing ballot designs, and faulty machinery. African Americans made up 16 percent of voters on Election Day, up from 10 percent four years earlier, and favored Gore by a margin of nine to one. Yet their votes, as the U.S. Commission on Civil Rights later estimated, were close to ten times more likely to be disqualified than those of other racial groups.[9]

At Miami-Dade County's Precinct 255, housed inside an elementary school, the punchcard machines failed preliminary testing and missed 13 percent of the votes cast on Election Day. In black-majority Gadsden County, near the Georgia state line, the ballot was so confusing that 12.33 percent of voters spoiled their vote for president. (They were instructed to "Vote for Group," meaning candidates for both president and vice president, but many misunderstood and opted for more than one presidential candidate. Some filled in every circle except Gore's. Others picked all ten presidential candidates.) In Duval County, which includes Jacksonville, the names of the presidential candidates were laid out over two pages, even though the instructions on the sample ballot were to "vote each page." More than 22,000 ballots, the bulk of them from four black-majority city council districts, were thrown out because of double voting.

It was not only African Americans who cried foul. In Palm Beach County, thousands of distraught Jewish voters reeled at the realization that they might have accidentally voted for the right-wing, explicitly anti-Jewish, Reform Party candidate, Pat Buchanan. Their undoing was the infamous "butterfly" ballot layout, which aligned the names of candidates for each race on either side of a central bar of punch holes. The butterfly ballot had caused problems everywhere it was tried, but Palm Beach County's miserably incapable elections supervisor, Theresa LePore, thought the county's disproportionately elderly voting population would like the larger type. Buchanan won an improbable 3,424 votes, way out of line with his dismal percentages elsewhere in the state. A Berkeley political scientist subsequently calculated that at least 2,000 of these had been meant for Gore.[10]

Across the state, the Votomatic punchcard machines showed every sign of the decrepitude elections professionals had been warning about for years. Overall, Florida lost 2.93 percent of its vote total, representing a steady increase from 2.5 percent in the 1996 presidential election and 2.3 percent in 1992. The Votomatics' discard rate was 3.93 percent, although in the big urban counties it was considerably higher—4.37 percent in Miami-Dade, 6.39 percent in Palm Beach, 9.23 percent in Duval.[11] One of the Gore campaign's misfortunes was that some of the counties most favorable to his party had the highest incidence of lost votes, while those using an optical-scan system, where the discard rate hovered just above 1 percent, leaned Republican. Some Florida counties had systems that notified voters if they cast an invalid ballot and offered them a second chance. But only 26 percent of eligible black voters lived in those counties, compared with 34 percent of nonblack voters.

Conventional wisdom, as it has evolved since 2000, would have us believe that the punchcard ballots were *the* key obstacle to resolving the election, an impression bolstered by the hordes of lawyers who descended on Florida and focused their efforts almost exclusively on whether, and how, the votes should be recounted. The media also played a role in the pop culture demonization of pregnant, hanging, and swinging chad, especially after canvassing-board members in the southern Florida counties were paraded on national television staring cluelessly at nearly indecipherable 12 x 26 cards with flashlights and giant magnifying glasses.

But it wasn't the Votomatics that turned Florida into such a mess. Whatever the flaws in the machinery were, it should have been possible to agree on standards for counting and recounting the ballots, along the lines of the Gorton-Cantwell race in Washington State. Instead, recounts became one more football to kick around. Florida was something much more elemental and vicious, a *political* fight in which the win-at-any-cost mentality ingrained in the system over two centuries became visible in ways that a modern electorate found jarringly unfamiliar. Some of that visibility took the form of physical symptoms, as an angry boil erupted on George W. Bush's face and Dick Cheney was rushed to the emergency room with his fourth heart attack. Politicians found it convenient to blame election officials and voting machine manufacturers for the unfolding debacle, but really they were driving the fight themselves. The Republicans had an entrenched advantage in the state and chose to exploit it well beyond the usually understood rules of fair play. That said, if the Democrats had found an effective way to counterattack, they would have leaped on it. Neither camp, in the end, was as interested in democratic accountability as it was in beating the other by all and any means.

Many people sought to rationalize the shameless grab for power as a one-off, or else they pretended it was not a power grab at all, just a misunderstanding that would be sorted out to everyone's satisfaction in the fullness of time. The media, which had a direct interest in spinning out the drama for as long as possible, refused to call the race—politically or morally—for one side or the other, no matter how much evidence came in about suppressed or mangled Democratic votes. Some pundits took refuge in statistics to justify this stance. "Whatever happens," the mathematician John Allen Paulos wrote as the struggle was reaching its climax in the Supreme Court, "the margin of error is greater than the margin of victory or defeat."[12] In a perfect mathematical universe, he might have been right: Florida's voting machines missed almost 3 percent of the electorate, while the 537-vote margin by which Bush was eventually declared the winner represented less than one ten-thousandth, or 0.01 percent, of the vote total. But this was an election about much more than mathematics, and almost every indicator pointed to Gore, not Bush, as the rightful victor.

How do we know this? Let's start with the narrow, technical question of how the count would have gone if the votes had been assessed as accurately as possible. We have a trove of information on this, because two different media consortia gained access to the ballots under Florida's so-called Sunshine Law and conducted their own recounts. The conclusion (much misreported at the time): in a full statewide manual recount, incontrovertibly the fairest and fullest approach, although it was spurned by both major parties, Gore would have come out ahead. Ironically, the four Democrat-leaning South Florida counties at the heart of the lawsuits were not, on their own, enough to give Gore the votes he needed. A statewide recount of "undervotes"—votes recorded the first time around as having shown no vote for president—as ordered by the Florida Supreme Court would not have sufficed either, except under the laxest of counting standards. In a statistical quirk that could hardly have been predicted, least of all by Democratic Party lawyers, Gore in fact made up the decisive ground in eighteen predominantly Republican-leaning counties, which buckled to pressure from Tallahassee and secretly decided not to conduct machine recounts the day after the election.[13]

Gore also fell short in the count of overseas military ballots, whose admissibility was treated so lackadaisically the *New York Times* subsequently concluded that 680 of them, cast for Bush, should never have been included.[14] That alone could have overturned the official 537-vote Bush margin.

Still, we're talking about a difference of just a few hundred votes. So let's ask a slightly broader question: Which candidate did Floridians who turned out on Election Day *intend* to vote for in greater numbers? Again, the evidence overwhelmingly favors Gore. An unknown number of African American voters either spoiled their ballots, were wrongly turned away at the polls, or were intimidated before they got there. Their number is likely to have been in the thousands, perhaps even the low tens of thousands, and most would have voted Democrat. That figure would have dwarfed any possible disadvantage Bush suffered in the Panhandle. In Palm Beach County, the butterfly ballot did more than cause Gore supporters to vote for Buchanan by mistake; it also created a statistically anomalous rash of nineteen thousand "overvotes," ballots spoiled because more than one vote was cast for president. The *Palm Beach Post* went through these one by one and concluded that they represented a net loss for Gore of about 6,600 votes. (Ballots double-marked for Gore and Buchanan were counted by the paper for Gore; ballots marked for Bush and Buchanan were counted for Bush.)[15]

All these numbers point to one logical conclusion: Al Gore won the 2000 presidential election. But can we say the election was stolen? There were certainly plentiful instances of Republican dishonesty, under-handedness, and foul play. The Supreme Court's decision to halt manual recounts in early December and hand the election to Bush only added to the impression that GOP partisans were determined to keep the outcome as far out of the hands of the voters as possible. Whether it was a *premeditated* theft is a more complicated question. The Republican Party operatives who swooped in after the election were as discombobulated by the shortcomings of Florida's voting machinery as anyone and had no way of knowing which candidate deserved to prevail. The point is that they never troubled themselves with the question. All they saw was that Bush had a slim lead in the provisional count on the morning of November 8, and they did everything in their power to keep it that way. They did not steal the election so much as grab hold of it and refuse to let go.

The groundwork laid by the Florida Republican Party gave a crucial boost to their efforts. It didn't hurt that Bush's brother Jeb was governor, or that the co-chair of his state election campaign, Katherine Harris, was secretary of state, the official responsible for overseeing and certifying the vote. Neither was shy about showing partisan colors before, during, or after the election. Harris campaigned for Bush in New Hampshire and drafted a known Bush supporter, the retired Gulf War commander Norman Schwarzkopf, to record get-out-the-vote public service announcements. Despite the supposed "firewall" that existed between the secretary of state and governor's office, public records requests made by the *Miami Herald* demonstrated that Harris and Jeb Bush were in regular e-mail contact during the recount.[16]

It didn't hurt, either, that the Republicans were in charge of a majority of Florida's sixty-seven counties. In two central counties, Seminole and Martin, elections supervisors permitted Republican Party operatives, and Republicans only, to go through absentee ballot applications and make sure the paperwork for registered party members was squared away. This not only gave the Republicans a partisan advantage; it was also a violation of Florida election law. In Martin County, the GOP representative was even authorized to take the application forms home with him.[17]

Most egregious, however, was Katherine Harris's endorsement of a contentious, error-ridden voter purge list that later became the subject of a lawsuit by the NAACP. Ostensibly, the list was intended to help counties rid their electoral rolls of known felons. In practice, it was a scattershot disenfranchisement mechanism aimed disproportionately at African Americans. Not only did it have the effect of depressing the Democratic Party vote, it was also a distasteful throwback to the days of Jim Crow in a state that had elected its first black member of Congress only eight years earlier.

The purge list had its origins in a contested 1997 election for mayor of Miami, in which the incumbent, "Crazy Joe" Carollo, managed to convince a judge that his rival, Xavier Suarez, had stolen the race through massive absentee ballot fraud. Carollo's lawyer Kendall Coffey—later employed by the Gore campaign—produced evidence of voters who had no idea they had voted, voters who did not live within the Miami city limits, voters who were paid $10 apiece to cast their votes for Suarez, and, inevitably, voters who were stone-cold dead. The case had many eye-popping elements, not least a ruling by the U.S. Third District Court of Appeals that absentee voting was a privilege not a right, and that the entire block of absentee ballots, fraudulent or not, could therefore be discarded with a clear conscience.[18] The takeaway for Florida's state elections officials was that county voter registration rolls were in disarray and there was a risk of nonresidents, felons, and dead people influencing the outcome of all state elections, not just local ones. The Republicans were, naturally, more worried about fraudulent Democratic votes than about fraud in general and were disinclined to mess with the Cuban vote, which tended to go heavily in their favor. So they focused exclusively on the felon question, which they knew would have the biggest effect on African Americans, the Democratic Party's most reliable constituency.

The purge list was initiated by Katherine Harris's predecessor, Sandra Mortham, and subcontracted to a private Atlanta firm called DBT/ChoicePoint, which cast its net so broadly it failed to cross-check names with other identifying data, like dates of birth and known addresses.[19] It also included the names of ex-felons who had done their time in other states and were known to have had their voting rights restored. Black Floridians were in no doubt these oversights were deliberate, one more outrage to add to a litany of discriminatory public policy decisions aimed at curbing their democratic rights. Florida was already an outlier state (and remains so to this day) for refusing to restore the voting rights of convicted felons on completion of their sentences—a law dating back to 1868 when white plantation owners were urgently looking for ways to repress newly freed Negro slaves. By 2000, Florida was locking up a higher proportion of its African American population than any other state; so many had been through the prison system that 31 percent of black men had lost their right to vote.[20]

By the time Katherine Harris took over from Mortham, her office was inundated with complaints about the purge list, but she pursued it anyway. The Division of Elections sent the counties a list of 173,142 names, equivalent to almost one-third of the total number of felons and ex-felons in the state. Those listed as convicted criminals included Linda Howell, the elections supervisor of Madison County on the Georgia state line, and a smattering of other government employees from around the state. None had criminal histories. In Tallahassee, Leon County elections supervisor Ion Sancho went through all 694 people on his list and confirmed only 33 as convicted criminals—an error rate of 95 percent.[21] One of those wrongfully listed, a local church minister named Willie Whiting, said he felt "slingshotted into slavery."[22] Sancho and a handful of other county supervisors repudiated the list, but many others implemented it, causing unknown thousands of eligible voters to lose their rights.

As soon as Bush's slim lead was established the day after the election, one of Florida's savviest political operators, the lobbyist and lawyer Mac Stipanovich, took charge of Katherine Harris's office and directed her every move. Every morning he would walk through an underground passageway beneath the state Capitol building to enter Harris's office unseen by the media.[23] His oft-repeated mantra was to "bring this election in for a landing." That meant, in essence, resisting all efforts to recount votes and enforcing the strictest possible certification deadlines. Stipanovich and Harris persuaded the eighteen Republican counties not to conduct machine recounts the day after the election; they also chose to make political hay of the state's overseas military ballots. According to state law, these needed to be postmarked by Election Day to be considered valid, but Harris's staff put out statements suggesting it was enough for the signature on the ballot application *inside* the envelope to be dated November 7 or sooner. The number of military ballots from overseas swelled in the wake of these declarations. Just 446 were received between Election Day and November 13. By November 16, the number had reached 2,575, and by November 17 it was 3,733. The decision on what to do with these fell to the lone Democrat holding statewide office in Florida, Attorney General Bob Butterworth, who buckled under pressure and agreed—to widespread consternation—to allow missing or illegible postmarks as long as the date accompanying the signature was in order. Enough military votes slipped through this way to give Bush a net gain of 176 votes. One Republican operative described these as "Thanksgiving stuffing."[24]

The Republicans were adept at whipping up outrage by suggesting it was the Democrats, not them, doing the stealing. The party stayed relentlessly on message, delivering one set of talking points after another that managed to make right look like left and up like down. "Make no mistake," said Tom DeLay, the House chief whip who would later be indicted for election law violations in Texas, "we are witnessing nothing less than a theft in progress, and the American people, the Constitution and the rule of law are all potential victims." David Horowitz, the consultant and commentator, called it "an ill-advised and reckless post-election coup." Grover Norquist, the antitax campaigner, said the furor over President Clinton's impeachment in 1998 had already shown "the rule of law means nothing to these people." George Will, the bow-tied columnist and noted skeptic about the usefulness of mass political participation, came up with the much-repeated formulation "slow-motion grand larceny."[25]

The overseas military ballots became a subject with particular public relations potency. "The man who would be their commander-in-chief," one Bush lawyer, Jim Smith, argued, "is fighting to take away the votes from the people that he would command." The fact that Smith had argued for a strict application of the postmark rule just one day earlier was quietly forgotten in the mounting foment against the Gore-Lieberman ticket, or "Sore Loserman," as it was now renamed. The Republicans sent Marc Racicot, the Montana governor and a former military prosecutor, to act as chief public relations man, and Racicot reeled off lists of irregularities allegedly marring the recount process in Palm Beach and Broward Counties. "What in the name of God is going on here?"[26]

he asked. Soon, stories were circulating of Democrats pushing chad out of punchcards, taping other pieces on, and stuffing squares in their mouths. All this was pot stirring, nothing more. There *were* cases of loose chad taped onto ballots, but in every known instance it was the voters who had done the taping to rectify a mistake.

The Republicans' ugliest stunt was to burst into the Miami-Dade elections supervisor's office the day before Thanksgiving and reduce it to such turmoil that the recount begun there was abandoned for good. The so-called Brooks Brothers riot was spun by the Republicans as a spontaneous expression of disgust by citizens fearful for the future of their democracy. Really, it was a carefully planned exercise in intimidation, staged by elected Republican officials with paid party sympathizers and designed to prevent any new Gore votes from surfacing. Days later, with the election now in the hands of the Florida State Supreme Court, six of whose seven members were appointed by Democrats, black-clad police snipers took up positions on the roof of Tallahassee's City Hall and a state senate office complex. Their guns, as seen in an aerial photograph taken at the time, were pointed not at the state legislature or at the streets, but at the building housing the justices in whose hands the fate of the election temporarily rested.[27]

The Democrats liked to think they were the more principled party, and overall they certainly played fairer. They argued more than once that their post-election strategy was about taking the moral high ground and fighting for small-d democracy. In truth, though, their ground was at once too high and not high enough. Party officials often seemed stunned, even hurt by the ruthlessness of their opponents, but they had no answer for it except chronic indecisiveness and halfhearted grabs for whatever seemed most easily attainable. And that led them only to be beaten up more by their opponents.

The trouble began, as it often does, with the lawyers. It's not that the Democratic lawyers were worse than Republican ones, or vice versa; rather, they all shared the same defect, which was to shift the emphasis away from who really won and reduce the contest to a tug-of-war in which the so-called will of the people was yanked this way and that for partisan advantage. These lawyers knew each other from previous stand-offs and had all but rehearsed each other's lines. All of them, at some point, had taken the side that said recounting the votes was the only way to serve democracy, and all of them had also argued that re-examining the ballots would be a grotesque exercise in selective vote hunting after the fact. The determining factor in every case was never which party they were representing, only which had come out ahead in the initial count.

David Boies, the Gore lawyer who argued in favor of manual recounts in Tallahassee and before the Supreme Court, had taken the opposite tack when he defended Congresswoman Jane Harman of California against allegations of absentee ballot fraud in a 1994 House race. The Republican chair of the House Oversight Committee who adjudicated Harman's fitness to be seated was Lincoln Diaz-Balart, a prominent Miami Cuban, and he had been in no hurry to agree that Harman won fair and square. Now, however, he was one of the chief instigators of the Brooks Brothers riot, arguing that no good could come of allowing the Bush-Gore election to go on even one day longer.

The gospel of the Democratic lawyers in Florida was *The Recount Primer*, which three party operatives with plentiful experience of contested elections had written in 1994.

> The posture a campaign takes with regard to punch card problems will depend on whether the candidate is ahead or behind. . . . If a candidate is ahead, the scope of the recount should be as narrow as possible, and the rules and procedures for the recount should be the same as those used election night. . . . If a candidate is behind, the scope should be as broad as possible, and the rules for the recount should be different from those used election night.[28]

In other words, all is fair in love, war, and elections. It was Gore's lawyers who came up with the idea of requesting manual recounts in four counties, not the whole state, in the belief that this was the most efficient way to find the votes needed to wrest back the lead. After the Republicans filed suit to challenge this, Gore briefly considered backing off from the selective recounts and pressing for a bipartisan commitment to do a hand recount in all sixty-seven counties. If he had gone through with this, not only would he have served the cause of democracy, he would also have stood a much better chance of winning. His decision to take the lower, seemingly more expedient route was the single worst move of the entire election, condemning him to a moral and political hell entirely of his own making. Gore himself seemed to realize his mistake, because on November 15, four days after deciding to press ahead with the selective recounts, he tried to backtrack. By that stage, though, his offer of a statewide recount as a possible Plan B looked pusillanimous and insincere, and the Bush campaign turned him down flat.

From that moment on, the Gore campaign was crucially stripped of moral authority. When the candidate argued toward the end of November that ignoring votes meant "ignoring democracy itself," the Republicans were not stung but elated to have such an easy opportunity to take him down. "Al Gore is not interested in counting every vote," the party's talking points for November 27 read, "he's simply interested in selectively recounting the votes he thinks will help him overturn the results of this election."[29] Intriguingly, the Florida Supreme Court indicated as late as December 7 that it would entertain the idea of a statewide hand recount. But by that time neither side was interested.

The adviser who ultimately talked Gore out of a statewide recount was his running mate, Joe Lieberman, who played a curiously ambivalent role throughout the thirty-six days in Florida. Lieberman had refused to drop his Senate reelection campaign in Connecticut when he became the vice presidential candidate, making him look from the get-go like a man hedging his bets. After the election, he seemed a little too willing to countenance defeat. At the height of the overseas military ballot controversy, he told NBC's *Meet the Press* he would give "the benefit of the doubt" to ambiguously postmarked ballots. "We ought to do everything we can to count the votes our military personnel overseas," he said.[30] That statement alone cost the ticket hundreds of votes. In early December, Lieberman told reporters he was "proud of the race we ran,"[31] as if it were now in the past. It might have been a verbal slip, but it also added to the very thing the Republicans were trying to establish, an aura of inevitability.

Bush's final triumph was, of course, sealed not in Florida but in the Supreme Court. The *Bush v. Gore* decision, which ended the election with a snap of the fingers, has rightly been condemned as a scandalously partisan intervention that robbed the voters of any notion of democratic accountability. The five justices who formed the deciding majority concluded that the possibility of "irreparable harm to petitioner"—that is, Bush losing the election—was of greater legal consequence than counting the votes. It may be, as some constitutional scholars have argued, that the decision will come to be regarded as a "self-inflicted wound" every bit as damaging as the *Dred Scott* decision upholding slavery in 1857. That was certainly Justice John Paul Stevens's fear when he wrote in his dissent that the loser in the election was "the Nation's confidence in the judge as an impartial guardian of the rule of law." [32]

From a long-term standpoint, the most alarming aspect of the Supreme Court decision was not the outcome itself, which the majority, in an apparent acknowledgment of the dirty work they were doing, limited to "present circumstances"; rather, it was the suggestion, made in oral argument and again in the majority opinion, that voters are not the final arbiters of presidential elections. Technically, Justice Antonin Scalia was correct when he asserted that "there is no right of suffrage under Article II [of the Constitution]." As we have seen, the framers left it to individual state legislatures to pick their electors. In the early years of the Republic, some states did indeed prefer to appoint their electors instead of consulting the voters. But we are talking about the preindustrial age, when universal suffrage was still viewed as a dangerous eccentricity, not the norm of civilized societies. Since the Jacksonian era, it has been an article of faith that U.S. democracy is founded on the will of the people. The right to vote may have been restricted, manipulated, and abused, but the fundamental notion that political leaders should be elected, not appointed, has never been questioned. Or it wasn't until the meltdown in Florida.

The first person to suggest taking the decision out of the hands of the voters was not a Supreme Court judge but Tom Feeney, the Republican Speaker of Florida's lower house, who reread Article II sometime in November and realized the crisis could be resolved if the state legislature simply appointed the twenty-five electors on its own. Feeney was essentially playing a game of political brinksmanship with the Florida Supreme Court, warning the justices that if they leaned too far in Gore's direction he had the means to retaliate. This was dangerous enough ground to be treading—"playing with fire," in the words of the former Nixon White House counsel Leonard Garment. [33] Even Feeney, though, must have been surprised that the U.S. Supreme Court backed him so vigorously. "The individual citizen has no federal constitutional right to vote for electors for the President of the United States," the majority opinion read, "unless and until the state legislature chooses a statewide election as the means to implement its power to appoint members of the Electoral College. The state . . . after granting the franchise in the special context of Article II, can take back the power to appoint electors." Was this the sort of close literal reading of the Constitution Bush had in mind when he expressed a preference for "strict constructionists" as judicial nominees? If so, the *Bush v. Gore* decision offers an ominous warning to combatants in future close elections.

Florida may have been where the 2000 election was fought most vigorously, but it was far from the only state to witness problems or near-catastrophic breakdowns. Had the electoral college arithmetic outside of Florida been closer, we could have seen knock-down fights in as many as half a dozen states. The Sunshine State was one of four where the official margin of victory was slimmer than the number of ballots discarded as undervotes. Two others, New Mexico and Oregon, were carried by the slimmest of margins by Gore while the fourth, New Hampshire, squeaked into the Bush column. In Oregon, which voted entirely by mail, a pilot study conducted shortly after the election suggested as many as 36,000 ballots statewide were filled in by someone other than the signatory. That alone could have been grounds for a debilitating lawsuit, since Gore's margin in the state was just 6,765.

Other states were spared machine-related problems only because the outcome happened to be decisive. Several, including Georgia, Idaho, Illinois, South Carolina, and Wyoming, had higher rates of rejected or uncounted ballots than Florida. The Democratic staff of the House Judiciary Committee, led by Representative John Conyers of Michigan, found that more than 1.2 million ballots in thirty-one states, plus the District of Columbia, had been rejected as undervotes. (The other nineteen states kept no records of their discarded ballots.)[34] Since it seems unlikely that more than a tiny fraction of the electorate would have deliberately left the presidential ballot blank—exit polls and other data suggest that figure should have been somewhere around 0.5 percent— we can say with some certainty that the number of uncounted votes was at least twice as large as Al Gore's 500,000 official margin in the popular vote.

A 2001 report by the Voting Technology Project, a joint venture between Cal Tech and the Massachusetts Institute of Technology, painted an even gloomier picture. It estimated that somewhere between 4 million and 6 million presidential votes were lost. Roughly 2 million of these were rejected as overvotes or undervotes. Somewhere between 1.5 million and 3 million were never cast because of bureaucratic difficulties with the registration process—a problem that is with us still. Another million or so were lost either because voters could not locate the correct precinct, or because polling hours were inconvenient, or because the lines were too long.[35]

The Cal Tech/MIT report did not even attempt to quantify the number of absentee and overseas ballots that went missing. But we know many of them did, sometimes in strange and mystifying ways. The votes of Steven and Barbara Forrest of Bellevue, Washington, turned up several days after the election in the Danish city of Odense. They had somehow been slipped into an envelope containing navigational charts sent by a company on Shaw Island, fifty miles north of Seattle. The Danish couple who received them, Brian and Helle Kain, called the U.S. embassy in Copenhagen, only to be told that it was too late for the stray votes to be counted.[36]

Other, more brazen forms of electoral chicanery were alive and well in 2000, including a thriving vote-buying business in Alice, Texas, the origin of the infamous Box 13 that gave Lyndon Johnson his decisive last two hundred votes in the stolen 1948 Texas Senate race. The *Los Angeles Times* found women known as "vote whores" who took money from the political parties to talk people into abdicating control of their absentee ballots. "Last I heard," the town's police chief told the *Times*, "it was $20 a vote."

Perhaps no state outside Florida was more questionable than New Mexico, which had its own tarnished tradition of electoral malfeasance. In Rio Arriba County, a sparsely populated area between Santa Fe and Taos with a reputation as the dirtiest county of all, one precinct registered 203 voters but 0 votes for president, Senate, or the House. The glitch was later ascribed to an electronic voting machine malfunction. In Bernalillo County, encompassing Albuquerque, an agonizingly slow count gradually transformed a narrow statewide lead for Gore into a tantalizingly thin 134-vote edge for Bush. Then, six days after the election, an extra five hundred Democratic votes materialized in Doña Ana County, on the Texas border, and Gore's 134-vote deficit became a 366-vote victory.[37]

The Republicans were deeply suspicious of the miracle five hundred, particularly since the local elections clerk, Rita Torres, was a Democrat in a notoriously dirty county. (Two years later, Torres's successor was prosecuted and convicted on five criminal charges of violating state election laws.) But it emerged that it was a Republican volunteer, not a Democrat, who noticed the discrepancy during the vote-canvassing process. He'd joked about it with his Democratic counterpart, who quickly pounced on it and reported it to a higher authority. A precinct worker had scribbled down the number 620 to denote the running vote total for Gore, but the six looked like a one, causing the number to be transcribed into the provisional results as 120.[38]

After years of grumbling and dropping dark hints, the Republicans came around and acknowledged the transcription error. The party's local vote fraud expert Bill Wheeler called it an "honest mistake." The Democrats, however, had their own qualms about what had happened. After years of being on the defensive, they came to suspect that the poll worker who made the six look like a one was a Republican sympathizer who created the confusion on purpose. Naturally, there is no way to know for sure.

As a postscript, it's worth noting the fuzzy math that popped up when New Mexico's Democratic governor Bill Richardson took two state constitutional amendments to the people in September 2003. The second amendment, regarding education funding, was particularly close, and the numbers changed almost daily from election night until certification three weeks later. At one point, the amendment was down by two, only to finish 195 votes ahead. In one county, the yes and no numbers were switched—canvassing officials concluded they had been transposed by accident. Republicans, already alarmed in the wake of their narrow defeat in the 2000 presidential election, called for a recount, but were told that under New Mexico law only candidates could request recounts. Since this was a ballot proposition, not a candidates' race, they had no recourse.

When the final vote tabulations were published, Richardson's opponents noticed that two counties, Cibola and San Juan, had more votes for Amendment 2 than voters.[39] More accidental transpositions, perhaps? Or proof that, when it comes to electoral malfeasance, the two parties are separated not by democratic scruples but by access to power and the opportunity it affords one of them, in an appropriately degraded political culture and a tight enough circumstance, to do its very worst?

10

MIRACLE CURE

I always say, out of something bad, something good happens.

—*Theresa LePore, Palm Beach County elections supervisor*[1]

There are many ways to manipulate paper elections, but the scope of such an attack is limited to one precinct or one county. . . . The danger of a software attack is that, while it takes a little more skill (but nothing extraordinary), it can affect hundreds of counties simultaneously.

—*David Jefferson, Lawrence Livermore National Laboratory*[2]

When Palm Beach County's elections supervisor Theresa LePore was struggling with her abortive post-election recount in November 2000, her reputation in as many tattered pieces as the chad littering the counting-room floor, a reporter asked how much it would cost to install a new voting system. "A lot of millions," she answered sharply. "And if you go to a new system, it has its own inherent set of problems."[3]

Five months later, however, LePore was in Riverside County, California, to observe the nation's first county-wide touchscreen computer voting system and fell instantly in love.[4] The Sequoia Pacific AVC Edge machines, she enthused, did almost all the work—for voters who could flit from race to race and double-check their choices on a summary screen before giving final approval, and for election administrators who didn't have to count or tabulate anything. Best of all, no chad and, because the machines used no paper, no recounts.

LePore was not the only one to be impressed. Riverside's registrar of voters, Mischelle Townsend, had attracted national attention with her seemingly prescient decision to go all-electronic. "If the U.S. State Department is looking for a way to restore America's good name," Wired News enthused, "it ought to let the world know about Mischelle Townsend's bold experiment."[5] Townsend was happy to bask in the glory. "I've been counting my blessings for the last 24 hours that I'm not Theresa LePore," she crowed at one point during the Florida recount fiasco.

Neither LePore nor Wired News reporter Farhad Manjoo (soon to evolve into a thoughtful and trenchant critic of electronic voting) knew that election night in Riverside had been a near disaster. A couple of hours after the polls closed, the tabulation software overloaded and started deleting votes from the tallying system instead of adding them.[6] Sequoia sent in an emergency resuscitation team and claimed to have put everything right, but when the dust settled, one candidate for a local school board who had been comfortably in the lead when the machines went down found herself unaccountably trailing. Bernadette Burks demanded an explanation but received none.[7] Townsend told her there had been no computer crash, only a problem with a server that needed to be "manually expanded" after it reached capacity. Townsend refused to acknowledge even that Burks had been ahead in the count, although her own figures clearly showed that she was.[8] The election, Townsend liked to tell people, had been "flawless."

"Flawless" was the catchword LePore used to cajole the Palm Beach County commissioners into spending $14.4 million on their own Sequoia system. The new touchscreens were deployed in time for the March 2002 local elections, and they, too, failed at the first hurdle. A respected former mayor of Boca Raton, Emil Danciu, was flabbergasted to discover he had finished third in a race for a seat on the city council, since an opinion poll taken shortly before the election put him seventeen points in front. Supporters flooded his campaign office with stories that every time they tried to vote for him, the machine lit up the name of one of his opponents. Danciu discovered that fifteen cartridges containing the vote totals from machines in his home precinct had been removed by a poll worker on election night, causing an unexpected delay in the final results. Some of the cartridges were subsequently found to be empty. Armed with a fistful of affidavits, Danciu sued for access to the Sequoia source code, only to be told the code was a trade secret under Florida law. Even LePore and her staff were not authorized to examine it on pain of criminal prosecution.[9]

Two weeks after the Danciu election, a runoff for mayor in the inland town of Wellington was decided by just four votes. Another seventy-eight votes, however, did not register at all. Since the runoff was the only race on the ballot, that meant—assuming the machines were not lying—that seventy-eight people had jumped in their cars, driven to the polls, *not* voted, and gone home again. LePore touted this very scenario with a straight face and insisted the machines had worked fine.[10] "She treated us as though we were sour-grapes sore losers and basically blew us off," Danciu's daughter Charlotte, a lawyer who represented him in court, complained.[11]

Computers might have seemed like the providential response to the fiasco in Florida, but county officials who rushed to spend millions on new systems almost all ended up regretting it. They should have known better. Computer scientists had been warning for years that touch-screeen direct recording electronic (or DRE) machines were inherently unsafe, vulnerable to software bugs, malicious code, or hacking.[12] Even the best-designed system could not guarantee that data entered into the computers during an election would be the same as the data the machines spat back out. Hence, the strong recommendation of experts—largely ignored in the early going—to generate a paper receipt for each voter to serve as a backup and provide a basis for meaningful recounts.

County officials also chose to overlook that fact that the DREs on the market after 2000 were poorly programmed by their manufacturers—in some cases shockingly so—and were inadequately tested by the government-contracted private laboratories charged with certifying them. Vendors teased public officials with grandiose claims about the machines' miracle-working powers but also refused to give up the secret of the proprietary software, so the assurances they gave about ballot security had to be taken on trust. As we saw with AVM's lever machines, the sales pitch was all about the convenience of the administrators—many of whom *liked* the idea of elections without recounts or second-guessing—and hardly at all about the needs of the voters. When the grave problems with DREs became more widely known, many administrators like LePore and Townsend preferred denial to any acknowledgment of error of their part.

Curiously, DRE machines were *not* the recommendation of a blue-ribbon panel established by Florida governor Jeb Bush in the aftermath of Hurricane Chad.[13] Bush's Select Task Force on Election Procedures, Standards, and Technology found that only the optical-scan machines already in operation in a number of Florida counties met acceptable standards of cost, accuracy, and convenience. The panel recommended picking one system, making it uniform across all sixty-seven counties, and ensuring that tabulation occurred precinct by precinct, not at county headquarters, to maximize the number of checks and balances.

This didn't happen, largely because of one person. Sandra Mortham was Katherine Harris's predecessor as secretary of state, the one who instigated the notorious felon purge list. Now she was a lobbyist for Election Systems & Software, the largest voting machine maker in the United States, which was anxious to push a new product to replace its now untouchable Votomatics. Mortham was also a lobbyist for the Florida Association of Counties, which meant she was in the happy position of being able to sell the new machinery to members of her own organization. She was also eminently well connected in Tallahassee and sweet-talked the state legislature into endorsing her plans. The upshot: ES&S sold its iVotronic electronic touchscreen system to twelve counties for a total of $70.6 million. Miami-Dade spent $24.5 million, Broward $18 million. ES&S paid a percentage of its profits to the FAC and a commission fee to Mortham personally.[14]

The results were predictably disastrous. When the iVotronics made their debut in a Democratic Party primary election in September 2002, they took so long to boot up—especially in precincts requiring Creole-language services as well as English and Spanish—that many polling stations in Miami-Dade did not open until lunchtime. When a freak storm caused power blackouts, the battery backup on many machines failed. One Miami precinct reported 900 percent turnout; another showed just one ballot cast. Governor Bush declared a state of emergency in Miami-

Dade and Broward and extended the opening hours of polling stations by two hours. Janet Reno, the former U.S. attorney general now running for governor, strongly suspected that the eight-thousand-vote deficit separating her from her challenger was inaccurate, but she was forced to concede after a week of uncomfortable back-and-forth because recounts were impossible. "It turned out the county had purchased a prototype," said Lida Rodriguez-Taseff, a gutsy lawyer and founder of the Miami-Dade Electoral Reform Coalition. "This was an invention that had never been tested. We were the guinea pigs."[15]

For the general election in November, Miami-Dade switched on its seven thousand voting machines twelve hours ahead of time and had police standing guard outside each precinct. Still, things did not run smoothly. Broward County, which spent $3.5 million to fix the problems that arose in the primary, lost a hundred thousand votes for twenty-four hours after the election—which deputy elections supervisor Joe Cotter later blamed on "a minor software thing."[16]

It was a similar story in Maryland, where Secretary of State John Willis rode roughshod over the recommendations of his own advisory panel and bought a statewide DRE system from Diebold Election Systems. The September 2002 primary saw the kind of problems that would soon become epidemic around the country: machines that refused to fire up and screens that froze or assigned votes to the wrong candidates. The administrator of the State Board of Elections, Linda Lamone, didn't find fault with the machines; she blamed Diebold's training teams, who were supposed to show poll workers what to do but were "not responsible people," as she told a government oversight committee. Months later, undaunted, she doubled down on the state's original $13.2 million investment and spent another $55.6 million on Diebold touchscreens.[17] "Why would anyone want to buy first-generation technology which is a lot more expensive than established technology?" Baltimore County's information technology chief, Tom Iler, asked. "You don't want to be on the bleeding edge with critical systems."[18]

Maryland was not the only state where such sound advice was ignored. In Georgia, Secretary of State Cathy Cox rushed into a $54 million contract with Diebold and later ran for governor boasting that her state was the first to go all-touchscreen. One of her advisers, Brit Williams of Kennesaw State University, had previously told officials in

Maryland "he would not choose a touch screen DRE to replace existing inadequate systems for the 2002 election."[19] But three months later, under contract to Cox, he told the Georgia Technology Authority he saw no problem in rushing Diebold's AccuVote touchscreen system through state certification in time for the 2002 midterms.[20]

In June 2002, six brand-new Diebold tabulation machines and a touchscreen voting terminal were stolen from a training session in a Macon Ramada Inn, which was doubling as a halfway house for recovering drug addicts. It was a serious security breach that risked giving the thieves access to Georgia's election-management software, and with it the means to alter the outcome of any race. State officials wouldn't even acknowledge the theft for two years, then said it was of little consequence because the machines were probably "at the bottom of the Chattahoochee [River]."[21]

Then the computers malfunctioned, forcing Diebold to come up with three separate software patches in the run-up to the midterms, which, as far as anyone can tell, were never put through the state certification process. (When activists asked the Georgia Technology Authority, an official said he was "not sure what you mean by the words 'please provide written certification documents.'")[22] "If the machines were not certified," Georgia activist Denis Wright said, "then right there the election was illegal."[23]

The November elections didn't just cause terminals to freeze and screen alignments to go out of whack. There were also serious concerns about the results. The races for both governor and U.S. Senate saw wild double-digit swings in favor of the Republican candidates—at variance not only with the final exit polls but also with the open primary that had taken place on older voting machines just two months earlier. Part of the late Republican momentum was undoubtedly due to a viciously personal television ad campaign launched against Max Cleland, the incumbent senator, and to a campaign appearance by President Bush— then still popular—on behalf of his opponent Saxby Chambliss. But the math was crazy, any way you looked at it. In twenty-seven counties in Republican-dominated north Georgia, Cleland unaccountably scored fourteen percentage points higher in the general election than he had in the primary, while in seventy-four counties in the Democrat-heavy south, Chambliss improved by a whopping twenty-two points.[24] In

Dooly County, the two major candidates for governor received the same number of votes—an oddity in a poor, predominantly African American county with a history of strong support for Democrats. When the county probate judge in charge of elections was presented with evidence that the figures derived from a test run, not the election itself, he declined to comment.[25]

In a prescient survey of voting systems written in 1988, Roy Saltman of the National Bureau of Standards identified four problem areas in verifying the outcome of computerized elections—the absence of a proper audit trail, poor program design, trade secrecy provisions, and inadequate administrative oversight. The new DRE systems introduced in the wake of the 2000 election suffered from every one of these defects. Saltman cited a handful of other dangers, including inadequate poll-worker training and insufficient financial resources to maintain and operate the machines. The risk, he wrote, was that these oversights would be tantamount to an "abdication of control over elections to vendors."[26]

That abdication became all the more apparent as counties kept purchasing electronic systems. Administrators in smaller jurisdictions were happy to admit the machines were too complicated, and they were more than willing to have the nice representative from Diebold help out, much as they might call in a technician to fix a home PC. But Diebold had no allegiance except to its own bottom line, while the officials had a duty to the public that they were failing to fulfill.

Since it was in neither side's interest to conduct manifestly fouled-up elections, they often colluded in allowing the outward appearance of efficiency, speed, and mathematical exactitude to cover up whatever flaws, miscalculations, or worse were concealed within the machines' hermetic electro-universe. As the Miami lawyer Lida Rodriguez-Taseff put it, "We have thrown millions and millions of dollars at correcting the outward signs of problems, without correcting the problems themselves."[27] Chances were, the next bona fide instance of "slow-motion grand larceny" would go entirely undetected.

Theoretically, the incoming Bush administration was committed to finding federal solutions to the Florida debacle. Yet nothing happened until the second Florida meltdown in 2002, at which point the White House moved with such haste to pass the long dormant Help America

Vote Act (HAVA) it ended up showering county administrators with hundreds of millions of dollars for electronic voting systems while providing little or no regulatory oversight. The two biggest practical improvements created by HAVA—encouraging early voting and giving voters the right to cast provisional ballots in cases where their eligibility was in doubt—had no bearing on the voting machinery itself; what power the act provided to regulate voting equipment was largely undercut by Congress's slowness in funding the requisite oversight bodies.[28]

Meanwhile, the major players in the new e-voting market—Diebold, ES&S, and Sequoia—raced to ingratiate themselves with local and state officials, offering campaign contributions and throwing lavish conferences. They hired well-connected present and former public officials as lobbyists and sales employees. Deborah Seiler, California's former elections division chief, became Diebold's West Coast representative. Sequoia snapped up election officials from California and Nevada, as well as the head of the Denver Election Commission, which had spent $6.6 million on Sequoia machines two years earlier. After Bill Jones, who served as California's secretary of state from 1995 to 2003, told Sequoia he saw no need to fit each touchscreen terminal with a printer—despite a provision in his state's new Elections Code to create a paper backup system—he too was rewarded with a lucrative consultancy with Sequoia on leaving office.[29]

This revolving door wasn't just ethically dubious; in some instances it was downright crooked. In 2002, Arkansas secretary of state Bill McCuen pleaded guilty to taking bribes and kickbacks in a scheme involving a precursor company to ES&S. In Louisiana, Sequoia's southern regional sales manager Phil Foster was indicted in a $40,000 kickback scheme involving his brother-in-law, a voting equipment salesman from New Jersey, and Louisiana's state commissioner of elections Jerry Fowler, previously mentioned in chapter 8. Foster was given immunity in exchange for testimony against the others, who all pleaded guilty.[30]

Perhaps such corruption was inevitable when a small number of companies were able to shift fabulous quantities of substandard product at scandalously high prices. The old Votomatics had cost between $125 and $300 per machine. Optical-scan technology was even cheaper. The price of a single touchscreen voting terminal, by contrast, was around $3,000—and even more with a printer attached.[31] (Another reason why administrators didn't like the idea of paper trails: they felt they'd spent enough already.) Los Angeles County gave serious consideration to replacing its $3 million InkaVote optical-scan system with $100 million worth of Diebold DREs, which would have meant ditching one of the better performing elections systems with what experts from Cal Tech and MIT have described as one of the worst—*for 33 times the price.* LA's registrar-recorder, Conny McCormack (a veteran of the 1985 mayoral election in Dallas), relented only because of the blizzard of bad publicity that whipped up around Diebold as time went on. She insisted, however, that her long-standing friendship with Deborah Seiler, the Diebold West Coast rep, did not play into her calculations.[32]

The federal government just sat back and watched. The Help America Vote Act called for a federal oversight agency, the Election Assistance Commission (EAC), with a dedicated technical panel to determine standards for new voting machinery. The EAC, however, proved toothless and woefully underfunded and did not even come into being until almost a year after the deadline laid down by the act.[33] In the run-up to the 2004 presidential election, the EAC was struggling with just a handful of full-time staffers and, after spending three months waiting for funding for an office, had to abandon plans to develop a national voting machine testing system. One unusually blunt EAC commissioner, DeForest "Buster" Soaries, was so appalled he tendered his resignation within a week of his appointment and stayed only because he was afraid of the consequences of leaving before the 2004 election.[34] One of the legislative aides who drafted HAVA later acknowledged "the EAC was designed to have as little regulatory power as possible."[35] The National Association of Secretaries of State, which never fancied being regulated in the first place, took advantage of a growing mood of budgetary austerity in Washington to join the first of many calls for the commission's abolition.

By that time, national debate over election management had—incredibly—degenerated into a partisan dogfight, in which critics of electronic voting were dismissed as Democratic Party whiners (even though Diebold's biggest champions in Georgia and Maryland were all Democrats), and most elected Republicans felt compelled to insist the DREs, and almost every other aspect of election management, functioned just fine. When the U.S. Commission on Civil Rights convened an expert panel to discuss HAVA implementation in April 2004, the Republican delegation walked out before the proceedings even began.[36]

It didn't help that many of the noisier amateur voting rights activists were partisans of the political left who saw electronic voting as a Republican-inspired plot. They pointed to the election results in Georgia—with much suspicion but no proof that the Republicans had messed with the machines—and to the fact that Chuck Hagel, then a Republican senator from Nebraska, had previously been chief executive of a precursor to ES&S and thus, in their view, came into office with votes counted by his own company.[37]

Most egregious, in the activists' eyes, were the ties all three major vendors had to the Republican Party, mostly through campaign contributions. In June 2003, Diebold's chief executive, Walden O'Dell, threw a $600,000 fund-raising party for Vice President Dick Cheney, earning himself an invitation to the presidential ranch in Crawford, Texas, and subsequently sent out a fund-raising letter in which he declared himself "committed to helping Ohio deliver its electoral votes to the president next year." It was an unfortunate choice of words, to say the least, at a time when O'Dell's company was vying for consideration as a preferred vendor in Ohio, his home state. When his letter was leaked to the *Cleveland Plain Dealer* it lit a firestorm across the country and probably did more than any other incident to tarnish Diebold's name in the voting rights community.[38]

There is a difference, however, between carelessness and conspiracy. For all the overheated fears of a Republican plot to steal all elections from here to the end of time, the political allegiances of the voting machine companies and their top executives were never the root problem; it was the reliability of their products. As the computer-voting expert Rebecca Mercuri put it, "If the machines were independently verifiable, who would give a crap who owns them?"[39] Diebold, Sequoia, and ES&S were hardly on a par with the Big Three from Detroit's auto manufacturing heyday. They were middle-ranking corporate structures of negligible interest either to the Republican campaign apparatus or to legislators on Capitol Hill. With a few notable exceptions they, and the elections administrators they did business with, were just small-timers, glad-handers, chancers, and dimwits who couldn't have organized an effective political conspiracy if their lives depended on it. Their behavior didn't point to connivance or grand-scale dastardly thinking so much as to shabbiness, complacency, laziness, backscratching, small-town networking, conflicts of interest, petty ambition, even pettier revenge, and an appalling lack of basic critical thinking.

Take, as an example, a January 2004 meeting between a Diebold sales representative and members of the Texas Voting Systems Examination Board, which was captured on videotape and obtained by the Austin chapter of the ACLU.[40] It's oddly compelling viewing, in a soufflé-deflating, car-wreck-ogling sort of way. The state board members seem vaguely bored, more interested in making small talk about timetable changes at Southwest Airlines than asking tough questions about ballot security, even though Diebold's national reputation was going through the shredder at the time.

"Is that okay with everyone, the tally on that vote isn't going to match?" one board member asks.

To which the Diebold representative Don Vopalensky replies, unreassuringly, "That's what we did last time." And the conversation goes no further.

When it transpires that a single person is able to cast multiple provisional ballots using the same assigned voter number because of a flaw in the software, Vopalensky suggests using paper stickers to check off voter numbers—hardly a fail-safe method. "Slap it on there," he says. "They [poll workers] should do that."

Another board member interjects: "Forget provisional, I just want to make sure this machine can add. Remember we've had machines recently that didn't add?"

When Adina Levin of the Texas ACLU's Cyber Liberties Project first obtained the tape through a public records request, she could scarcely believe what she called "the stunning lack of rigor." The Systems Examination Board ended up recommending conditional certification of the Diebold system for one year, even after the company tried and failed to fix the provisional ballot problem and even after it transpired that the operating system was vulnerable to manipulation while an election was in progress. Levin commented, "This is like the lock on your front door being broken and saying, 'We'll have a locksmith come by in a year and fix it.'"[41]

There was abundant evidence to suggest things were this unedified most of the time, at least until the public sat up and took notice. As soon as the Texas ACLU saw the tapes, it sued for access to the next Voting Systems Examination Board meeting. In response, the state first tried to argue that the board was not a formal governmental body, just a random collection of individuals. When that argument went nowhere, the meeting was postponed indefinitely.

The death blow to paperless electronic voting was delivered surprisingly early on; it just took several years for everyone to recognize it. In January 2003, a Seattle-area grandmother and ardent anti-electronic-voting activist named Bev Harris stumbled on a trove of forty thousand Diebold computer documents that had been left on an open File Transfer Protocol site on the Internet. The documents included the source code for Diebold's AccuVote-TS touchscreen machine and program files for the company's election-management software—everything a competent computer scientist would need to understand how the machine worked, and how it didn't.

Harris, whose day job was to run a small public relations firm, did not have the expertise to assess the trove in full, but she did figure out it was possible to enter the voter database using Microsoft Access and change votes without leaving a trace.[42] A more thorough assessment came six months later when Avi Rubin, a computer scientist at Johns Hopkins University, and Dan Wallach of Rice University went through the files line by line. Rubin and two of his graduate students found the first gaping flaw within half an hour—the fact that the password unlocking the system's encrypted data was written directly into the source code. Not only did this mean that anyone with access to the source code had the means to break into the system at will; it also meant that every single Diebold machine was crackable by the same means.[43] As David Jefferson, an elections security expert at the Lawrence Livermore National Laboratory and a frequent consultant to the California secretary of state's office, later described it, "What [Diebold] did is create a big complex building, put locks on every door, use the same key for every lock, and then publish a picture of the key on the wall."[44]

And it got worse. The full report produced by Rubin's team showed a number of ways to alter the outcome of an election undetected. It was relatively straightforward, for example, to produce homemade replicas of the system's voter smart cards and use them to cast multiple ballots. It was also easy to intercept communications between individual precincts and county headquarters—so-called man-in-the-middle attacks. "Cryptography, when used at all, is used incorrectly," the report went on. "[W]e see no evidence of disciplined software engineering processes . . . no evidence of any change-control process that might restrict a developer's ability to insert arbitrary patches to the code. Absent such processes, a malevolent developer could easily make changes to the code that would create vulnerabilities to be later exploited on Election Day."

The report left Diebold reeling. At first, the company tried to cast doubt on the authenticity of the code, saying it was just a test version and was more than a year old. This was later contradicted by a company spokesman who told Wired News it was in fact the code used in the previous November's midterms.[45] Diebold then sought to nitpick Rubin's work and suggested he had a conflict of interest because he served on the technical advisory board of another computer-voting company. Finally, Diebold acknowledged that there might be a problem but assured nervous clients it had been addressed and corrected.[46]

The Rubin-Wallach report wasn't just an indictment of Diebold; it also cast a troublesome light on the three testing labs tasked with passing voting software for federal certification. These labs—Wyle, Ciber, and SysTest Labs—were nominally independent, but they were paid directly by the voting machine companies and competed for their business, giving them a financial incentive to go easy on their clients. They worked in secret and were subject to no oversight. It was impossible, barring leaks or court orders, to make even a minimal assessment of their competence.[47]

When the Federal Election Commission first drew up technical standards for electronic voting machines in 1990, it omitted to give any direction on how those standards should be tested and enforced. That administrative hole was filled by the Election Center, a Houston-based nonpartisan lobbying group representing state and local elections officials, which took it upon itself to accredit and oversee the labs. But the Election Center never wielded any formal congressional authority, giving rise to a deeply unsatisfactory situation in which the integrity of the country's election machinery depended on a system that was both impenetrable and publicly unaccountable. It didn't help that the Election Center had close ties to the voting machine manufacturers, accepting sponsorship and direct donations from Diebold, Sequoia, and ES&S.[48]

The FEC published new standards in 2002 to take account of the giant leaps in computer technology—the rise of the Internet, the growing sophistication of code-writing languages and encryption techniques, and the proliferation of worms, viruses, and other security liabilities. But the timing was awkward, because the country was in the throes of a DRE-buying frenzy and HAVA was about to redefine, however unsatisfactorily, the architecture of voting equipment accreditation and approval. No vendor wanted to review its product line in the middle of a sales boom, and no elections official wanted to be kept waiting for supposedly flawless systems for which they'd paid top dollar. So the Election Center and NASED, the National Association of State Election Directors, fudged it. Any new product *components*, they said, would have to conform to the 2002 standards, but vendor companies would not be required to update entire *systems*.

The question of what constituted a new component was left vague. Did a patch on a software program qualify, or only a new software package? According to an official who helped draw up the FEC standards, the understanding was that the testing labs would have "a bit of leeway" to decide such questions for themselves. In practice, though, key computer-voting system components used in the 2004 presidential election were still meeting only the 1990 benchmark—about as effective, in digital terms, as assessing a modern washer-dryer by the standards of a tub and washboard.[49]

This was a system primed for failure. The thing that most stunned Doug Jones, Iowa's top voting-machine examiner, about the Rubin-Wallach report was that he had found exactly the same flaws and encryption problems when he inspected the software of Diebold's precursor company, I-Mark Systems, in 1996. At the time, Jones forwarded his discoveries to both I-Mark and the testing authority Wyle Laboratories, believing the software as it stood should not be certified for use. But Wyle didn't just ignore him. It wrote, "This is the best voting system software we've ever seen."[50]

Diebold came in for further embarrassment when a large batch of internal company e-mails, leaked in March 2003, painted a picture of company employees working largely on the fly with clients, government testing labs, and each other. Software engineers made clear they preferred to keep security access lax so county officials could get "out of a bind" when necessary. They even made their operating system compatible with handheld devices, raising yet another possibility for election tampering, or what one e-mail referred to as "stupid things." The leaked e-mails also included a 2001 resignation letter from an employee, Brian Clubb, who deplored "the practice of writing contracts to products and services which do not exist and then attempting to build these items on an unreasonable timetable with no written plan, little no time for testing, and minimal resources."[51]

The first state to express buyer's remorse was Maryland, which commissioned two technical studies to find out if the $55.6 million voting system it had just bought was even usable. The first study, by SAIC International, identified 328 security weaknesses, 26 of them critical.[52] The second, by Raba Technologies, included a "Red Team" exercise to break into the system during a simulated election.[53] "We could have done anything we wanted to," one of the Red Team members, William Arbaugh of the University of Maryland, reported. "We could change the ballots [before the election] or change the votes during the election."[54] Another team member concurred: "Diebold basically had no interest in putting actual security in this system. . . . It's not like they did it wrong. It's like they didn't bother."[55]

Amazingly, both Diebold and Linda Lamone, the state's top elections official, took the Raba report as vindication. Raba had said that the system could be used in the primary election, but only as a stopgap measure and only if certain security issues were addressed first. Lamone's State Board of Elections said the SAIC and Raba reports confirmed "the accuracy and security of Maryland's voting procedures and our voting systems as they exist today," and she gave Diebold the all clear.[56]

Such doggedness was typical. Cathy Cox's supporters in Georgia dismissed e-voting critics as "crazies and skeptics" and said the new voting system was something "to brag about."[57] R. Doug Lewis, the director of the Election Center, told a Senate Judiciary Committee hearing in September 2003 that it was misleading to think computer voting could be manipulated. "The real question," he said, "is whether there are sufficient and proper safeguards to make it highly improbable. And the answer to that is yes. . . . Like time travel (which is theoretically possible), it is highly unlikely at this time."[58]

Then reality hit. In California, where one of the "crazies and skeptics" was now secretary of state, Diebold kept promising that federal certification of its AccuVote-TSx was imminent, when in fact the machine was nowhere near ready. In February 2004, with less than a month to go before a primary election in which seventeen counties were counting on certified software or machines or both, Diebold finally acknowledged the problem and suggested, lamely, that its clients resort to paper ballots instead. Secretary of State Kevin Shelley and his staff hit the roof, complaining that Diebold was "stringing us along . . . jerking us around . . . [and] doing a bait-and-switch on software that has resulted in the disenfranchisement of voters."[59]

On primary day itself, there were equipment meltdowns in Oakland and San Diego, causing hundreds of polling stations to open late and forcing election workers to turn away unknown thousands of voters because they did not have more than a handful of backup paper ballots. A key problem was a device used to generate individualized computer cards for each voter, which was still in development and suffered significant battery drainage problems, even when the device was switched off. "We were caught. We apologize for that," Diebold's election systems chief executive Bob Urosevich later told a heated investigative hearing in Sacramento. "We did not realize that when we have an off button on this machine, that it does not turn the system off."[60] Shelley subsequently banned the TSx from use in California and issued a twenty-three-point security checklist for counties to follow if they ever wanted to use DRE equipment again.

Shelley also triggered a national movement to demand an independently verifiable paper audit trail for all election equipment. He set 2006 as the deadline in his own state, and others either followed suit or, in Nevada's case, sped the timetable up further. In theory, "a permanent paper record with a manual audit capacity" had already been mandated by HAVA for federal elections starting in 2006,[61] but that provision was regarded as so weak that bills were introduced in the House and Senate to address its flaws and broaden the scope.[62] In Florida and Maryland, activists sued for the introduction of an independent paper trail.

In Ohio, already shaping up to be the key battleground of the 2004 presidential election, Secretary of State Kenneth Blackwell canceled plans to introduce DREs statewide, in part because of concern about the lack of auditability.[63] Over time, touchscreen voting machines were banned, phased out, or fitted with a recountable paper receipt system in thirty-nine of the fifty states. Where they remained in use, age became a problem compounding the others; by 2015, many of the machines were reaching the end of their natural life, but counties that had relied on HAVA funding to purchase them in the early 2000s had no money for replacements.[64]

In some quarters, county officials who had staked their all on electronic voting continued to champion them long after the problems had been exposed. In Los Angeles, Conny McCormack, furious with Kevin Shelley for throwing off her timetable for HAVA compliance (in other words, her qualification for federal funding), argued there was nothing wrong with using uncertified software. In fact she had done just that with her Diebold early voting machines in the October 2003 recall election that made Arnold Schwarzenegger governor of California. "We have not been dotting every *i* and crossing every *t* to certify all the software," she said, and poured scorn on Shelley and others for insisting on such a thing.[65]

In Riverside County, Mischelle Townsend sued Shelley and four other California counties in federal court to argue that a paper trail and other new security stipulations were unreasonable, if not also unconstitutional. Her suit was quickly tossed. By then, however, Townsend was embroiled in fresh scandal over a March 2004 county supervisor's race in which one candidate was doing unexpectedly well until the count ground to a halt (much as it had in November 2000) and fared much less well after. The losing candidate's campaign manager spotted two Sequoia employees in the vote tabulation room during the count and saw one of them again two days later as the controversy hit the local media.[66]

Townsend was so intransigent in handing over what little data the system provided that she attracted renewed national attention[67]—the wrong sort this time—and appeared headed toward litigation without end. Local activists started bombarding the county with public records requests and showed that Townsend had far exceeded Riverside's gift limit in accepting a free trip to Florida on Sequoia's tab; had failed to file public declarations of financial interest in four of the previous six years; and had circumvented county protocol in hiring expensive Sacramento lawyers to defend her questionable actions.[68]

The upshot: Townsend resigned. She denied her departure had anything to do with the growing disquiet over her job performance. Rather, she said, she was taking early retirement to nurse her father-in-law through knee surgery.[69]

11

ELECTION 2004:
THE SHAPE OF THINGS TO COME

Welcome to Ukraine

> —*Republican protest banner in Olympia, Washington, during
> the Gregoire-Rossi gubernatorial recount, December 2004*

The word now is, if someone gives you a provisional ballot, turn
around and run.

> —*Bess McElroy, African American voter organizer, Miami*[1]

In June 2004, the Florida Department of Law Enforcement sent plain-
clothes officers to the homes of more than fifty elderly black residents
in Orlando and told them they were under investigation for conspiracy
to steal an election. The residents were nonplussed; they had relied on
the help of a well-known community organizer to obtain absentee ballots in a mayoral election three months earlier, as they had many times
in the past, and didn't think they had done anything wrong. But they
were also terrified, especially when the officers removed their jackets
and exposed their firearms. One officer crossed his legs and tapped a
9mm pistol in an ankle holster as he quizzed an old lady on why she saw
the need to vote absentee at all. The residents felt threatened, embarrassed, and disinclined to vote absentee again.[2]

From a strict law enforcement standpoint, it was a perplexing investigation. The election *had* given rise to a fraud allegation by the unsuccessful Republican candidate, Ken Mulvaney, who argued that since

the community organizer was working for Mayor Buddy Dyer's reelection campaign, the absentee ballots he distributed and witnessed were somehow tainted. But the allegation had already been investigated by the Orlando city attorney's office and the FDLE and was deemed to be without merit. "The Florida Department of Law Enforcement considers this matter closed," a May 13 letter to the state attorney read.[3]

Why was the state police deployed at all? The FDLE suggested it was based on a paragraph in the Florida statutes declaring it illegal to receive or offer "something of value" for absentee ballots. The only things of value to come to light, though, were the stamps that the community organizer, a grizzled seventy-three-year-old charmer named Ezzie Thomas, offered to facilitate the voting process. "A 37-cent postage stamp is a very interesting definition of racketeering," Thomas's lawyer, Joe Egan, commented.[4]

Egan and the local Democratic Party were convinced the house visits had nothing to do the integrity of the March mayoral election and everything to do with suppressing black votes ahead of the November presidential race. Dyer was mayor of *the* swing city in *the* swing area—the so-called I-4 corridor—in one of *the* swing states George W. Bush had to win if he wanted a second term in the White House. Unseating Dyer was always going to be a long shot for the Republicans—he won more than 50 percent of the vote against Mulvaney—but tainting his reputation and strangling his political machine was a plausible Plan B. That was certainly the upshot: Dyer was subjected to a grand jury investigation, indicted, and briefly suspended by Governor Jeb Bush before the case against him collapsed.[5] Thomas, meanwhile, dropped from sight for the duration of the presidential campaign, and his neighborhood group, the Orlando Voters' League, lapsed into inactivity.

Thomas Alston, a former leader of the Orange County branch of the NAACP, put it succinctly: "We elected Buddy, and now they're taking our vote away."[6] Much local anger focused on Guy Tunnell, Governor Bush's appointee as state police chief, who had previously been upbraided by a federal judge for "racial animus" when, as a county sheriff in the Florida panhandle, he had conducted a series of raids and arrests against the only black nightclub in Panama City. Now the local critics saw him as Jeb Bush's henchman, abusing his position to pursue a political agenda. (Bush, for his part, called Tunnell "as good a cop as this state has.")[7]

Around the time of the house calls, the FDLE opened a second investigation into the political activities of the Orlando firefighters' union, which had supported George W. Bush in 2000 but was now switching allegiance to John Kerry. Within days of the Kerry endorsement vote, the FDLE raided City Hall, television cameras in tow, and confiscated several computers. They said they were concerned that a "leave bank" established to give union officials time away from their firefighting duties was tantamount to a Democratic Party slush fund. The charge seemed questionable at best, since the leave bank had been established by Dyer's Republican predecessor as mayor, Glenda Hood, and raised no eyebrows until the political calculus shifted. A grand jury was convened and, while expressing disquiet at the political use of time paid for out of public funds, found no evidence of criminal wrongdoing.[8] By then, though, the damage had been done. Union officials who'd received less-than-friendly home visits from FDLE officers, just like Ezzie Thomas's elderly charges, grew fearful of engaging in political activities of any kind. The get-out-the-vote campaign they would ordinarily have organized for November was canceled. The head of the union, Steve Clelland, didn't dare attend a Kerry rally in his off hours for fear of being accused of abusing his office.[9]

Such was the tone set for the 2004 election. Far from shying away from the strong-arm tactics they had deployed in Florida four years earlier, the Republicans doubled down. They weren't taking any chances; this time they were going to fight their political battles before Election Day.

Glenda Hood, who had graduated from mayor of Orlando to succeed Katherine Harris as secretary of state, made clear from the get-go she was giving the other side no quarter. First, she sought to revive the notorious felon purge list, subcontracting the job to Accenture, which had donated $25,000 to Republican candidates in Florida, and relying on the FDLE to provide most of the information. Hood's office was confident that the new list—48,000 names in all—was error-free, but it proved not to be. CNN and the ACLU, which sued for access to the names and won, found that it included two thousand ex-felons who had had their voting rights restored. The list was disproportionately weighted toward African Americans and unaccountably light on Latinos, especially Cubans, who in Florida tend to lean Republican. With a major scandal brewing, the list was abandoned.[10]

Hood made a number of other decisions that carried the whiff of partisanship. She insisted that Ralph Nader's name appear on the ballot as an independent candidate, despite a court order declaring his candidacy papers invalid and despite concerns that he could split the Democratic vote, just as he had four years earlier when he ran on the Green Party ticket. She directed county election supervisors to throw out registration forms if applicants confirmed less than twice that they were U.S. citizens. The form called for them to sign a sworn statement and, elsewhere, to check a box—a bureaucratic hurdle most likely to trip up recent immigrants and lower-income voters, all of whom leaned Democrat. And she campaigned hard to get rid of what limited manual recounts Florida's DRE machines could provide. When the courts told her she couldn't simply ban recounts, she agreed to allow analysis of the computerized machines' internal audit logs, but ruled that if there was a discrepancy the counties should go with the original count. In other words: we will do recounts, but if the recounts change the outcome we will disregard them. Since the fifteen counties using DREs were predominantly urban and Democrat-leaning, this too was seen as a one-sided maneuver.[11]

"She is the political mouthpiece of Jeb Bush, a true partisan using her office to the best possible advantage of the Republican Party," the Democratic congressman Robert Wexler said shortly before the election. "She is the mechanism Jeb and George Bush have employed to do everything in their power to make Florida a Bush state. And she doesn't care what people think, because she's not accountable to them." Unlike Katherine Harris, Hood was appointed, not elected.[12]

Similar suspicions of blatant partisanship swirled around Ohio's secretary of state, Kenneth Blackwell, who came to be known in some quarters as the Katherine Harris of 2004. He, too, was a Republican election manager in a closely fought, Republican-run state. He, too, was co-chair of George W. Bush's state campaign team. To compound the conflict of interest, he spent quite a bit of election season, when his role called for him to be *super partes*, mustering support for his own prospective run at the Ohio governorship in 2006. But Blackwell proved a smarter and more sophisticated strategist than Harris—and less inclined to toe the party line at every turn. He hadn't rolled over for Diebold's electronic voting machines, and he didn't allow Ralph Nader on the Ohio ballot, to the frustration of some fellow Republicans who wanted to split the anti-Bush vote.

Some of Blackwell's decisions, though, were real peaches. In early September, he ordered county elections officials to reject voter registration forms unless they were "printed on white, uncoated paper of not less than 80 lb. text weight." Since many lower-income, urban new voters (read: Democrats) were pulling forms out of newspapers whose pages were neither white, nor uncoated, nor as heavy as he specified, the directive was viewed as a crude mechanism to trip up supporters of the opposing party. Blackwell rescinded the order after three weeks, but that was long enough to trash an unknown number of otherwise valid registration forms. He also decreed that provisional ballots would be counted only if they were cast in the correct precinct, a measure likely to suppress the voices of poorer, more transient voters who tended to favor Democrats. The impact of Blackwell's ruling was made worse by the fact that door hangers and flyers printed on official-looking paper with the wrong information on where to vote started circulating in Democrat-leaning urban areas. Some people received phone calls saying their polling place had been changed when it hadn't. A federal district court struck down Blackwell's ruling in late October, saying the secretary of state "apparently seeks to accomplish the same result in Ohio in 2004 that occurred in Florida in 2000," but Blackwell refused to comply, calling the judge a "liberal . . . who wants to be co-secretary of state." He won the fight on appeal.[13]

Across the country, the presidential election campaign was orders of magnitude more rancorous and partisan than it had been four years earlier. Both sides believed the political stakes to be higher, now that American troops were engaged in bloody, expensive, increasingly futile wars in Iraq and Afghanistan and the sheen was coming off Bush's War on Terror. Nobody now took the electoral system for granted; it became its own partisan battleground, as Democrats pushed to increase registration among young people, minorities, and the poor, and Republicans countered them with allegations of rampant fraud and calls to tighten the qualifications for voting. Nobody knew it at the time, but this rhetorical back-and-forth would set the electoral pattern for the next decade or more.

Every day, newspapers recounted stories—largely serving the Republican cause—of registration forms being found in garbage cans, or voter rolls being padded with the names of noncitizens or non-people. Students at Democrat-leaning campuses were reported to be registering twice, once at their college address and once at their family's home, although it was unclear how many people, if any, cast more than one ballot. The *Chicago Tribune*, in a throwback to its prize-winning work on the Daley machine, found 181,000 dead people on the registration lists of six key battleground states.[14]

Every day, too, newspapers carried stories about Republican attempts at stifling the voices of legitimate voters. A Republican state senator in Michigan came in for a roasting after announcing his party's intention to "suppress" Detroit's overwhelmingly African American vote.[15] In Nashville, African Americans were reported to be receiving phone calls and flyers giving out erroneous polling station locations or the wrong election date. In Miami's Little Haiti, voters complained they were sent no registration card at all or that duplicate cards arrived without warning with the wrong party affiliation.[16] In many of Miami's black neighborhoods, the assumption was that if people had been left off the voter rolls it was no accident, and the prospect of their provisional ballots being recognized was zero—a fear that was at least partially borne out when post-election figures showed a wild variance around the country in the rates of provisional ballot acceptance.[17]

In Las Vegas, a former employee of a pro-Republican voter outreach firm triggered an FBI investigation after he testified that he had seen a supervisor systematically tear up and discard completed registration forms from declared Democrats, while continuing to process forms submitted by Republicans. The company was run by Nathan Sproul, a former head of the Republican Party in Arizona and a prominent member of the Christian Coalition, who was never charged with any crime but was put through the media ringer as reports from Oregon to West Virginia suggested his employees were passing themselves off either as nonpartisan get-out-the-vote activists or as opinion pollsters who revealed themselves as registration drive workers only after they established that they were talking to Republicans.[18] Similar anecdotal evidence emerged on the other side: a disenchanted volunteer for a pro-Democratic group in Colorado, Moving America Forward, alleged that she and her fellow volunteers were instructed to ask voters whether they supported Ken Salazar, a Democrat, for Senate, or his Republican opponent, Pete Coors. If the answer was Coors, they were to say thank-you and walk away. If the answer was Salazar, they were to offer an absentee ballot form.[19]

The cutthroat electioneering went all the way to the wire. A Republican election lawyer in Denver, Scott Gessler, admitted that his party routinely called up supporters who had requested absentee ballots and suggested they go to the polls and cast a provisional ballot as well, the hope being that at least a handful of them would have their votes counted twice. This he called "gaming the system"—one tiny but significant step away from out-and-out illegality.[20] Across the country, voters reported being called by operatives of both parties and urged to throw away their absentee ballots, citing bogus administrative reasons. In Milwaukee, the Democratic mayor put in a request for 260,000 extra ballots in anticipation of a high turnout for Kerry, especially in the black-majority wards, only to be rebuffed by the county executive, the future Republican governor of Wisconsin (and shortlived presidential candidate) Scott Walker, who said—in another glimpse of things to come—that having extra ballots on hand would be an invitation to fraud.[21]

Election Day saw armies of voting rights activists, party workers, and paralegals stationed outside polling stations in the most hotly contested precincts, ready to advise voters they suspected were being denied their rights and to lodge complaints if the problems could not be sorted out on the spot. Again, this would prove to be the pattern of the next several election cycles. The Republican Party mounted mass challenges to the eligibility of more than five hundred thousand voters in nine states, most commonly by sending unforwardable postcards to addresses associated with individual voters and using any returned mail as a reason to push for their disqualification.[22] At the height of the civil rights movement this practice, intended to perpetuate Jim Crow–style discrimination even after the end of Jim Crow, had been given the name "caging," and it never quite died out, despite numerous laws circumscribing its use.[23] In Ohio alone, the Republican Party sent out 230,000 postcards to overwhelmingly African American neighborhoods in Cleveland, Cincinnati, Dayton, Toledo, and Akron and mounted challenges to more than 35,000 of them. In almost every case, in Ohio and elsewhere, the challenges were thrown out by election administrators or the courts, despite pressure from a highly politicized Justice Department to accept them.[24]

That still left plenty of voter abuse to go around. Across the country, voters in urban, heavily African American precincts complained their polling places had too few voting machines to accommodate the crowds, creating lines as long as seven or eight hours and deterring an unknown number of voters. The *Charlotte Observer* said some places in the Carolinas looked "like Soviet bread stores, with lines spilling onto sidewalks and wrapping around buildings."[25] In some precincts, voters were given a time limit—three or five minutes—or else were pestered by election workers to hurry up, which surely led to mistakes and parts of the ballot unwillingly being left blank.[26]

In Ohio, some precincts had more votes than voters. Others showed anomalous totals for lower-order candidates or obscure third parties. In Columbus, a computer glitch in one precinct, later corrected, gave four thousand votes too many to President Bush. Miami County found an extra nineteen thousand unexplained votes after asserting that 100 percent of its precincts had reported their results.[27] The widespread fear was of "another Florida"—a second meltdown that would fail to produce a conclusive presidential winner and perpetuate the preelection combat indefinitely.

That such a meltdown did not materialize was largely because, as election lawyers like to say, the margin of victory exceeded the margin of litigation. Many voting rights activists, especially Democratic partisans, complained after the election that the Republicans had stolen tens of thousands of votes in Ohio, the closest and most intensely fought of the battleground states. Understandably, they were more inclined to believe the election-night exit polls showing Kerry far in the lead in several battlegrounds than the actual results, and felt that the disparity had to be connected to what they saw as massive voter suppression efforts.[28] The Democratic staff of the House Judiciary Committee, led by John Conyers of Michigan, later produced a report laying out what were overwhelmingly legitimate grievances in Ohio—not the least of which was that the networks had called the election for Bush while voters were still waiting in line to cast their ballots. But Kerry, who conceded the day after the election, recognized that dirty electioneering told only part of the story. President Bush's 118,000 vote margin in the Buckeye

State, and his 3 million vote margin in the national popular vote, were just too big to overcome or explain away.

In some quarters, this was a big pill to swallow. Many Americans clung to the belief that they lived in the world's greatest democracy, and they found the dysfunctions now laid bare to be jarring and frightening—an emotional response shared by Republicans and Democrats alike, even if they disagreed sharply about the reasons. A headline a couple of days after the election asserted "Kerry Won,"[29] to which the Republican antitax guru Grover Norquist responded with spectacular disdain that Democrats should calm down and stop "peeing on the furniture." "Any farmer will tell you that certain animals run around and are unpleasant," he said, "but when they've been fixed, then they are happy and sedate."[30]

In many ways, what the country witnessed was *American democracy as usual*, the most significant departure from established practice being that the ugliness was now out in the open and visible to all. The big lesson of 2004 was that Florida had not been a one-off. The system was beset with problems, and in the absence of a bipartisan consensus on how to fix them they were likely to persist indefinitely—if not worsen now that all pretense of democratic well-being had been dropped and gentlemanly restraint in the pursuit of partisan victory set asunder.

Everything in this sharper-elbowed political environment, even matters of national security, was ripe for partisan exploitation. For months before the election, the Bush administration issued warnings about potential terrorist attacks disrupting the elections, but without offering specifics. Tom Ridge, the director of Homeland Security, even suggested postponing the election altogether in the event of an attack.[31] The theme was taken up in some of the most contentious and most tightly fought races around the country. In late August in Florida, Palm Beach County sheriff's deputies surrounded the elections supervisor's office with men and crime-scene tape, citing the risk of a major terrorist attack—even though this was more than two months before the presidential election and the highest profile candidate on the ballot that day was the hapless Theresa LePore. No credible threat was ever substantiated, and LePore lost, but not before voting rights activists accused her of violating the election code and disenfranchising "walk-in" absentee voters who were planning on dropping off their envelopes at her office.[32] In

Warren County, Ohio, outside Cincinnati, officials locked down their administration building and barred reporters and independent observers from watching the vote count, citing a terror alert they'd supposedly received from the FBI. The FBI later denied any knowledge of it.[33]

The war on terror even became an excuse—in Georgia and other states—for election officials to keep audit logs and other data generated by electronic voting machines away from the public.[34] Cathy Cox claimed Georgia had witnessed its most accurate election ever, with only a 0.39 percent undervote, although voting rights activists found official documentation casting serious doubt on both those claims.[35] (Cox became an unexpected convert to the cause of voter-verifiable paper audit trails shortly after.) The Sequoia system in Riverside County, California, was seen crashing several times on Election Day;[36] in Cartaret County, North Carolina, a tabulation system made by Unilect lost 4,500 ballots because of a server capacity problem.[37] The voting rights group Verified Voting, founded by David Dill of Stanford University, tracked more than 23,000 complaints about e-voting on Election Day, and another 11,000 complaints thereafter. As in previous elections, many voters said they pressed the button for one candidate, only to have the name of another pop up on screen. Others complained of screen freezes, machines abruptly taken out of service, and other breakdowns, leading them to fear their votes were either improperly recorded or lost. No evidence emerged—in Ohio or anywhere else—that these problems changed election results. But, as Kim Alexander of the California Voter Foundation commented, "People shouldn't confuse the absence of a meltdown with a success."[38]

Two episodes in the election's aftermath illustrated how far the atmosphere had soured since 2000. The first was another impossibly close statewide contest in Washington, where the Republican candidate for governor, Dino Rossi, found himself 261 votes ahead of his Democratic challenger, Christine Gregoire, after the initial count. A machine recount narrowed that lead to 42 votes, and a manual recount put Gregoire ahead by 129 votes out of more than 2.9 million cast.

The civilized tone that had marked the Gorton-Cantwell Senate race in 2000 (Gail Collins of the New York Times joked that in Washington they like to age their ballots in oak casks[39]) was noticeable this time only by its absence. Both sides hired lawyers and crisis communications consultants. Rossi formally contested the election and, while helpless to prevent Gregoire from taking office, did not formally concede for seven months. As long as Rossi was ahead, his staff argued he had already won, and it was time to put the electoral process where it belonged— in the past. As soon as he found himself trailing, however, he became inordinately interested in the niceties of balloting procedure, count- ing rules, and the competence of the state's elections administrators. Gregoire, naturally, took the diametrically opposed tack, finding all kinds of irregularities to complain about until she realized the race was breaking in her favor.

The integrity of the state's elections administration did not fare well under withering scrutiny, especially in Seattle, where it turned out 660 provisional ballots had been fed into the vote totals without the voters' eligibility being checked first. The county official responsible for absen- tee ballots admitted having falsified a report in which she'd claimed that all absentee ballots were accounted for—when ninety-four had not been. The judge who oversaw the election contest found a total of 1,678 illegal votes—far more than Gregoire's margin of victory. Of these, the majority had been cast by disenfranchised felons or ex-felons whose cre- dentials were never checked. There were six instances of double-voting, nineteen votes cast by dead people, and a number of provisional ballots cast by ineligible voters. None of these findings altered the outcome, because there was no way to show which candidate these illegal ballots had favored.[40]

Such was the progress of four years. In 2000, neither side could be totally sure who really won but accepted the flawed outcome anyway. In 2004, they fought like dogs, and the result remained every bit as uncertain.

To partisan Republicans moved to paroxysms of rage, the uncertainty became its own rallying cry. Seattle was a liberal bastion and, as far as they were concerned, the liberals had stolen the race out from under them—whether they could prove it or not. The party faithful amassed outside the state Supreme Court in Olympia and made unflattering comparisons between the gubernatorial race and Ukraine's so-called Orange Revolution then dominating the news headlines.[41] Rossi's frus- tration was understandable after what amounted to an administrative coin toss, and it was redoubled when he lost to Gregoire in a rematch four years later. The Bush administration took notice, too, wondering why the U.S. attorney for western Washington, John McKay, was not pursuing a criminal investigation into voter fraud.[42] McKay was fired in 2006, along with six other U.S. attorneys who displeased the administration.

The second symptom of the souring national mood was the reception California senator Barbara Boxer received when she lodged a formal protest against the Ohio election results and forced a two-hour Senate debate before the results were certified. The move was largely symbolic, as Boxer was not disputing the outcome of the election, only the manner of its conduct. Four years earlier, no senator had dared object to the more dubious assignment of Florida's crucial twenty-five electoral votes, and Boxer felt it was important not to whitewash the system a second time. But the Republicans refused to take her objections seriously, painting her as some off-the-planet lunatic from what Tom DeLay, in the House of Representatives, described as the X-Files wing of the Democratic Party. Ric Keller, a Republican congressman from Florida, told Boxer to "get over it"—the twenty-first-century equivalent of Boss Tweed gloating to his enemies about his electoral victories in 1860s New York.[43]

One of the few Republicans who bothered to respond to Boxer on the Senate floor, Mike DeWine of Ohio, called her complaints "wild, incoherent [and] completely unsubstantiated." Vice President Dick Cheney spent much of the two hours talking and laughing in a corner. The Democrats looked uncomfortable, too, and none joined Boxer's side in the end-of-debate vote. John Kerry, the most directly interested Democrat, was not even present.

Such was the response of the two-party system to the breakdown of America's democratic apparatus. The Republicans, giddy on three electoral cycles' worth of victories, believed that winning provided its own validation, no matter what it took to get there. And the Democrats, when push came to shove, did not feel much different. Rather than dwell on a defeat they could not alter, or advocate for voters whose voices had not been heard, they preferred to lick their wounds and hope for better luck next time. The problems themselves were left to fester and deteriorate.

12

THE 3 PERCENT SOLUTION

As there is no evidence that voter-impersonation fraud is a problem, how can the fact that a legislature says it's a problem turn it into one? If the Wisconsin legislature says witches are a problem, shall Wisconsin courts be permitted to conduct witch trials?

—*Judge Richard A. Posner, Seventh Circuit Court of Appeals*[1]

Even before he entered the White House as George W. Bush's trusted political consigliere, Karl Rove knew all about the power of voter fraud as a rallying cry for the Republican Party faithful because he'd used it to devastating effect to win an election most other consultants would have given up for lost. Back in 1994, Rove had been hired by Perry Hooper, a Republican running for chief justice on the Alabama Supreme Court against a popular incumbent. The odds were long to begin with, in a state where no Republican had been elected to the supreme court in more than a century. Then Hooper fell behind on Election Day and remained stuck in second place for close to a year.

Rove had been hired because he seemed to understand how the political winds in the South were shifting, and he'd already begun turning an all-Democrat Texas Supreme Court into an all-Republican one. First, he created an aura of dishonesty around the incumbent, Sonny Hornsby, with negative campaign ads insinuating he was in the pocket of litigation-happy attorneys with "jackpot justice" cases pending before his court. The insinuations were distorted and in some cases flat-out untrue, but they made the race close, which was all that mattered.

When the initial count had Hooper trailing by a few hundred votes, Rove was not discouraged. Having tarnished the incumbent, he now set about tarnishing the people who voted for him. "Our role," one of Rove's staffers later told Joshua Green of *The Atlantic*, "was . . . to undermine the other side's support by casting them as liars, cheaters, stealers, immoral—all of that."[2] Campaign staffers and private investigators spread into Alabama's farthest-flung counties to look for signs of impropriety. Soon they were telling stories of poll watchers threatened with arrest, county election managers mysteriously locking themselves in their offices, and Democrats copying names off tombstones to enlist a ghost army of mail-in voters. A number of county probate judges (who run elections in Alabama) then started finding pockets of undiscovered votes for Hooper, and the count slowly turned in his favor.

The decisive issue was a batch of two thousand absentee ballots from heavily Democratic counties that had been signed but not notarized or witnessed. The practice of Alabama's courts was to admit such ballots as long as the voter intent was clear, but Rove understood he might obtain a different outcome if he could create a bad enough odor around them. Newspaper ads started running anti-Hornsby ads saying, "They steal elections they don't like." Hooper's campaign sued every probate judge, circuit clerk, and sheriff in Alabama, accusing them of blanket discrimination. The Alabama courts determined that the disputed absentee ballots should be counted, but Rove successfully appealed to the federal court of appeals to overturn that decision, and Hooper ended up prevailing by a 262-vote margin. Once installed as chief justice, he remarked, "That Karl Rove was a very impressive fellow."[3]

Another member of the Bush administration with a keen interest in voter fraud was John Ashcroft, who became attorney general in early 2001 after narrowly losing his Senate seat to a dead man, the recently deceased governor of Missouri, Mel Carnahan. Ashcroft conceded the race graciously as Carnahan's seat was taken up by his widow, but Missouri's other senator, Kit Bond, called for a criminal investigation. Bond, like many Republicans, was aggrieved that the polls had stayed open forty-five minutes longer in Democrat-leaning St. Louis than in the rest of the state to accommodate long lines in underserved African American neighborhoods. "I think the evidence points very strongly to a major criminal enterprise," Bond thundered. He later claimed to have found evidence of votes from "people who registered from vacant lots, dead people on the rolls, even a springer spaniel."[4]

Where Bond led, Ashcroft followed. Barely a month after his confirmation as attorney general, Ashcroft announced he was adding eight new lawyers to the Justice Department's civil rights division to pay closer attention to what he called "voter access and voter integrity."[5] The idea did not come from the head of the voting section, a career lawyer named Joe Rich who was told about it just twenty minutes before Ashcroft informed the media, but rather from his political staff, who believed—like Bond—that in-person voter fraud was *the* core issue requiring action.[6] A similar project had been proposed twenty years earlier under the Reagan administration but never went anywhere because the department's career lawyers saw it, correctly, as a remedy to a nonexistent problem.

For many Republicans, the idea of rampant voter fraud was an appealing one. Royal Masset, a longtime political director of the Texas Republican Party, described how, after every election, he'd receive calls from as many as fifty unsuccessful candidates and campaign workers who believed they had been cheated of what was rightfully theirs. "Human beings do not accept defeat easily," Masset said. "They would talk about illegal aliens mass-voting . . . or Jesse Jackson marching illegal voters to early voting locations." The problem was, there was almost never any proof—no sworn testimony, no names of illegal voters, nothing. Masset would tell his disappointed interlocutors, "Losing an election does not prove election fraud."[7]

The lack of evidence was no deterrent to the Bush administration, which chose to take the issue with the utmost seriousness. When the career lawyers at the Justice Department objected, they were shown the door and, in a stark departure from previous practice, replaced with more reliable Republican loyalists. "There is nothing funny about winning an election with stolen votes," Ashcroft intoned from the Great Hall of the main Department of Justice building as he formally rolled out his Ballot Access and Voting Integrity Initiative on the eve of the 2002 midterms. "All of us pay the price for voting fraud."[8] Hans von Spakovsky, a Georgia lawyer with a long history of support for voting-roll purges and crackdowns on in-person voter fraud, was recruited to the voting section and used his position to insert a voter ID requirement into the Help America Vote Act, albeit in the limited circumstance of a first-time voter who shows up at the polls after registering to vote by mail.[9] Kit Bond, one of HAVA's co-sponsors in the Senate, had wanted to go much further and institute a national voter ID requirement.[10] Still, the more modest victory was landmark enough, because it set a precedent that advocates of state-by-state voter ID laws could later cite as justification for their own actions.

The most insidious aspect of the Republican campaign was that it *sounded* like a good idea. Who wouldn't be opposed to stamping out voter fraud in a country where cheating in elections has been the great undeclared national sport for two centuries? Many rank-and-file Republicans genuinely believed in the righteousness of the cause. As John Feehery, a Republican consultant and former aide to Tom DeLay and Dennis Hastert, put it, "There was a general sense that when we were losing, fraud was the reason. It was hard not to be pretty cynical about it [the system]."[11]

The problem, though, was that they were chasing the wrong target. Study after study has shown in-person voter fraud to be a rarity in the modern era—"more rare than getting struck by lightning," in the words of one report from the Brennan Center for Justice[12]—because it is difficult to get away with and even more difficult to organize on any scale. On the handful of occasions when ineligible voters have tried to cast ballots, it has usually been because of a misunderstanding or a clerical error. Absentee ballot fraud is a more pervasive problem, as is corruption by elections officials, but with rare exceptions none of the legislation pushed by Republicans over the past fifteen years has addressed these issues. Shifting the onus of suspected fraud onto individual voters can *only* have a partisan purpose, because the members of the vote-eligible population most inconvenienced by a photo ID requirement—the 10 percent or more without a driver's license—are predominantly poor, transient, nonwhite, and more likely to vote Democrat if they vote at all.[13] For them, obtaining an alternate ID becomes a form of double registration, if not also a backdoor poll tax because of the costs involved. That's why, when election officials considered the matter in the past, they almost always opted to double-check the signature on file as a way of verifying a voter's identity. Voter ID is not only a remedy to a nonexistent problem; it doesn't even cover one of the central Republican concerns, voting by noncitizens, because in most states noncitizens can obtain driver's licenses as easily as Americans can.[14] Of course, IDs can be—and often are—faked too.

On rare occasions, Republican officials have come clean about the party's underlying agenda, which is to use ID laws to shave as much as 3 percent off the Democratic vote total in any given election. Masset, the former Republican Party political director in Texas, said as much in an interview with the *Houston Chronicle* in 2007.[15] And Dick Armey, the former House majority leader, also from Texas, confirmed it in a talk to Republican Party supporters in California in 2010—although in his case he characterized the 3 percent as fraudulent votes rightfully being taken *away* from the Democrats. "I'm tired of people being Republican all their lives and then changing parties when they die," Armey said, trotting out what by then had become a well-worn GOP trope to justify the party's voter ID obsession.[16]

The first place Ashcroft's task force went looking for fraud in 2002 was on Indian reservations in South Dakota in the wake of a closely fought Senate race in which Tim Johnson, the Democratic incumbent, held on to his seat by just 532 votes. Republican lawyers took several dozen affidavits, but only one of them made a serious allegation of criminal activity, and the matter went no further. Two years later, however, when the Republicans were gunning for South Dakota's other Democratic senator, minority leader Tom Daschle, hundreds of GOP poll watchers followed Native American voters to and from the polls and wrote down their license plate numbers in a clear attempt at intimidation. When Daschle went to court to put a stop to it, he was accused of trying to steal the election himself.[17]

A major ambition of the Republicans of the early 2000s was to complete their takeover of the Solid South, and they weren't content to wait for the naturally evolving shifts in the electorate to take their course. In 2002, the party ran a breathtakingly vicious campaign against Senator Max Cleland of Georgia, a Vietnam war veteran and triple amputee, running his photograph alongside images of Osama bin Laden and Saddam Hussein in a television ad to suggest he was on the side of the enemy because he'd voted against President Bush eleven times on national security issues. It was a classic case of the Republican machine (inspired by Rove and Ralph Reed, then the chair of the Georgia party) attacking a candidate where he was strongest. In fact, Cleland was widely regarded as a safe pair of hands on national security who had co-sponsored the legislation that led to the creation of the Department of Homeland Security earlier that year. The contested votes were mostly about the collective bargaining rights of federal workers. Nevertheless, the ads, together with possible problems with the state's new electronic voting machines, were effective in torpedoing his career.[18]

That same year in Alabama, the incumbent Democratic governor, Don Siegelman, saw a narrow lead in his reelection race slip away after a probate judge in rural Baldwin County found what he called a computer error in the vote count late on election night and deducted seven thousand votes from Siegelman's total—enough to upend the result statewide. The error was discovered after poll watchers and most of the judge's staff had gone home and was never explained except in the barest of terms or investigated further. One account attributed it to a lightning strike.[19] The judge, a Republican, refused to conduct a recount or allow an independent inspection of the ballots, and the state's attorney general, also a Republican, concurred. James Gundlach of Auburn University later wrote: "There is simply no way that electronic vote counting can produce two sets of results without someone using computer programs in ways that were not intended. In other words, the fact that two sets of results were reported is sufficient evidence in and of itself that the vote tabulation process was compromised."[20]

Siegelman had been a particularly juicy target for Republicans, a dynamic Southern governor seen as a strong potential challenger to President Bush in 2004. Alabama's attorney general, Bill Pryor, had begun gunning for him long before the election with a corruption investigation that went nowhere but nevertheless attained the strategic goal of making the race close. Rove was also involved, according to an opposition researcher who said she was given instructions to catch Siegelman cheating on his wife, much as Nixon had tried to catch Ted Kennedy in 1971. (The effort failed.)[21] After the election, a federal prosecutor married to one of Rove's closest political associates in Alabama initiated a four-year hunt for evidence of corruption against Siegelman and eventually mounted a case that stuck—thanks in part to a judge, a Bush appointee, who restricted the evidence he allowed Siegelman to present in his defense and gave the jury an unusually broad definition of corruption that made it much easier to find him guilty.

Nobody ever alleged that Siegelman put a cent in his own pocket. The most he was accused of was appointing a campaign contributor to a state oversight board, the sort of thing that happens in American politics every day. But it was enough to sink him. The trial alone scuttled Siegelman's hopes of winning the governor's office again. By the time he appealed his conviction, Bill Pryor had been elevated to the federal court of appeals and was instrumental in sending him to prison for six and a half years—despite the protests of dozens of former attorneys general from around the country who saw Siegelman as the victim of an ugly political witch hunt. "Rove came after me because he wanted me out of the way," Siegelman later said. "I was a Democrat they could not beat fair and square."[22]

The 2002 midterms were good to the Republicans all around: they took control of the Senate, expanded their majority in the House, and extended their grip on state offices across the South. But they weren't content to stop there. In Texas, where they took control of the state legislature for the first time in 130 years, they decided to redraw the boundaries of congressional and state legislative districts for the second time in two years—an anomalous and unprecedented maneuver explicitly designed to transform what was still a Republican minority in the state's congressional delegation into a majority and lock in those gains for the foreseeable future.

The scheme was concocted by Tom DeLay, the Texan House majority leader who spent several days in his home state to make sure it passed in the face of furious Democratic opposition. And the Republican establishment in Washington cheered on. Fred Barnes, the executive editor of the *Weekly Standard*, happily characterized the redistricting as a "gerrymander," placing partisan advantage over any notion of democratic fairness. He even used the words of the eminent historian Walter Dean Burnham to tell his fellow Republicans, "If you control the relevant institutions you can really do a number on the opposition."[23] Sure enough, the new electoral map changed a 17–15 Democratic edge in the Texas congressional delegation into a 21–11 Republican advantage after 2004.

The Justice Department had an opportunity to intervene, using its powers under the Voting Rights Act to deny Texas "preclearance" for the new map on the grounds that it violated the minority rights of black and Hispanic voters. The career lawyers in the voting section wanted to do just that. They wrote a memo detailing their concerns about two of the newly drawn districts, but they were overruled by the political appointees—another anomalous and unprecedented occurrence—and placed under a gag order preventing the memo from becoming public. (It was leaked in defiance of that order two years later.)[24] Not until 2006 did the Supreme Court rule that one of the two districts in question, carving out a swath of West Texas between Laredo and San Antonio, needed to be redrawn.

This was far from the only instance when the Justice Department's voting section suffered from political interference. The unit devoted to preclearance was cut from twenty-five lawyers to about ten, leaving it "shot to hell," in the words of Joe Rich, the veteran section chief who finally left in 2005.[25] Soon after, the section initiated the Justice Department's first-ever investigation into discrimination against *white* voters in black-majority Noxubee County, Mississippi. Rich's political overlords had no problem with redistricting plans that benefited Republicans, but they encouraged an investigation into Georgia's 2001 round of redistricting, which had been done under Democratic majority control. When Georgia came up with one of the country's first voter ID laws in 2005—including a provision that voters without a driver's license would have to pay to obtain an alternate identification document—the department leadership once again squashed the objections of the rank-and-file career lawyers. John Tanner, the new voting section chief, insisted the law would not be discriminatory, telling the Georgia NAACP with an entirely straight face that black people in Georgia were more likely than whites to carry government ID because they were used to trouble from the police. He also suggested that elderly people without a driver's license were more likely to be white than black or Latino because "minorities don't become elderly the way white people do . . . they die first."[26]

The Georgia voter ID law was eventually modified after a federal judge found, as the Justice Department lawyers had, that payment for a government ID was tantamount to an illegal poll tax. But the law itself was allowed to stand, despite the suspicions of the same federal judge that it was more broadly discriminatory against anyone who did not already have a government-issued document such as a passport or a driver's license.[27]

The federal courts generally seemed to underestimate the political calculus behind the voter ID movement. It didn't help that the Justice Department had chosen not to block the laws itself or that a 2005 bipartisan commission on electoral reform co-chaired by Jimmy Carter and James Baker endorsed voter ID—as long as it was introduced over a long enough period (they recommended two federal election cycles, or four years) and gave the elderly and the poor a chance to obtain their documentation free of charge.[28] Carter has since distanced himself from that position, which seems in retrospect to have been an ill-considered piece of political horse trading in the context of a much broader report. Unfortunately, the commission's findings gave voter ID advocates everywhere the opportunity to argue for years after that *even Jimmy Carter supports us.* It wasn't until 2013 that Carter made clear he did not.[29]

When a suit challenging Indiana's new ID law was heard by the Seventh Circuit Court of Appeals in 2007, Judge Richard Posner—later to undergo a change of heart and become perhaps the country's most scathing critic of voter ID—wrote a dismissive opinion suggesting that the only people likely to have their voting rights curtailed were too marginal to be taken seriously. "A great many people who are eligible to vote don't bother to do so," he said. "The benefits of voting to the individual voter are elusive . . . and even very slight costs in time or bother or out-of-pocket expense deter many people from voting, or at least from voting in elections they're not much interested in." In other words: what possible harm could one more obstacle do?[30]

The tone was similar when the Indiana case reached the Supreme Court. John Paul Stevens, writing for the majority, bought the premise that the law was intended to protect "the integrity and reliability of the electoral process," even though he acknowledged there was no recorded case of in-person voter fraud in Indiana's history and very few anywhere else in the country. The only examples he could cite in his extensive footnotes were a single proven case from the Rossi-Gregoire race in Washington State in 2004 and the repeat voting scams run by Boss Tweed's Tammany Hall machine *in the 1860s.* Stevens did cite instances of absentee-ballot fraud, including one episode in Indiana, but appears not to have noticed that the law under review did not address this problem.[31] And so the floodgates to voter ID laws nationwide were opened.

When John Ashcroft's Ballot Access and Voter Integrity Initiative struggled to find voter fraud cases to prosecute—the program, characterized as a "top priority," led to just thirty-eight prosecutions and twenty-four convictions in its first three years[32]—the Justice Department doubled down and rewrote the rulebook on pursuing election-related crimes. Federal prosecutors previously had been instructed not to intervene in elections until they were over, thereby avoiding the suspicion that their actions could in any way sway the outcome. But a new rulebook issued in 2007 merely cautioned them to hold off "in most cases."[33]

By then, one particularly aggressive and partisan U.S. attorney, Bradley Schlozman of the western district of Missouri, had already broken the old protocol. Just days before the 2006 midterm election, Schlozman issued indictments against four former voter-registration organizers for the community organizing group ACORN in Kansas City, accusing them not only of turning in fraudulent registration forms—something ACORN itself had acknowledged when it fired them—but of being part of a broader registration scam.[34] The charges landed in the middle of a contentious and closely fought Senate race in Missouri, and they were taken, by both parties, as a last-ditch attempt by Schlozman to save the incumbent Republican, Jim Talent. (Talent still lost, by two points, to Claire McCaskill.)

Schlozman had been part of the Republican legal team that fought against the extended polling station hours in St. Louis in 2000, and he'd been spoiling for a fight ever since. After Bush became president, he joined the Justice Department's civil rights division and quickly joined battle against the career staff, describing them in e-mails as "commies" and "mold spores," questioning their judgments and systematically issuing poor performance reviews. "My tentative plans are to gerrymander all of those crazy libs rights out of the section," Schlozman wrote in a 2003 e-mail later revealed in a Justice Department investigation.[35] Joe Rich called him "the most difficult, vindictive person I've ever worked for," and others in the voting section concurred.[36] In 2005, still with the Justice Department, Schlozman was determined to sue Missouri's Democratic secretary of state, Robin Carnahan, on the grounds that she'd failed in her duty to purge the registration lists of ineligible voters. When the then U.S. attorney for western Missouri, Todd Graves, told him there wasn't enough evidence to go after Carnahan, Schlozman filed suit anyway. (The case was later thrown out.) Four months later, Graves was fired, and Schlozman took over his job.[37]

ACORN, the country's largest network of community organizing groups, was already in the Republicans' crosshairs because it was viewed as a partisan organization, in practice if not in theory, that was flagrantly abusing the federal grant money it received to push an explicitly political agenda. (ACORN, for its part, pleaded that voter registration was not a partisan activity.) It—along with groups like the NAACP National Voter Fund and America Coming Together—had registered hundreds of thousands of new voters in 2004, most of them poor and thus more likely to vote for the Democrats. In certain parts of the country, these groups ran into trouble over the behavior of their low-wage registration workers, some of whom skimped on the work of finding real people to register and submitted bogus forms under a variety of fictitious names ranging from the innocuous to the ridiculous. No evidence ever emerged of a Dick Tracy or a Mary Poppins attempting to cast a ballot, but that did not stop a short-lived Republican front group, the American Center for Voting Rights (ACVR), from alleging that the registrations were part of a Democratic Party plot to inflate the voter rolls and steal elections around the country. ACVR, headed by yet another Republican lawyer from Missouri, Thor Hearne, even filed a racketeering suit in Ohio, accusing ACT, ACORN, and the NAACP Voter Fund of involvement in the drug trade on the basis of a single rogue NAACP volunteer who was found to have offered a Toledo-area man crack cocaine in exchange for a list of a hundred fictitious voters.[38]

When Schlozman told Missouri voters there was a "national investigation" into ACORN, he was presumably referring to ACVR's activities, because the Justice Department—despite the wishes of its political overlords—had no ongoing investigation of its own. The U.S. attorney for New Mexico, David Iglesias, was under pressure to mount a prosecution against ACORN in his state, but he refused because he lacked sufficient evidence. Likewise, John McKay, the U.S. attorney for western Washington, considered a grand jury investigation into the Rossi-Gregoire gubernatorial race but couldn't justify it on the merits. Both

Iglesias and McKay were fired in late 2006, along with five other U.S. attorneys deemed to have committed a variety of political sins against the administration.[39]

The ensuing scandal and investigation suggested to many observers that the Bush administration had pushed its luck too far. One thing going into the 2008 campaign season, though, remained constant: ACORN was still viewed as a piñata ripe for the pummeling. The goal was no longer to push for maximum partisan advantage in close races—the Republicans knew they were in for a rough year—but rather to cast a pall of illegitimacy over the Democrats, in particular over the unprecedented grassroots movement that ended up sweeping Barack Obama to victory over Hillary Clinton in the party primaries and thence into the White House. John McCain, the Republican nominee, repeatedly drew a link between ACORN and Obama, who had spent time as a community organizer in Chicago. During one of their preelection debates, McCain charged that ACORN was "on the verge of maybe perpetrating one of the greatest frauds in voter history in this country, maybe destroying the fabric of democracy."[40] Obama did not grace his accusation with a response.

In reality, ACORN was having a typically successful and chaotic year—boasting that it had registered 1.3 million new voters only to discover that at least four hundred thousand of those registrations were not valid. The Republicans went nuts, accusing ACORN of being a "quasi-criminal organization" and even "a multi-million dollar, multi-national conglomerate" responsible for the subprime mortgage lending crisis and the collapse of the global economy.[41] The hysteria did little to dent the Democrats' success at the polls that year, although the scrutiny did eventually lead to the demise of ACORN after the group was shown to have a number of troubling internal problems, some related to its registration efforts and some not. That, in turn, contributed to an atmosphere of barely repressed rage among grassroots Republicans that soon gave rise to the Tea Party movement and a new, even more startling round of voter suppression.

On the eve of the 2008 primaries, a conservative lobbying group named Citizens United wanted to air a ninety-minute film lambasting Hillary Clinton over DirecTV's satellite television network. The Federal Election Commission ruled that the group was in violation of the 2002 Bipartisan Campaign Reform Act, which prohibited any "electioneering communication" mentioning the name of a candidate on the airwaves within thirty days of a primary. Citizens United argued that the film was a documentary, not a campaign ad, and sued.

The Supreme Court, unusually, heard two separate rounds of argument and, by the time it ruled, had greatly expanded the scope of the case beyond *Hillary: The Movie* to encompass the question of money in politics in the broadest possible terms. The upshot was the lifting of all previous limits on so-called independent expenditures—money spent on political advertising by corporations or other outside parties in support of, but not in conjunction with, a particular candidate or campaign. In its 1976 decision *Buckley v. Valeo*, the court had already ruled—controversially—that money was a form of speech protected by the First Amendment, but imposed limits on what it considered legitimate support for a campaign as opposed to out-and-out corruption. The most radical departure in the *Citizens United* case was to narrow the definition of corruption almost to a vanishing point. If there was no explicit quid pro quo, the court ruled, it was not corruption. "Ingratiation and access" were no longer of concern; neither were "the corrosive and distorting effects of immense aggregations of wealth." Anthony Kennedy, writing for the majority, declared: "The appearance of influence or access . . . will not cause the electorate to lose faith in our democracy. . . . The fact that a corporation or any other speaker is willing to spend money to try to persuade voters presupposes that the people have the ultimate influence over elected officials."[42]

This was, to put it mildly, a tendentious point of view. The legal scholar Lawrence Lessig (later to make a run for the 2016 Democratic presidential nomination on the single issue of campaign finance) likened it to South African president Thabo Mbeki's pronouncement that the HIV virus did not cause AIDS. "Upon what authority did the Justice make this claim? On what factual basis did the Court rest this factual judgment?" Lessig asked. "The answer is none."[43]

The available evidence suggested that the electorate was, contrary to Kennedy's assertions, losing faith in the system, and losing it fast. In 1964, before the modern era of big-money politics inaugurated by *Buckley*, 64 percent of the American electorate believed the government was run for the benefit of all and only 29 percent believed it was for the benefit of a few big interests. By 2008, those numbers had almost exactly flipped.[44] Campaign finance reformers like Russ Feingold, the Wisconsin senator who co-authored the 2002 act disputed in *Citizens United*, had been complaining for years that the system was no better than "legalized bribery." Bernie Sanders, the independent senator from Vermont, used the same term during his campaign for the 2016 Democratic presidential nomination. And it wasn't just the left talking in these terms. Jack Abramoff, the disgraced former super-lobbyist, also called it "legalized bribery." So did David Rubenstein, the co-founder of the Carlyle Group, which enjoyed close ties to the Bush administration. The fact that the money was going to politicians' campaign war chests and not directly into their pocket may have made, in the words of former Louisiana senator Russell Long, no more than a "hairline's difference."[45] Lessig again: "We don't excuse a bank robber if he donates the money he stole to an orphanage. Neither should we excuse a political system that bends itself because of its dependency upon funders just because it donates the proceeds it collects to funding political speech."

It was remarkable that a decision reached by a group of originalists—justices supposedly devoted to determining the intent behind the wording of the Constitution—could have taken the political system so far from the vision of the country's founders. The push for American independence had been motivated, after all, by disgust at the systemic corruptions of British rule. Yet *Citizens United* gave virtually free rein to the "monied interests" that Jefferson and others had hoped to curtail; it was closer in spirit to the view of avowed anti-democrats like John Jay and Alexander Hamilton that the country was best governed by those who owned it.[46] The 2010 ruling did not invent the problem of money in politics, of course. Jefferson was merely the first in a long line of political leaders to warn against its corrupting power.[47] The aftermath of the *Buckley* decision had already revealed how campaign contributions distorted policy making in both major parties—away from the interests of the poor and the working class and toward the interests of the elite. Now, though, that distortion risked running out of control entirely.

In the short term, at least, *Citizens United* proved to be a partisan windfall for the Republicans. A University of Alberta study of 38,000 state legislative races in the 2010 and 2012 cycles showed a correlation between political spending and electoral outcomes, meaning that the Republicans, whose super PACs were able to raise and spend significantly more money than their Democratic counterparts, reaped the greater benefits. The study suggested that direct and indirect campaign contributions had increased the probability of a Republican candidate prevailing by about 4 percent. In hard-fought states like North Carolina and Tennessee, the increase was as high as 15 percent.[48]

The flood of new, unregulated money acted as a turbo boost to the rise of the Tea Party, contributing to a Republican sweep of state legislatures and governorships over the next three election cycles and pushing the party's candidates significantly to the right. Was that an accurate reflection of the will of the people? In some states, perhaps. But in North Carolina, a state that went for Barack Obama in 2008 and came close to doing so again in 2012, it was difficult if not impossible to accept that Republicans touting the most radical agenda in a generation could be taking over every branch of state government *solely as a matter of popular choice*. Something altogether less democratic appeared to be afoot—and indeed it was.

13

POPE AND ABBOTT: THE NEW RELIGION OF BUYING AND SUPPRESSING VOTES

The law is going to kick the Democrats in the butt. . . . If it hurts a bunch of college kids too lazy to get up off their bohunkus and go get a photo ID, so be it. If it hurts a bunch of lazy blacks that want the government to give them everything, so be it.

—*Don Yelton, Buncombe County, North Carolina, Republican Party, on the state's HB 589, also known as "the monster law"*[1]

In the fall of 2010, John Snow, a retired judge from western North Carolina, thought he was cruising to a fourth term in the state senate when a barrage of hostile television ads alerted him that the Republicans were after his hide. He was one of the most conservative Democrats in the state legislature, but now he was being lambasted as a profligate spender, an elitist, and a coddler of murderers on death row. Almost every charge against him was distorted or untrue, but he didn't have the wherewithal to fight back on equal terms. At first Snow couldn't understand where his neophyte Republican opponent was getting his money. By the time he understood that all previous rules of campaigning had been upended by *Citizens United* and that he and twenty-one other Democrats in state legislative races were now facing an all-out assault from foundations and political lobbying groups financed largely by one man, the North Carolina discount store magnate and conservative ideologue Art Pope, it was too late. He'd lost his race by 199 votes.[2]

Republicans picked up eighteen of the twenty-two seats they targeted in North Carolina that year, winning control of both chambers of the state legislature for the first time since Reconstruction. Many of the attack ads used to push their candidates over the top were bankrolled, directly or indirectly, by Pope, his family, or one of a number of independent groups to which Pope had close ties. These groups included Civitas Action, which received 97 percent of its annual income from the Pope family foundation; Real Jobs NC, a new, supposedly nonpartisan entity started with $200,000 in seed money from Pope's Variety Stores; and Americans for Prosperity, a national group founded by the Koch brothers to which Pope's family foundation had contributed $1.3 million. (Pope also sat on the board.) One attack ad that attracted national attention characterized state senate candidate Margaret Dickson as a floozy with bright lipstick, garish jewelry, and a fat wad of $100 bills.[3] She also lost.

Pope and his network poured just $2.24 million into the 2010 election cycle, a relatively small investment that nevertheless blew away the opposition because it was allocated in places nobody had thought to invest before. The $265,000 thrown at unseating John Snow, for example, was more than Snow's entire war chest. Before *Citizens United*, such independent expenditures would have been both illegal and inconceivable. When the state Republican Party put up another $320,000 against Snow, including a large direct contribution from Pope, it proved overwhelming. Shell-shocked Democrats accused Pope of buying the election, and Pope made only a token effort to bat the accusation away. "Acknowledge and proud of it," he said of the money he and his network had spent. "If that helped them win, especially in the close elections, then wonderful."[4]

Pope's focus on state races didn't mean he'd forgotten about the Democrats' slim advantage in the state's congressional delegation. He was merely warming up for the next round of combat two years down the road. The most important impact his money made in the 2010 cycle was to give the new Republican majority in the state legislature control over redistricting—redrawing the boundaries of both congressional and state legislative districts based on data from that year's U.S. Census. Pope didn't need to spend lavishly on congressional races because, after redistricting, the political makeup of the congressional delegation would largely take care of itself. The 1991 and 2001 rounds of redistricting in North Carolina, run by Democrats, had been some of the most bruising and litigious in the country's history, and now the Republicans were ready for payback.[5] With some expert technical advice, powerful computer technology, and a suitably cynical approach to carving up the electorate, they could settle the next several cycles of voting before the campaigning even began.

This wasn't just Pope's project. The Republican Party made redistricting a priority nationwide and sensed that 2010 could be a very good year, as midterm elections often are for the party in opposition to the president. Ed Gillespie, a former chair of the Republican National Committee, repurposed the anodyne-sounding Republican State Leadership Committee (RSLC), which had previously offered logistical support to state legislators on policy issues, as a strategic and fund-raising powerhouse for what became known, tellingly, as Project REDMAP, short for the Redistricting Majority Project. To maximize its fund-raising potential in the wake of *Citizens United*, the party treated the RSLC as an independent organization entirely separate from the Republican National Committee—a legalistic work-around that created what some critics described as a dark money conduit. In North Carolina, an estimated $1.25 million in donations to the RSLC was funneled through Real Jobs NC, one of the groups established by Art Pope.[6]

After the election, Pope became a special adviser to the mapping team, and they went far beyond anything the Democrats had done when they were in charge. They broke down the population neighborhood by neighborhood, even street by street, to separate out Democrats from Republicans—and, in many cases, blacks from whites. On the congressional level, they created three spectacularly misshapen districts to cram in as many Democrats as possible and dilute their support elsewhere. At the state legislative level, they targeted candidates as well as voters; where they saw progressive Democratic women representatives in neighboring districts they collapsed their constituencies and forced them to compete against each other for the single remaining seat—a practice they nicknamed "double bunking."[7]

The goal of Project REDMAP was to turn a 7–6 Democratic majority in North Carolina's congressional delegation into a 10–3 edge for the Republicans, and make it all but voter-proof. Mission accomplished; in the 2012 election, North Carolina voted 51 percent to 49 percent in favor of Democratic congressional candidates, yet the GOP took nine out of thirteen seats. (The Republicans clinched the tenth seat they wanted in 2014.) One of the new districts looked like a gesticulating monkey; another—the much contested 12th district, which had been subject to litigation twenty years earlier because of a Democrat-imposed gerrymander—was long and straggly, stretching like an elongated rubber band from parts of Greensboro and Winston-Salem 120 miles southwest to Charlotte.

The Republicans were not the only gerrymandering party in 2011. The practice has always been a matter of opportunity in American politics, not party ideology, and Democrats were hard at it in Maryland and other states where they held an advantage. Still, Project REDMAP marked a new departure because of the money, the sophisticated mechanisms the RSLC devised to distribute it, and the party's willingness to play dirty in state races where nobody had previously paid much attention. The Democrats were simply steamrollered.[8] The biggest imbalances in the GOP's favor came in six crucial presidential states all won by Barack Obama in 2008—Michigan, Ohio, Pennsylvania, Virginia, North Carolina, and Florida—but the impact was felt beyond even these. Of the ten most gerrymandered states, seven favored the Republicans and just three favored the Democrats. By the time 2012 rolled around, the Republican Party had a seven-point voting edge in those ten states but won 76 percent more House seats.[9]

North Carolina was, in many ways, ground zero for the Republican effort, with its peculiar alignment of special-interest money, aggressive party strategizing, and ugly segregationist history. North Carolina's Republicans, mindful of the restrictions imposed by the Voting Rights Act, argued that they were *increasing* the number of safe districts for black representatives. Really, though, what they were doing was engaging in the old practice of "packing" the black vote and curtailing its overall influence. Tom Hofeller, the Republicans' trusted map specialist, acknowledged as much in an e-mail about North Carolina's first congressional district that came to light two years later.[10]

After redistricting, African Americans were 50 percent more likely than whites to live in a split precinct, meaning that their voting area now straddled at least one boundary line, so different voters within the same jurisdiction would be voting for different races. Split precincts are, more or less by definition, an indication of gerrymandering and, in the

South, have long been associated with packing or cracking black votes. Bob Hall of the voting rights group Democracy North Carolina called it "computerized apartheid."[11]

From the RSLC's perspective, discrimination was not the primary intent; North Carolina was just a promising state where the party could hope to make gains.[12] But for the state party, the fight was more visceral and more laden with history. Obama had been the first Democratic presidential candidate to win North Carolina since Jimmy Carter, and the first black candidate ever to win a statewide election; not even the mixed-race Fusionist alliance of the 1890s had matched his achievement. Obama did it with an astonishingly successful ground game that took advantage of early voting, same-day registration, and other improvements in voter access made in the wake of the Help America Vote Act. The improvements had been attained despite some initial resistance from Democrats as well as Republicans; both major parties worried that the other side might benefit or that they could lose strategic control of their supporters.[13] As things transpired, voter participation in 2008 leapt to 70 percent, up from 64 percent in 2004. The higher turnout included 2.4 million North Carolinians who voted early, roughly 10 percent of whom registered on the spot. The black vote was key: turnout among African Americans jumped from 59 percent in 2004 to 72 percent in 2008.[14]

Right away, Republican strategists in North Carolina knew they had to do something to stem this tide. "The liberals . . . were motivated, well-financed, and united," the former state party chair Jack Hawke wrote in a postmortem two weeks after Obama's election. "Until conservatives can say the same, our country will continue sliding toward socialism."[15] Hawke zeroed in on two areas of concern, the black vote and the youth vote—the very groups who would be most heavily affected by suppressive new voting legislation in the ensuing years. "They had to reverse the Democrats' 2008 achievement and cripple the high turnout of black and young voters," Democracy North Carolina's Bob Hall commented. "The partisan goal became intertwined with an antiblack, antiyouth electoral strategy, and they did it intentionally, purposefully."[16]

The 2012 electoral year in North Carolina was another close one in terms of vote totals (Obama lost the state by just two percentage points), but still proved to be a Republican blowout because of the distorting effect of the redrawn district boundaries and what the state political analyst John Davis characterized as overwhelming advantages for the GOP in "power, money, maps, message, momentum."[17] In addition to its gains in the congressional delegation, the party won a supermajority in both houses of the state legislature and captured the governorship. Art Pope once again proved to be the engine of a huge fund-raising advantage for Republicans and was rewarded first by being named head of incoming governor Pat McCrory's transition team and then by being appointed state budget director. "In North Carolina," the *Raleigh News & Observer* later lamented, "the ideal of one person, one vote is giving way to one person who rules the vote. And his name is Art Pope."[18]

McCrory had been a pragmatic, business-friendly mayor of Charlotte before taking the governorship but now found himself surrounded by forces pushing a far more radical agenda. Some of the more eye-catching proposals from the state legislature included drug testing for welfare recipients, prosecuting thirteen-year-olds as adults, allowing lobbyists to shower lawmakers with gifts without restriction, and making Christianity the state religion. Pope, playing a similar role to Mark Hanna in President McKinley's administration, or Karl Rove in George W. Bush's, wasted no time pushing his pet causes, including the elimination of public campaign financing for judicial races. The measure had acted as a bulwark preventing wealthy campaign donors from influencing judges who heard their cases, but it was dismissed by Pope as "candidate welfare."[19] The party also wasted no time putting together what would eventually become one of the most restrictive voting laws in the country—cutting back the number of early voting days, eliminating same-day registration, obliging voters to vote only in their own precinct, cutting a preregistration program for sixteen- and seventeen-year-olds, making it easier for poll observers to challenge voters, and, of course, introducing a strict photo ID requirement.

Many of these proposals took direct aim at the surge in black voter turnout. African Americans made up 22 percent of North Carolina's voters but more than 40 percent of those who had used same-day registration in 2008, 2010, and 2012. They were also twice as likely as white voters to cast a ballot in a precinct other than their own.[20] Republicans in the state legislature—inspired by the intellectual groundwork laid by Art Pope's think tanks—had pushed for a crackdown right after the 2010 election, but they couldn't muster the handful of Democratic votes they needed for a veto-proof supermajority. Now that the governorship had switched party hands, the only thing holding them back was the Voting Rights Act, and even that obstacle appeared to lift as the Supreme Court gutted the preclearance requirement in June 2013. The chair of the state Senate Rules Committee wasted no time announcing, "So, now we can go with the full bill."[21] HB 589 cleared both houses of the legislature and was signed into law less than two months after the Supreme Court's *Shelby* decision.

North Carolina's African American community was incensed. The chair of the state NAACP, Rev. William Barber, initiated regular weekly protests outside the Capitol that became known as Moral Mondays and were so successful they spawned copycat protests in other Southern states where voting rights were under threat. "This is our Selma," Barber said. "We refuse to accept the revival of Jim Crow tactics used to block access to the ballot for African American and Latino voters."[22] Hundreds of protesters were arrested over the course of the first several Moral Mondays for nonviolent offenses like trespassing on state property (the Capitol) or refusal to disperse. Pope's Civitas Institute responded by creating an online "pick the protester" game on its website, in which users were invited to decide which of three detainee mugshots picked at random matched information the institute had dug up—name, race, age, arrest record, employer's name, "interest group affiliations," or some discrepancy in the voter registration records like a mismatch between a current address and a registration address.[23]

It was difficult not to see this as red-meat politics at its crudest, intended to reinforce conservative prejudices about blacks and liberals and stir the Republican base to new heights of indignation and hostility. The Institute for Southern Studies said the list was reminiscent of the openly racist White Citizens' Councils, which, at the height of the civil rights movement, had published the names of NAACP supporters in local newspapers to encourage retaliation.[24]

The NAACP also went to court, in concert with many other voting rights groups and with the support of the Justice Department. A few weeks before the 2014 midterms, a federal appeals panel struck down HB 589's bans on same-day registration and out-of-precinct voting, agreeing that these measures would have an adverse impact on minority access to the ballot box. When the matter went up to the Supreme Court, however, the bans were reinstated so the elections could go ahead without officials having to contend with the upheaval of a last-minute rule change.[25]

By the time HB 589 returned to a full hearing in federal court the following summer, proponents were arguing that black turnout in the 2014 midterms was higher than it had been in 2010—true—so nobody's voting rights had been harmed. Opponents countered that the turnout comparison was not meaningful, because the two elections attracted vastly different levels of public interest.[26] More significant, they said, was a study showing that at least thirty thousand voters had been prevented from casting a ballot by the new restrictions, with African Americans disproportionately affected.[27] "The North Carolina General Assembly *knew* that this law would discriminate against African-American voters," the state NAACP charged, "but passed it anyway."[28]

The lawmakers themselves were not impervious to such arguments, because on the eve of the trial in July 2015, they took the precaution of watering down HB 589's voter ID requirement, due to take effect in 2016, and thus removing it from judicial debate. Under the modified rules, voters in certain categories would have to produce only a utility bill or a voter registration card—neither of them government-issued photo ID—to qualify for a provisional ballot.[29]

This did not indicate that North Carolina's all-powerful Republicans had undergone a change of heart or that they had suddenly woken up to the needs and sensitivities of black voters; their very next move, in fact, was to pass a law to protect the state's Confederate memorials, which the NAACP and others found deeply offensive.[30] But they were aware of the affidavits piling up against them and the exposure HB 589 was receiving nationally and internationally. They also heard testimony that voter ID would be onerous and expensive to administer and was hampered by bureaucratic problems at the state Department of Motor Vehicles. And so they erred on the side of caution.[31]

No such restraint has so far been in evidence in Texas, where in 2011 state Republicans bent and finagled every rule possible to pass the most repressive, most nakedly partisan voter ID law in the land. Under the new rules, a state student photo ID did not qualify as adequate documentation, but a concealed-carry weapons permit did. Military ID passed muster; state employee cards did not. The partisan tilt was unmistakable. Anyone needing an "election identification certificate" could not obtain one from their local voter registration office. They had to go instead to the Texas Department of Public Safety, which had no presence in about one-third of the state's 254 counties and only part-time offices, some of them open just one day a week, in forty others. If an applicant for an election identification card needed to obtain a replacement birth certificate first, that required a visit to yet another office and a minimum fee of $22, not including the cost and inconvenience of traveling what in more remote parts of Texas can be dizzyingly long distances.[32]

The law was turned down for preclearance by the Justice Department but was revived the very day that the Supreme Court issued its *Shelby* ruling. When it reached U.S. District Court, it was savaged as "an unconstitutional burden on the right to vote . . . imposed with an unconstitutional discriminatory purpose" but, like North Carolina's law, was waved through by the Supreme Court for the 2014 midterms because the lower-court ruling came down just a few weeks before Election Day.

Two factors pushed Texas to this extreme, and both were tinged with racial animus. The first was Barack Obama's election as president, which prompted voter ID to jump from a second- or third-tier political issue to the very top of the Republicans' priority list. "Everything else—roads, transportation, schools, health care—was now insignificant by comparison," the then chair of the Texas House Committee on Elections, Todd Smith, recalled. "Somebody had whipped up the grassroots and the perception was that illegals were voting by the busload and swaying elections."[33]

The Tea Party was now in the ascendant, and talk of noncitizens voting in Texas dovetailed with a national conversation in which Tea Party activists were casting doubt on Obama's own citizenship, religion, and birthplace—as well as the legitimacy of the voters who swept him into office. "You didn't see this sort of polarization of the conservative electorate until Obama got elected," observed Chad Dunn, a Houston lawyer and former Democratic Party operative who later spearheaded the legal challenge to voter ID. "It woke up a lot of deep-seated feelings about race in the South."[34]

The second reason was the rapidly changing demographic makeup of Texas itself.

The 2010 Census showed that minorities accounted for a staggering 89 percent of the state's population increase over the previous ten years; the school system was now majority Hispanic for the first time. "These were astronomical metrics of demographic growth," the Democratic state representative Trey Martinez-Fischer later testified. [35]

Texas is not a swing state like North Carolina, but the Republicans there understood they could lose their dominance at any time. Like the earthquake that Californians call the Big One, the political shift is forecast often and viewed as inevitable—it's just a matter of when. Many people, on both sides of the aisle, thought the shift might come in the wake of the highly competitive primary race in Texas between Obama and Hillary Clinton in 2008, which caused turnout to jump by more than two *million* votes above the Texas average for Democratic primaries, including a sharp uptick in Hispanic turnout to 32 percent, up from 24 percent in the 2004 primary. [36]

There is nothing automatic, of course, about Hispanic voters being anti-Republican, especially not in Texas. When George W. Bush was governor, he made efforts to broaden the Republican Party's appeal among Hispanics and ended up hitting a high-water mark of 49 percent of the Hispanic vote in his 2004 presidential reelection bid. Those numbers have seesawed since: Mitt Romney captured just 27 percent of the Hispanic vote in 2012, while Greg Abbott won 44 percent in his 2014 gubernatorial campaign, despite his hard line on immigration issues, by playing up his wife's Hispanic heritage. [37]

Both parties believe Hispanic voters will skew Democratic over time; they just need to start voting in larger numbers. The 2008 Democratic primary was not, in the end, a breakthrough moment. By 2012, the number of eligible Hispanic voters who did not vote was back up to 60 percent, a horrifying statistic that harkened back to the pre–civil rights era when African Americans could not vote at all and "Mexicans," as they were generally described, were deemed to be for sale to the highest political bidder. [38]

That rotten history did not cease with the end of Jim Crow. For years after the passage of the Voting Rights Act, Texas obliged voters to re-register every year, a maneuver denounced by one newspaper as a "poll tax without the tax" but praised by Governor John Connally in scarcely disguised racial language as "the most logical means of preventing fraud and guaranteeing the purity of the ballot box."[39] Every round of redistricting undertaken since—by both parties—has featured minority voter suppression serious enough to warrant the intervention of the Justice Department or the federal courts. Intimidation of minority voters remains common, especially in the smaller rural counties, as does the Jim Crow–era practice of creating at-large districts to dilute minority representation on city councils and county boards.[40]

To that inglorious tradition, the cancers of modern politics have now been added. The Obama-Clinton primary proved that voters can be motivated if campaigns sense real competition and spend their money accordingly. Most of the time, however, minority voters in Texas find themselves in noncompetitive gerrymandered districts and struggle to find a reason to vote even in statewide political races. Overall, turnout in Texas tends to be lower than almost anywhere else in the country because of the lack of competition, and because of enduring restrictions on absentee voting and out-of-precinct voting that affect rural counties in particular. The Democrats have certainly courted minorities, but the perception that the party is the perennial underdog has hampered its fund-raising and get-out-the-vote efforts. "It's a chicken and egg thing," Dunn said. "Democrats could certainly do more to mobilize these communities, but if Texas was more competitive there would be more money for mobilization."

The Republicans have had their own struggles with voter apathy, but they have also been much better funded and have pounced on red-meat issues like immigration and fear of voter fraud because they know these will stir the passions of the party's increasingly right-wing base, even as more moderate voters stay away. The much-predicted takeover of Texas politics by minority groups may not have happened yet, but the *fear* of it has proven a potent political motivator to the other side.

Nobody in the past fifteen years has invoked the specter of voter fraud or pushed for tough voter ID restrictions more loudly than Greg Abbott, who served three terms as Texas's attorney general before ascending to the governorship and has personified the rightward drift of his party. In 2006, Abbott described voter fraud as "an epidemic . . . infesting the electoral process" and announced he'd secured $1.5 million in federal grant money to train local law enforcement officials to root it out.[41] The initiative, predictably, was a bust: Texas secured just two convictions for fraudulent voter impersonation in the years leading up to passage of the voter ID law in 2011, out of roughly 20 million votes cast. But Abbott remained undeterred. "It doesn't matter that the cheating is in-person voter impersonation or absentee ballot," he told the *Dallas Morning News* in 2013. "What matters more is the integrity of the election system. . . . Anyone who thinks there isn't cheating going on at the ballot box is wrong."[42]

In the early running, Abbott's main judicial weapon was a bipartisan 2003 law intended to crack down on a form of absentee ballot manipulation known as vote harvesting—a category including the "vote whores" in the San Antonio hinterlands discussed in chapter 9. The problem was a genuine one, but the wording of the law was problematic, and Abbott soon came under fire for applying it in ways that were said to be both discriminatory and tilted toward Republican partisan interests.

A lawsuit filed in 2006 and later settled out of court alleged that Abbott's office had indicted a dozen elderly black or Hispanic women solely because they carried absentee ballots to the mail on behalf of infirm friends and forgot to sign the envelope, as the law required.[43] At the same time, Abbott took no action to investigate an election in the Dallas suburb of Highland Park in 2005 in which two Republican election judges were suspected of personally distributing about a hundred ballots without following standard procedure on checking eligibility. "While Greg Abbott's office has prosecuted minority seniors for simply mailing ballots," the lawyer spearheading the suit, Gerry Hebert, told the Texas House Committee on Elections in 2008, "he has not prosecuted anyone on the other side of the aisle for what appears to be open-and-shut cases of real voter fraud."[44]

Minority-vote organizers in poorer areas of the state complained that Abbott's actions had made them fearful of doing their jobs—whether or not the state had found evidence of irregularly cast votes. In 2010, armed police acting for the attorney general's office swooped in on the offices of the voter registration organization Houston Votes and seized computers and documentary records, ostensibly on suspicion of some sort of voter fraud. No charges ever surfaced, but by the time the investigation was dropped a year later, Houston Votes had lost its funding and closed its doors. Abbott's office never returned the materials it seized; instead, it obtained a court order to destroy them.[45]

Abbott's 2006 warning about the voter fraud "epidemic" coincided with the first efforts by Texas Republicans to push for a voter ID law. In 2005 and again in 2007, they tested the waters with a bill that did not even insist on photo ID—utility bills, bank statements, and pay checks were acceptable alternatives. But the political appetite to enact something was already voracious. When the Houston-area Democratic state senator Mario Gallegos underwent liver transplant surgery in 2007, the Republicans saw an opportunity to seize a supermajority and ram through a voter ID law. (With Gallegos, they were one vote short of that supermajority and couldn't bring the issue to the floor.) They failed only because Gallegos, going against his doctor's orders, had his hospital bed moved to the state Capitol in Austin and so managed to keep the issue off the agenda for the rest of the legislative session.[46]

By 2009, the atmosphere had changed entirely. Voter ID was now the ultimate wedge issue, actively encouraged by national political consultants not just because it was a means of suppressing Democratic votes, but also because it was a vehicle for turning out conservative Republicans. Tea Party activists and their allies in elected office flooded the airwaves with paranoid talk about illegal immigrants coming to the polls en masse, and they accused anyone who challenged them—moderate Republicans as well as Democrats—of favoring voting rights for noncitizens. Their assertions bore no relationship to reality, but it didn't matter. Their voters, especially primary voters, believed the stories about busloads of immigrants, and that was enough.

The Republicans still did not have a supermajority in the state senate, but they passed a special order exempting voter ID from the usual two-thirds rule (viewed in some quarters as a "nuclear option" overturning decades of bipartisan tradition[47]). When the Democrats reacted by running out the clock on the legislative timetable—a Texas variant on the filibuster known as "chubbing"—they were punished with a barrage of campaign ads accusing them of obstructionism and illegal immigrant coddling and promptly lost twenty-one seats in the Texas House. Before the 2010 elections, they had been just a seat or two away from a majority, but afterward they commanded barely one-third of the chamber. Such was the political power of voter ID: even *before* it became law, it worked powerfully in the Republicans' favor.

After 2010, the party went into overdrive—"trying to rocket this bill out of there," in the words of the Democratic senator Rodney Ellis. There was no question now of going with the older, softer legislation. The GOP had the most conservative state legislature in half a century, perhaps since Reconstruction, and was determined to take full advantage before the bloom faded. Moderates like Todd Smith—who had held hearings and was genuinely interested to know which voters might be adversely affected by the ID requirement—were kicked out of their committee positions and challenged in primary races. Governor Rick Perry declared voter ID an "emergency matter for immediate consideration," meaning that it qualified for the first sixty days of the 2011 legislative session. He never explained what the emergency was. The draconian new bill, known as Senate Bill 14, was thrown together so hastily its own sponsors didn't seem conversant with its contents.[48] No Republican dared question it, much less vote against it. "Any of us would've been lynched," Smith said, "if we hadn't passed the version the party apparatus wanted us to pass."[49]

When the backlash came, first from the Justice Department and then from the federal courts, the Republicans amped up their rhetoric about Democrats coddling illegal immigrants, this time taking aim at Washington, D.C., as well as their adversaries across the aisle back home. The party didn't seem to care what happened to the law; as an engine of indignation and outrage to stir up their supporters it was already unbeatable. Abbott, who was gearing up for his run for governor, made sure he was front and center of the counterblast. "The president is using the legal system as a sword to wage partisan battles rather than a shield to protect voting rights," he charged in a 2013 piece in the *Washington Times*, conveniently forgetting Texas's fifty-year history of confrontation with previous presidential administrations, Republican as well as Democrat. "Crying 'voter suppression' is nothing but a cynical scare tactic. . . . The administration's absurd claim that this common-sense fraud prevention device is actually a racist plot to prevent minorities from voting would be comical if it weren't so depressing to see an American president stoop to that level."[50]

Abbott had, of course, flipped the truth almost entirely. Interestingly, he was no longer calling in-person voter fraud an "epidemic"—and had not for several years.

Before 2010, just two states, Indiana and Georgia, had voter ID requirements on their statute books. By the 2014 midterms, sixteen states were demanding that voters produce government-issued photo ID at the polls, and another sixteen required some lesser form of identification.[51] Many legislatures appear to have taken their cue from a model ID bill drawn up in 2009 by ALEC, the American Legislative Exchange Council, a conservative lobbying group that has pioneered the art of pushing copycat legislation in multiple states at once. "I very rarely see a single issue taken up by as many states in such a short period of time," Jennie Bowser of the bipartisan National Conference of State Legislatures told NBC News. "It's been a pretty remarkable spread."[52]

The push to restrict voter access hardly stopped at voter ID. Several states, including Ohio, Florida, and Wisconsin, cut back on early voting; in Ohio and Florida the restriction included the Sunday before Election Day, when black churches typically organize "Get Your Souls to the Polls" drives.[53] Florida attempted another voter purge ahead of the 2012 election, this time targeting noncitizens instead of felons, and once again it was forced to backtrack when it turned out that the list, culled from Department of Highway Safety and Motor Vehicles data, was close to 100 percent erroneous.[54] The state also cracked down on third-party registration drives, with a 2011 law so tough even schoolteachers helping to register their students received warning letters and fines. The League of Women Voters, which had operated in the state problem-free for seventy-two years, suspended its registration drives altogether, saying the law posed too great a risk to its volunteers.[55]

From one end of the country to the other, Republican politicians felt emboldened to belittle whole categories of voters, implying that they were, in and of themselves, an obstacle to the democratic process. The Speaker of the New Hampshire House, Bill O'Brien, told a Tea Party meeting that students were foolish because they lacked life experience; rather than being allowed to "vote their feelings," they should be barred from same-day registration, if not banned from voting at their campus precinct altogether. Doug Preisse, party chair in Franklin County, Ohio, freely acknowledged that restrictions on early voting would affect black voters but said it was better that way. "I guess I really actually feel we shouldn't contort the voting process to accommodate the urban—read African-American—voter-turnout machine," he told the *Columbus Dispatch* in an e-mail. "Let's be fair and reasonable."[56]

If, as the evidence strongly suggests, the goal of the new laws promulgated by Republicans was to suppress votes, the question then arises: how successful have they been? It's a maddeningly difficult question to answer, because people's motives for voting fluctuate from election to election, and the variables—the strictness of the ID laws, the socioeconomics of each state, the degree of political polarization and the closeness of any given election race—are almost limitless. Republicans and their lawyers like to argue that voter turnout has increased since the advent of voter ID, but that—even where true—is not the pertinent issue. What matters is the number of voters who *wanted* to cast a ballot but were unable to because of obstacles put deliberately in their way.[57]

On that question we are beginning to see some consistent data. Nate Silver, the statistics wizard who correctly predicted the outcome of the 2012 presidential election for the *New York Times*, calculated that voter ID laws suppress somewhere between 0.8 and 2.4 percent of the vote—not quite the 3 percent dreamed up by the Republicans in Texas, but heading in that direction.[58] The Government Accounting Office conducted its own study of six states, two with voter ID laws and four without, and concluded that new laws had most likely depressed turnout in the 1.9–2.2 percent range in Kansas and the 2.2–3.2 percent range in Tennessee, with African Americans, young people, and new voters most heavily affected.[59] If those figures are accurate, then they mean voter ID on its own was enough to change the outcome of the 2014 gubernatorial race in Kansas, which the conservative Republican Sam Brownback won in a squeaker, just as laws overturning same-day registration and out-of-precinct voting (even before voter ID) may have affected the outcome of the 2014 Senate race in North Carolina, in which the former state house Speaker Thom Tillis narrowly beat his Democratic rival, Kay Hagan.[60]

One wonders how all this will strike the Supreme Court once the lawsuits relating to voter ID and the Voting Rights Act work their way through the appeals courts and come back for renewed consideration. Already a federal appeals court has upheld the bulk of the lower court ruling in the Texas case. John Roberts, the conservative chief justice with a thirty-year history of skepticism about the act who was the swing vote on *Shelby*, acknowledged the importance of combating racial discrimination in his majority opinion in 2013 but said the law had to address "current conditions." That was the standard to which he held himself. Those conditions, in his view, did not come close to the "'pervasive,' 'flagrant,' 'widespread,' and 'rampant' discrimination that faced Congress in 1965." As he wrote in a 2009 ruling (and cited in the *Shelby* opinion), "Things have changed in the South. Voter turnout and registration rates approach parity. Blatantly discriminatory evasions of federal decrees are rare."[61]

Will he feel the same way when confronted with the fresh evidence of racial gerrymandering and minority vote suppression pouring in from Texas, North Carolina, and a number of other states?[62] A new generation of civil rights activists will be waiting anxiously for his answer.

14

THE SUPER-RICH AND
THE DEMOCRATIC FUTURE

Imagine a political system in which votes are bought and sold freely in the open market, a system in which it is taken for granted that people will buy all the votes they can afford and use their power to get more money in order to buy more votes, so that a single magnate might easily outvote a whole city. Imagine a situation in which elections have become a mere formality because one or a few individuals are owners of a controlling number of votes. Suppose that nine-tenths of the members of the community are unable to exert any appreciable influence. Suppose, moreover, that the minority is entitled to very little information about what is being done. That is what the political system would be like if it were run the way business is run.

—*E.E. Schattschneider*[1]

Does representative democracy have a future, or is it just a phase we've been going through? If by "representative democracy" we mean a system in which a majority of voters holds meaningful sway over policy outcomes, the game in the United States may already be over.

The corrupting influence of money hasn't just upended the priorities of elected officials, who now spend more time raising funds than talking to constituents or researching the issues they vote on. It hasn't just made campaigns more expensive, more media-saturated, and more vicious. The scenario that Schattschneider imagined in 1960 has largely come to pass. Magnates *do* outvote entire cities, at least in those cases—

the majority—where media coverage of political campaigns cannot keep up with the relentless flow of money. For many people living in noncompetitive or uncontested districts, elections have indeed become just a formality. Billionaires now sponsor presidential candidates (or run for president themselves) the way Renaissance popes and princes once patronized artists; where those candidates previously had to sway party committees and state delegates to become viable office seekers, now they need to win over an audience of just one. As the *Wall Street Journal* observed of the record crop of billionaire-backed Republican candidates for 2016, "The life of their candidacies is now divorced from their ability to directly raise money from voters."[2] Whether money alone can translate into electoral success remains to be seen, but it can certainly catapult presidential candidates over the first hurdle and into the public limelight.

Jimmy Carter has described the United States as an oligarchy, and a widely publicized academic study published in 2014 went a long way toward backing him up. "Our analyses suggest that majorities of the American public actually have little influence over the policies our government adopts," the political scientists Martin Gilens of Princeton and Benjamin Page of Northwestern wrote. "Americans do enjoy many features central to democratic governance, such as regular elections, freedom of speech and association, and a widespread (if still contested) franchise. But . . . if policymaking is dominated by powerful business organizations and a small number of affluent Americans, then America's claims to being a democratic society are seriously threatened."[3]

Journalists like to divide billionaires involved in American politics into simple categories of good and bad, depending on the point of view. Tom Steyer, the San Francisco hedge fund manager, is good if you're an environmentalist, bad if you think global warming is a hoax. Charles and David Koch, the Wichita industrialists and energy magnates, are good if you're a Tea Party Republican, brother devils incarnate if you're a liberal.[4] That coverage, however, is misleading, because the very rich really are different from you and me. Another recent study comparing the political views of America's top 1 percent with the electorate as a whole found the billionaire class to be far less committed to excellence in public school education (35 percent against 87 percent of all Americans), less committed to public-sector job creation, less committed to providing viable benefits to the unemployed, and less interested in increasing taxes to support universal health care—or for any other purpose. In short, they skew significantly to the right of the average voter and are generally skeptical about the public sector's power to generate jobs and beneficial social change. They favor tax cuts over programs for the poor, and deficit reduction over government stimulus plans.[5]

At the same time, the super-rich are far more active politically than most of us, taking full advantage of their wealth to contribute to campaigns and to enjoy the access that their money grants. Two-thirds of the top thousand campaign donors in the 2012 cycle favored Republicans, as one would expect given their overall political profile. Financial services was the sector that gave the most—helping to explain why both parties backed away from aggressive Wall Street reform in the wake of the 2008 economic collapse, despite overwhelming public support, and why the Justice Department under Obama failed to prosecute a single top financial executive.[6] Of those thousand top donors (making personal contributions of at least $134,000 each), 40 percent said they had contacted a U.S. senator, 37 percent a member of the House of Representatives, 21 percent a regulatory official, 14 percent someone in the executive branch, and 12 percent a White House official.[7] Most Americans can barely name their representatives, much less recall chatting with them.[8]

The way billionaires wield influence is rarely as crude and sinister as huddling with elected officials over cigars in some darkened room and plotting ways to subvert the public interest. It's about access and the flow of information. Long before *Citizens United* launched the money aspect of politics into the stratosphere, the one-term Georgia senator Wyche Fowler explained the basic problem. "The brutal fact that we all agonize over," he said in the early 1990s, "is that if you get two calls and one is from a constituent who wants to complain about the VA mistreating her father, for the 10th time, and one is from somebody who is going to give you a party and raise $10,000, you call back the contributor.... There's no way to justify it. Except that you rationalize that you have to have money or you can't campaign. You're not in the game."[9]

Nowadays, of course, it's unlikely that an ordinary constituent would get through to a senator even once, much less ten times. And, in a world where the Koch brothers are planning to raise almost $1 billion for the

2016 election cycle, $10,000 would barely buy a plate at a fund-raising dinner. Still, being *in the game* is what continues to drive American politics. Elected officials can disregard the public clamor for strict regulation of the derivatives market and still be *in the game*. But they can't turn their back on their Wall Street contributors and say the same thing. "The central point that emerges from our research is that economic elites and organized groups representing business interests have substantial independent impacts on U.S. government policy," Gilens and Page wrote, "while mass-based interest groups and average citizens have little or no independent influence."

The same imbalance of access and outcomes applies to longer-standing lobbying groups with specific policy interests, like the National Rifle Association (NRA) or the American Israel Public Affairs Committee (AIPAC). These groups don't just lobby for a particular point of view on domestic or foreign affairs; they use their campaign spending as leverage to close down debate before it can even begin. Congressional members aren't just afraid of losing their NRA or AIPAC funding if they step too far from the approved line—they are also afraid of how relentlessly these groups might back their opponents and flood the airwaves with negative advertising. The consequence is that the Israeli government endures a fraction of the scrutiny in Washington that it does at home, and even modest gun safety measures with broad popular support do not make it through Congress, no matter how many senseless mass shootings hit the headlines. One does not have to be a critic of Israel or of the NRA's tireless advocacy on behalf of gun manufacturers to see that taking issues off the table in advance and demonizing even the suggestion of discussing them is not a democratic way of conducting public business.[10]

Schattschneider argued that the genius of the American system, at its founding, was that it broke the monopoly stranglehold that economic elites had held over politics for much of the history of Western civilization and opened society up to vigorous competition between the economic and the political spheres. More conservative political theorists like to argue that capitalism and democracy are two sides of the same coin—that what benefits one will inevitably benefit the other. But Schattschneider took a different tack, one that went against Louis Hartz and other thinkers of his time but perhaps resonates more in our post–*Citizens United* world. "The public interest resides in the no man's land between government and business," Schattschneider wrote. "The public likes competitive power systems. It wants both democracy and a high standard of living and thinks it can have both provided it can maintain a dynamic equilibrium between the democratic and capitalist elements."

America has now lost that equilibrium and is in danger of being unable to recover it. Another political theorist from the baby boom years, Seymour Martin Lipset, wrote a famous paper arguing that middle-class stability, not just overall prosperity, was essential to a successful democracy. Wealth inequality was poison, he said, because it ate at the very core of that achievement: "A society divided between a large impoverished mass and a small favored elite would result either in oligarchy . . . or tyranny."[11]

The flood of corporate money that has taken over American politics since the Supreme Court's *Buckley v. Valeo* ruling in 1976 has coincided with a dramatic and continuing spike in exactly the kind of inequality that Lipset was talking about. The top 1 percent of Americans bring in more than 20 percent of the country's overall income, while the bottom 90 percent bring in less than 50 percent—a disparity unmatched even at the height of the Gilded Age. Between 1979 and 2012, the income of the top fifth of the population increased 48.8 percent in real terms, while the bottom fifth saw a 12.1 percent drop. Every income group except for the top 20 percent has lost ground in the last forty years, regardless of whether the economy has boomed or tanked and regardless, too, of which party has held the presidency or controlled Congress. The gap between rich and poor stopped widening briefly in the wake of the 2008 financial crisis, only to start growing again with a vengeance, with the top 1 percent snagging more than 90 percent of new income in 2010.[12]

How does this inequality affect political outcomes? How could it not? One recent econometric study found a direct correlation between the political activity of the super-rich and government commitment to quality public education, which billionaires tend to mistrust; conversely, countries with a greater commitment to public education see broader participation in politics across social classes.[13] In other words, the more billionaires influence the political process, the more they are likely to continue influencing it, because the broader electorate can only become more disengaged and ill-informed as a result of the policies they espouse.

The problem can only get worse in a more globalized economy where capital has become mobile in ways that classical economists like Adam Smith and David Ricardo never envisaged.[14] Multinational corporations are far more powerful now than they were in the era of the original robber barons because they have the power to bankroll politicians as long as they remain useful and to close down factories and move investments and jobs overseas if they do not. The history of democracy has been largely a history of the empowerment of the working class, but now we live in a world where much of that working class lives in another country, working in sweatshop conditions for minimal wages, with no voice whatsoever in our electoral process—or, often, their own. Where once industry stayed put and could be regulated, now, to a large extent, it regulates *us*.

That said, the mass electorate in the United States has hardly laid down and died. The 2008 Obama campaign showed that an insurgent candidate with charisma, the right message, and the right digital strategy can still mobilize a vast number of people. The 2016 campaign, meanwhile, has revealed an extraordinary anti-establishiment populism in both parties. The Internet and social media have changed the landscape of political activism more generally, and while it is too soon to say how effective they can be as a mechanism for countering the power of special-interest lobbyists over the long term, there are certainly promising signs. In 2014, the debate over net neutrality—the question of whether telecoms companies can create a tiered system of Internet access to enhance their own profitability at the expense of less powerful online players—was upended in startling fashion after John Oliver roused his audience to action in a segment on the HBO show *Last Week Tonight* and embarrassed the Federal Communications Commission into distancing itself from the corporate lobbyists—including a number of former FCC commissioners working for companies they once regulated.[15] Obama himself urged the young audience of *The Daily Show*, Oliver's alma mater on Comedy Central, to get involved in issues they cared about and not be daunted by "the money . . . the filters and all the polarization" in contemporary politics. "It doesn't take that much, I guarantee you," he said on the show in 2015. "If people are engaged, eventually the political system responds. Despite the money, despite the lobbyists, it responds."[16]

The barriers to sustained, grassroots involvement remain daunting, however, especially the sort of high-minded, fact-driven involvement Obama had in mind. Study after study has shown that the American public in general is dismally ill-informed, and that those who watch Fox News, the Republican Party's echo chamber and frequent outrage machine, not only learn nothing but actually become *less* informed the more they watch.[17] A particularly depressing University of Colorado study in 2012 demonstrated that voters will continue to express strong opinions about lightning-rod issues like health care reform or merit pay for teachers—the sort that Fox pundits love to feast on—even after they try and fail to articulate what the substance of those issues are.[18] In other words, the less voters and grassroots political activists know, the more they think they know. That helps explain the surface allure of Donald Trump's presidential campaign, say, but it's not a strong premise for mass political participation in anything.

The odds of progressive reform in the electoral arena are similarly steep, and for many of the same reasons. The system makes life so comfortable for incumbents they have little motivation to press for change. Many eligible voters are too disaffected to care, while a noisy minority of partisan activists—on both sides of the political aisle—prefers to resort to knee-jerk theories about cheating by the other side, with or without actual evidence, than to come together to demand a fairer system. One potential bright spot is Hillary Clinton's presidential campaign, which has placed voting rights front and center, especially with African American audiences whom she needs to keep fired up if she wants to repeat Obama's victories in Florida, Virginia, and North Carolina. Among Clinton's policy prescriptions are automatic voter registration nationwide, an expansion of early voting, and a repeal of lifetime voting bans on ex-felons—all solid ideas, if they ever came to fruition. Unfortunately, the prevailing view in Washington is that election management should be left up to individual states, and while that's an obstinate and irrational position given the failure of many states to police themselves to a standard worthy of the country's democratic ideals, it's unclear what even a sitting president could do to change it. It certainly does no harm that Clinton is throwing down the gauntlet to her Republican rivals and asking, "What part of democracy don't they understand?" But, for now, it's little more than campaign grandstanding.[19]

Finding solutions to the electoral woes besetting the United States would not be all that difficult if only the politics could be kept out of the way. The question has been studied many times, and the answers tend to look very similar: cut back the influence of special-interest money; depoliticize the administration of elections, including the drawing of district boundary lines; clean up the registration process; expand access to as many eligible voters as possible; impose appropriate standards for voting machinery, counting procedures, recounts, and contests; allow ex-felons and at least some classes of current convicts to exercise their voting rights; and consider other forms of voting than straight first-past-the-post to encourage greater electoral competition and outcomes that more fairly reflect voter choices.[20]

This book has dug deep into the historical roots of the obstacles that continue to beleaguer elections in the United States. None of that can be wished away. It's impossible to look back over the past two hundred years without seeing how race and racial discrimination have been hardwired into the American political consciousness. It's impossible, too, not to see the corrupting influence of the two-party system and the campaign money that has become its unrelenting master.

That said, it's important to have an idea of how things *should* look so others with more influence and insight than a mere author can one day figure out how to get there. My own wish list might look something like this:

- Roll back the notion, introduced by the Supreme Court in *Buckley v. Valeo*, that money is speech and that personal and corporate campaign contributors have a constitutional right to use their wealth to sway election outcomes. Candidates should be competing primarily for votes, not special-interest campaign contributions and super-PAC support. Elected officials should be paying attention to their constituents and the issues, not spending hours each day dialing for dollars. Public financing is one option that has been tried with some success at the state level. Lawrence Lessig has suggested a system of strict caps on campaign contributions—no more than a few hundred dollars per contributor—that would be matched by public funds. That way, candidates could reap the benefit of grassroots supporters willing to open their checkbooks, but without the risk of being outspent by an opponent backed by a single billionaire with a private agenda to pursue.[21]

- Don't just reinstate the Voting Rights Act in its entirety; extend the notion of preclearance to *all* voting laws and practices across the country and establish a dedicated nonpartisan agency with real enforcement power and a preestablished set of acceptable standards on *every* aspect of a free and fair voting system, not just racial parity. This agency would, essentially, be a do-over of the Election Assistance Commission, established by HAVA in 2002, only this time with funding, staff, and a founding charter that would limit if not eliminate the possibility of partisan mischief by future commissioners. Such a body could either negotiate bulk pricing for approved voting machines or, better still, hire experts to devise new machines to its precise specifications. How to fund such a body? A modest tax on campaign contributions could be one way to go. If elections are going to be flooded with private money, it makes sense there should be some public benefit too.

- Establish a professional training program for elections administrators. Nurses and CPAs have diplomas; so should the people who count our votes.

- Devise a system of incentives and penalties to ensure counties provide enough polling stations and voting machines to meet demand. Many counties are too poor to provide adequate coverage; they should be given a way to apply for federal grants to cover the cost if they meet performance benchmarks in other areas.

- Shift most if not all of the burden of registration from the individual voter to the government. Oregon has done this using driver's licenses, which do not capture the entire voter-eligible population but are a vast improvement on the previous system.

Creating a reliable database of voters with current addresses is a challenge in a society that is highly mobile and instinctively wary of the government tracking its movements. The Brennan Center for Justice and others have proposed making registration available at a variety of public assistance agencies, not just the DMV, to capture more of the voter-eligible population.[22]

- Establish uniform rules across the country on early voting, same-day registration, provisional ballots, and absentee ballots. That way, partisan administrators in key states won't have the option of playing with these rules from one cycle to the next to create obstacles for their opponents.

- Establish a national unit, made up of lawyers as well as law enforcement officials, dedicated to election security. The job of this unit would be to react to instances of fraud or malfeasance and also to come up with preventive measures to forestall them. If a state felt the need to beef up its voter-identification procedures, for example, it would turn to the unit for guidance—not ram through over-politicized voter ID laws that needlessly limit ballot access. It would then be up to the central preclearance agency whether or not to approve the resulting legislation.

- Move Election Day to the weekend. This is important, even if there is a long early voting period, because a ballot is fully secret only if it is cast in-person on election day, and people shouldn't have to compromise that secrecy because they are busy at work or weighed down by other responsibilities.

- Hold fewer elections. Voters can't possibly become properly informed on the profusion of races and ballot initiatives that confront them; the more they have to wade through, the more vulnerable they become to special-interest manipulation and/or apathy. Too many election days on the calendar are a turn-off too. Cities that hold mayoral elections in off-years should move them to coincide with big national races. More posts should be by appointment, not election—especially within the justice system—as long as an institution exists to make those appointments responsibly. One way to determine voter appetite for a race is to offer a "none of the above" option. If "none of the above" wins more votes than any candidate, perhaps the race shouldn't be on the ballot next time.[23]

- Institute automatic restoration of voting rights to felons who have completed their prison sentences. Consider allowing certain classes of felons to vote even behind bars, or leave it to the judge's discretion (but show no mercy to convicted election fraudsters).

- Get rid of the electoral college or, better still to avoid a constitutional showdown, circumvent it. In 2012, the presidential candidates ignored roughly 80 percent of the electorate who happened not to live in swing states—that's no way to run a democracy. The Stanford computer science professor John Koza came up with an unbeatably brilliant plan in 2006: an interstate compact under which signatories agree to award their electoral college seats to the presidential candidate who wins the national popular vote; the compact only comes into force once enough states have signed on to reach a majority in the electoral college. As of 2015, ten states plus the District of Columbia had signed, accounting for 161 electoral college votes, or just over 60 percent of the total needed to activate the compact. Not only is this a great idea, but sooner or later it will in fact happen.[24]

- Modify or at least rearrange the calendar of presidential primaries, so the small, unusually white states of Iowa and New Hampshire no longer get to set the pace. The parties could choose primary states the way baseball awards draft picks: they would go where turnout has previously been low, to help stimulate political participation. Based on the data from 2014, that could mean Texas and Nevada; say—why not?

- Liven up candidate debates. They need to be better television to get people interested, and they need to be less scripted and bloodless so voters can learn more about the issues as well as the candidates. Fox News deserves credit for lobbing tough questions at the Republican primary field and eliciting interesting answers in the first, unusually crowded debate in

August 2015; the other networks and local stations need to figure out something equally compelling, or else the entire drama will migrate to social media. Inviting third-party candidates, or getting one or more outspoken experts in a given field to moderate instead of some wizened journalist from the age of Cronkite, are possible ways to shake things up. The public interest here is in educating voters, and the only way that's going to happen is if they are also entertained. It's not an easy line to walk, but putting the voters to sleep is no answer either.

• Encourage experimentation with forms of voting other than first-past-the-post—and not just in municipal and county elections. The goal would be to increase competition in congressional and state legislative races from their current dismal levels, and thus increase voter engagement. To some degree, the states are taking care of this themselves; California, for example, now has an open primary system in which the top two vote getters move forward to the general election regardless of party. The jury is out on whether that entirely works, but the spirit of experimentation is spot-on. More ranked-choice voting would be good to see too—although incumbent politicians hate this idea, so it may have to wait for other reforms to kick in first.[25]

As the Obama presidency draws to a close, many of these ideas, especially the first two, seem such pie in the sky it's almost embarrassing to propose them. That said, dramatic and unforeseeable changes *have* taken place in the past, usually as a result of some major crisis or systemic breakdown. Think of the stolen presidential election of 1824 that inspired Andrew Jackson to embrace democratic populism, or the many profound injustices that stirred the civil rights movement to life after World War II. The extremism of the suppressive recent laws passed by state legislatures in North Carolina, Texas, Wisconsin. and elsewhere might yet trigger a counterreaction, including, perhaps, some rethinking of the Supreme Court's earlier rulings on voter ID and the scrapping of the preclearance provision under the Voting Rights Act.

On the other hand, history is full of depressing examples of disenfranchisement and voter suppression that were allowed to stand for generations. The meltdown in Florida in 2000 should have been a clarion call for progressive reform, but instead it was taken as an excuse to wage partisan political warfare at a whole new decibel level and stomp on the hard-won rights of the previous half century. America still adheres to the *form* of electoral democracy, but its content is being steadily hollowed out. Jimmy Carter, with whom we started this book, likes to say in his international mediation work that "peace is more than the absence of conflict"[26]; likewise, democracy has to be more than the ritual of holding regular elections, especially if those elections are just a rubber stamp for incumbents and the special-interest money that protects their seats like battlements around a fortress. The dirty truth explored throughout this book is that the United States is nowhere near as democratic a country as it likes to think. The more people understand that, and the angrier they get about the bill of goods the two-party system has been selling them for far too long, the higher the chance of defying the odds and changing things enduringly for the better.

ACKNOWLEDGMENTS

I t's gratifying that a book about democratic participation has been in large part a collaborative effort. Many people offered their time with remarkable selflessness, reflecting their commitment to fairer elections and their desire for greater knowledge and understanding. A few must remain anonymous, but my thanks are no less heartfelt for that. Most, however, were only too happy to be counted. Thanks, first, to my friend, neighbor, and favorite political scientist Chuck Noble, who acted as a felicitous combination of mentor, sounding board, interlocutor, and critic, suggesting all the right books for me to read and offering quite a few himself. His observation early on that free and fair elections in the United States are "almost an oxymoron" acted as an informal motto for the entire project. Rebecca Mercuri, Kim Zetter, Kim Alexander, David Dill, Eva Waskell, Robert Adams, Roxanne Jekot, and Jeremiah Akin were people on whose expertise and activism I relied in the early stages of this project. Waskell and Jekot in particular provided a large number of official documents they had amassed in the course of their own research. Bob Gumpert, Pierre Gervais, Tim Pershing, Rob Richie, Michael Pauls, Larry George, Gary Humphreys, Gioconda Belli, Sabeel Rahman, and John Taylor read portions of the manuscript and provided valuable comments. For the new edition, thank you in particular to Tova Wang, who responded at lightning speed to a first draft of the new material and helped me sharpen it in many important ways.

Thanks also to the Fair Election International team at Global Exchange, including Ted Lewis, Tim Kingston, Mat Rosen, Shannon Biggs, and Walter Turner, as well as their international monitors, especially Dr. Brigalia Bam and Neerja Choudhury. In Florida, thanks to Lida Rodriguez-Taseff, Courtney Strickland, Joe Egan, Steve Clelland, Lew

Oliver, Ion Sancho, Kevin Wood, Kendall Coffey, Robert Wexler, Jim Sebesta, Charlotte Danciu, Susan Van Houten, Echo Steiner, and Arthur Anderson. In Georgia: Denis Wright and Mark Sawyer. In Maryland: Linda Schade and Tom Iler. In North Carolina: Bob Hall. In South Carolina: Vernon Burton. In Texas: Todd Smith, Chad Dunn, Adina Levin, and the Austin ACLU office. In Ohio: Dan Tokaji, Peg Rosenfield, Ed Jerse, Kevin DeWine, and Catherine Turcer. In Montana: Tom Rodgers, Oliver and Barb Semans, and Bret Healy. In California: Ron and Bernadette Burks, Mike and Linda Soubirous, Art Cassel, Brian Floyd, Greg Luke, Fred Woocher, Bob Varni, Bill Rouverol, Paul Barbagelata, and Tony Miller. In Louisiana: Peppi Bruneau. In New Mexico: Mike Laurance, Al Solis, Bill Wheeler, Chuck Davis, and Bill Barnhouse. In Chicago: Jan Rieff, by way of Andrew Apter and Robin Derby. In Washington, D.C.: Gerry Hebert, Joe Rich, Larry Noble, Brett Kappel, Kristen Clarke, Jonah Goldman, Rob Richie, Bruce Fein, John Feehery, David Becker, and Toby Moore.

Back in 2003–5, my colleagues at *The Independent* were exceptionally accommodating about giving me the time and the assignments I needed to complete this project. Thank you to Dean Kuipers of the late lamented *LA CityBeat* for allowing me to make repeated mischief in both Los Angeles and Riverside Counties and to Katrina vanden Heuvel at *The Nation* for keeping me on the elections beat several years longer. My editors at *The Guardian* have also let me continue to explore and write on this topic. Thank you to the excellent library services of the cities of Santa Monica and Los Angeles, Santa Monica College, UCLA, Cal State Long Beach, and USC. Thank you to Carl Bromley, my editor who stuck with the project over twelve years and two publishing houses. Thanks to the rest of the spectacular team at The New Press, including Sarah Fan, April Rondeau, Don Kennison, Sharon Swados, Julie McCarroll, Bev Rivero, and Maredith Sheridan, and to Ed Davis. And thanks as always to my family: my wife Naomi, who knows politics better than I ever will and has been a great teacher, supporter, and partner in this as in all things, and my children, Max, Raffaella, and Sammy.

For any lapses or mistakes that may have crept into the manuscript—any repeating (of the obvious), floating (of dubious ideas), transcription errors, or faulty counting—I take full responsibility, of course.

NOTES

INTRODUCTION

1. From an unaired interview with a major network, published by Brad Friedman of BradBlog, October 17, 2006, www.bradblog.com.

2. Jimmy Carter, interviewed by Terry Gross, *Fresh Air*, NPR, October 21, 2004.

3. Since Carter gave his interview, the explosion of social media has of course made the question of equal, unpaid access to the media much more difficult to control, even in countries that previously had strict rules about media campaign coverage.

4. Sean Sullivan, "Jimmy Carter: Think of How King Would Have Reacted to Voter I.D. Laws," *Washington Post*, August 28, 2013.

5. Jimmy Carter, interview by Thom Hartmann, *The Thom Hartmann Program*, July 30, 2015.

6. Brigalia Bam, author interview, September 2004.

7. Christopher Uggen, Sarah Shannon, and Jeff Manza, *State-Level Estimates of Felon Disenfranchisement in the United States, 2010* (Washington, DC: Sentencing Project, 2012).

8. National Conference of State Legislatures (as of July 1, 2015).

9. On Oregon, see Shelby Sebens, "Oregon Governor Signs Sweeping Automatic Voter Registration into Law," Reuters, March 16, 2015. The state will send voter cards to anyone with state ID and offer an opt-out period to anyone who *doesn't* want to be registered. On California's similar law, which will not come into effect until a statewide voter database in completed, see Jim Miller and David Siders, "California to Register Voters Automatically at DMV," *Sacramento Bee*, October 10, 2015.

10. The six states are Alaska, Arizona, California, Idaho, Montana, and Washington (Alaska and Montana deal only with legislative boundaries as each state has only one representative in Congress). New Jersey has an independent commission for

congressional seats only; Iowa has its own system of using nonpartisan legislative staff and putting their proposals to a vote in the legislature. Source: Justin Levitt of Loyola Law School's "All About Redistricting" website, redistricting.lls.edu. Conservatives in the Arizona state legislature sought to prevent such anti-gerrymandering initiatives and take back the power to draw their own boundaries in a lawsuit that in 2015 reached the Supreme Court (*Arizona State Legislature v. Arizona Independent Redistricting Commission*, case no. 13-1314, heard March 2, 2015, decided June 29, 2015). The suit was rejected 5–4.

11. In 2004, the Pentagon abandoned a project to allow overseas military personnel to cast ballots online; many jurisdictions have since been deterred by a controlled "red team" hack conducted in Washington, D.C., in 2010. See, for example, Andrew Gumbel, "Oscars Vote Vulnerable to Cyber Attack under New Online System, Experts Warn," *The Guardian*, February 12, 2012.

12. As of 2015, Wisconsin has a voter ID law; Ohio does not. Ohio does not have same-day registration during the early voting period; Wisconsin does. Both have restricted early voting.

13. Robert A. Caro, *The Years of Lyndon Johnson: Means of Ascent* (New York: Knopf, 1990), 287. The book is a thrilling account of how Johnson bribed, stole, and cheated his way to victory against the odds. For years afterward, Johnson's nickname in the Senate was "Landslide Lyndon."

14. See Andrew Gumbel, "Anti-Theft Devices," *The Nation*, November 6, 2008. Plenty of examples are to be found later in this book.

15. Joseph P. Harris, *Election Administration in the United States* (Washington, DC: Brookings Institution, 1934), 1.

16. Quoted in Richard L. Hasen, *The Voting Wars: From Florida 2000 to the Next Election Meltdown* (New Haven, CT: Yale University Press, 2012), 150–54.

17. From the unaired interview published by Brad Friedman on BradBlog, October 17, 2006.

18. Quoted in Harris, *Election Administration in the United States*, 123.

19. Michael Finnegan et al., "A 'Modern' Democracy That Can't Count Votes," *Los Angeles Times*, December 11, 2000.

20. See, for example, what happened to Ion Sancho in Leon County, Florida, when he stood up for voter integrity against the wishes of the establishment. Andrew Gumbel, "Guardian of the Ballot Box," *The Nation*, November 6, 2006.

21. Ramona Kitzinger, quoted in Hasen, *Voting Wars*, 2.

22. Verifiedvoting.org. The statistics vary slightly for early voting and special-needs access voting.

23. Vernon material based on a column by the author that appeared in *LA CityBeat* in April 2006 (archive no longer available online). See also Sam Allen, "In Rebuff to Pérez, Senate Rejects Disbanding Vernon," *Los Angeles Times*, August 29, 2011.

24. Quoted in "Pérez's Bill to Ax City of Vernon Fails in State Senate," *Sacramento Bee*, Capitol Journal, August 29, 2011.

25. Montana and South Dakota material from Andrew Gumbel, "Montana's North-

ern Cheyenne Tribe Fighting to Secure Voting Rights," *The Guardian*, October 7, 2013. See also John S. Smith, "Montana Indian Voting Lawsuit Settled," *Great Falls Tribune* (MT), June 12, 2014; and Andrea J. Cook, "Jackson County Agrees to Open Satellite Voting Office," *Rapid City Journal* (SD), October 17, 2014.

26. Bob Egelko, "Judge Richard Cebull Sent Hundreds of Racist E-mails, Panel Says," *San Francisco Chronicle*, January 20, 2014.

27. On problems in San Juan County, Utah, see Stephanie Woodard, "Going Postal: How All-Mail Voting Thwarts Navajo Voters," *In These Times*, August 15, 2015.

28. A version of this theory can be found in Craig Unger's book *Boss Rove: Inside Karl Rove's Secret Kingdom of Power* (New York: Scribner, 2012), which in turn is based on Bob Fitrakis's work at the Ohio *Free Press*. The theory falls flat because few of Ohio's eighty-eight counties used electronic voting in 2004, and not one of them noticed a discrepancy in their vote tallies when the election was certified, as they would have done if a third party had messed with them. Mike Connell, who ran SmarTech in Chattanooga, might have been "Karl Rove's IT guru," but the guilt is by association only. No shred of evidence has emerged to suggest the private plane crash that killed Connell in 2008—a subject of particular speculation on anti-Bush websites—was anything but an accident.

29. Quoted in Mark W. Summers, *The Era of Good Stealings* (New York: Oxford University Press, 1993), 94.

30. John Feehery, author interview, 2015.

31. John Rondy, "GOP Ignored Black Vote, Chairman Says; RNC Head Apologizes at NAACP Meeting," Reuters, July 15, 2005.

32. On San Francisco in 1997, see, e.g., Lance Williams, "Illegal Votes Taint Ballot on Stadium," *San Francisco Examiner*, September 7, 1997; Lance Williams and Erin McCormick, "S.F. Voters Register Early and Too Often," *San Francisco Examiner*, October 24, 1999; and Philip Matier and Andrew Ross, "Elections Chief Says Tracking 'Dead' Voters a Tricky Task," *San Francisco Chronicle*, September 3, 1997.

33. On Tammy Haygood, see, e.g., Philip Matier and Andrew Ross, "Ex-election Chief's Intensely Personal Reason for Job Fight," *San Francisco Chronicle*, July 15, 2002.

34. I say "presumably" because they never seem to mention it. The 1975 election was overshadowed by the killing of Moscone and Supervisor Harvey Milk three years later, and has been largely forgotten.

35. On San Francisco in 1975, see Jeff A. Schnepper, "Jonestown Massacre: The Unrevealed Story," *USA Today Magazine*, January 1999; John M. Crewdson, "Followers Say Jim Jones Directed Voting Frauds," *New York Times*, December 17, 1978; Jeannie Mills, *Six Years with God* (New York: A. and W. Publishers, 1979); and Deborah Layton, *Seductive Poison* (New York: Doubleday/Anchor, 1998). Barbagelata material based on author interview with his son Paul Barbagelata, 2004.

36. OSCE Office of Democratic Institutions and Human Rights, *Existing Commitments for Democratic Elections in OSCE Participating States* (Warsaw: ODIHR, October 2003). The eleven paragraphs relating to problems within the United States are 2.4, 3.2, 3.3, 4.1, 4.2, .4.3, 5.2, 5.4, 7.3, 7.10, and 8.3.

37. Much of the narrative here is based on author interviews in 2005 and 2015 with present and former OSCE staff involved in election monitoring, who asked not to be named for reasons of protocol and/or diplomatic sensitivity.

38. Text of Lavrov's speech to OSCE ministers in Sofia obtained by author.

39. OSCE/ODIHR, "Preliminary Statement," November 2, 2004, and "Final Report," March 31, 2005.

40. Comment by the secretary-general of the Albanian foreign ministry, cited in OSCE paperwork seen by author.

41. In Texas, it was attorney general and future governor Greg Abbott—see chapter 13 for more on him—who made the arrest threat in a letter to the OSCE. On "United Nations" paranoia, see Jay Sekulow, "Opposition Growing to UN Monitors; Thousands Reject Election Day Intimidation Tactic," American Center for Law and Justice blog, aclj.org, 2012 (accessed July 2015).

42. Quoted in Julian Pecquet, "Russia Skewers US Election as Undemocratic, 'the Worst in the World,'" *The Hill*, November 4, 2012.

1: THE ANTIDEMOCRATIC TRADITION AND THE NEW RIGHT

1. Quoted in Steven Hill, *Fixing Elections: The Failure of America's Winner Take All Politics* (New York: Routledge, 2002), 278.

2. News conference, December 18, 2000, after meeting congressional leaders on Capitol Hill for the first time since being named president-elect.

3. Mona Charen, "Uninvited to the Polls," *Washington Times*, October 25, 2004.

4. Quoted in Tova Andrea Wang, *The Politics of Voter Suppression* (Ithaca, NY: Cornell University Press, 2012), 7.

5. Michael Crozier, Samuel P. Huntington, and Joji Watanuki, *The Crisis of Democracy: Report on the Governability of Democracies to the Trilateral Commission* (New York: New York University Press, 1975).

6. Quoted in Frances Fox Piven and Richard A. Cloward, *Why Americans Still Don't Vote and Why Politicians Want It That Way* (Boston: Beacon Press, 2000), 4.

7. Robert D. Kaplan, "The Future of Democracy," *Atlantic Monthly*, December 1997.

8. International IDEA has an interactive database at its website. It's worth noting that the figures are based on voting age population as opposed to the more precise voter eligibility population. The turnout figures looked a little better in 2004 and 2008, both intensely fought presidential election years, then sank in the 2014 midterms to just 36.6 percent of eligible voters, the lowest rate even by American standards since World War II. See Bernie Sanders, "US Voter Turnout Is an International Embarrassment. Here's How to Fix It," *The Guardian*, November 10, 2014. Local elections can be orders of magnitude worse: one mayoral election in Dallas in the 1990s saw 5 percent turnout; lower-order races for school boards or water boards can struggle to break the 1 percent barrier. See Hill, *Fixing Elections*.

9. Among the many books that touch on the subject of voter disaffection, see, e.g.,

Thomas E. Patterson, *The Vanishing Voter: Public Involvement in an Age of Uncertainty* (New York: Knopf, 2002); or Ruy E. Teixeira, *The Disappearing American Voter* (Washington, DC: Brookings Institution, 1992).

10. Zach Holden, "No Contest: 36 Percent of 2014 State Legislative Races Offered No Choice," *National Institute on Money in State Politics*, November 20, 2014, posted at www.followthemoney.org (accessed July 2015).

11. Mark McDaniel, quoted in J. Hoeffel, "Six Incumbents Are a Week Away from Easy Election," *Winston-Salem Journal*, January 27, 1998.

12. From Schwarzenegger's 2005 "State of the State" address. He proposed taking the redistricting process out of the hands of elected politicians, a proposal that eventually led to a successful 2008 ballot initiative to set up an independent redistricting commission.

13. An interesting discussion of these figures is found in Rob Richie, "Republicans Got Only 52 Percent of the Vote in House Races; How Did They End Up with 57 Percent of the Seats?," *The Nation*, November 7, 2014. Richie's organization, FairVote. org, has been crunching numbers from congressional elections for years and using them to argue for ranked-choice voting as opposed to first-past-the-post voting. Many of the statistics here were taken from FairVote.org's analyses.

14. Bertolt Brecht, "Die Lösung" (The Solution), written in 1953, in *Bertolt Brecht: Poems, 1913–1956*, ed. John Willett and Ralph Manheim (New York: Routledge, 1997), 440.

15. This narrative is expanded greatly in the following chapters. One book that makes the basic argument about the collapse of interparty competition and its effect on turnout is Piven and Cloward, *Why Americans Still Don't Vote*. The study cited is Raymond E. Wolfinger and Steven J. Rosenstone, *Who Votes?* (New Haven, CT: Yale University Press, 1980).

16. Per Bob Hall in interview with author, 2015. More on Democratic Party opposition to same-day registration in Jack Betts, "Why Take Voter Bill Off Agenda?," *Charlotte Observer*, June 19, 2007.

17. See Wang, *Politics of Voter Suppression*, 60–74.

18. One good example is Hasan Harnett, who became the chair of the North Carolina Republican Party in 2015 with broad Tea Party support and immediately sought to subvert race-related criticism of his party by likening Hillary Clinton's presidential campaign to the Ku Klux Klan. See Colin Campbell, "NC Republicans Pick First Black Leader," *Charlotte Observer*, June 6, 2015; and Mark Binker, "NC GOP Leader Links Hillary to KKK," WRAL, July 27, 2015.

19. More on the origin and popular history of the Atwater interview in Rick Perlstein, "Lee Atwater's Infamous 1981 Interview on the Southern Strategy," *The Nation*, November 13, 2012.

20. Weyrich's remarks, to a party meeting in Dallas in 1980, were captured on video and are now easily available on YouTube.

21. H.R. Haldeman, *The Haldeman Diaries: Inside the Nixon White House* (New York: Berkley Books, 1994), 66.

22. The paranoid style, as Richard Hofstadter memorably described it, was epitomized by Barry Goldwater and the backlash against the civil rights movement even before Nixon became president. See Hofstadter, *The Paranoid Style in American Politics, and Other Essays* (Cambridge, MA: Harvard University Press, 1965). Nixon himself launched his political career—as many Republicans would after him—by tapping into popular mistrust and envy of the monied classes. Nixon's defiance and fighting spirit were largely defined by his burning desire to be accepted by the East Coast establishment and his rage at feeling that he never could be.

23. Described in Jeffrey Toobin, *Too Close to Call: The Thirty-Six-Day Battle to Decide the 2000 Election* (New York: Random House, 2001), 44.

24. See, e.g., "How 'Normal' Is Newt?," *Newsweek*, November 6, 1994.

25. The Clinton-Gore ticket won both states in 1992 and 1996; neither state has voted Democrat in a presidential election since. Whether Gore lost these states because Clinton was viewed as damaged goods or because he was afraid to use Clinton as a campaign asset is difficult to assess. Reservations about Clinton's character, as expressed in opinion polls, also appeared to spill over into reservations about Gore's own probity, especially his political convictions on red-meat issues like guns and abortion. In any case, impeachment and the Lewinsky scandal proved a Democratic obstacle and a Republican boon in a part of the country where the GOP had been using similar wedge issues to appeal to conservative Democrats for a generation.

26. Matthew A. Crenson and Benjamin Ginsberg, *Downsizing Democracy: How America Sidelined Its Citizens and Privatized Its Public* (Baltimore: Johns Hopkins University Press, 2002), x and elsewhere. See also Ginsberg and Martin Shefter's earlier book laying out some of the groundwork, *Politics by Other Means* (New York: Basic Books, 1990). More on the Progressive Era in chapter 5.

27. Ilya Somin, "When Ignorance Isn't Bliss: How Political Ignorance Threatens Democracy," Cato Institute Policy Analysis, September 22, 2004.

28. Justice Scalia pointed out that Article II of the Constitution leaves the appointment of presidential electors in the hands of state legislatures, not the voters. Discussed in more depth in chapter 9.

29. See, e.g., Michael Waldman, "Heaven Sent: Does God Endorse George Bush?," *Slate*, September 13, 2004.

30. Nicholas Xenos, "Leo Strauss and the Rhetoric of the War on Terror," *Logos* 3, no. 2 (Spring 2004); John G. Mason, "Leo Strauss and the Noble Lie: The Neo-Cons at War," *Logos* 3, no. 2 (Spring 2004); Mark Lilla, "Leo Strauss: The European," *New York Review of Books*, October 21, 2004; and Lilla, "The Closing of the Straussian Mind," *New York Review of Books*, November 4, 2004.

31. For an extensive history of covert and often illegal actions by the national security establishment after World War II, see, for example, Tim Weiner, *Legacy of Ashes: The History of the CIA* (New York: Random House, 2007). The "city on a hill" image was used in public speeches by John F. Kennedy and Ronald Reagan, among others.

32. Quoted in Ron Suskind, "Faith, Certainty and the Presidency of George W. Bush," *New York Times*, October 17, 2004.

33. Bush joked after 9/11 that he'd envisaged deficit spending only in the event of war, recession, or national emergency. "Lucky me," he said, "I hit the trifecta." Quoted in Paul Krugman, "Hitting the Trifecta," *New York Times*, December 7, 2001. After 2002, Cheney pushed successfully for more tax cuts, despite the imminent prospect of war in Iraq. "Reagan proved deficits don't matter," he said. "We won the midterms. This is our due." Quoted in Ron Suskind, *The Price of Loyalty* (New York: Simon & Schuster, 2004), 291.

34. Allen Raymond, *How to Rig an Election: Confessions of a Republican Operative* (New York: Simon & Schuster, 2008), 1.

35. Lyndsey Layton, "Palin Apologizes for 'Real America' Comments," *Washington Post*, October 22, 2008.

36. Quoted in Wang, *Politics of Voter Suppression*, 3.

37. Gary L. Gregg, "Counting the Real People's Vote," *National Review Online*, October 27, 2004.

38. The electoral college arguably helped start the Civil War, because it elevated Abraham Lincoln to the presidency with just 39 percent of the vote, concentrated in the North. In 1888, the popular vote winner did not prevail, although it did not cause a crisis on that occasion. In 1948, Dewey almost captured the electoral college even though he lagged more than two million votes behind Truman. In 1960, Kennedy's razor-thin official margin in the popular vote was probably the only thing that saved the country from a protracted Florida-style dispute. In 1968, Nixon called Humphrey and tried to get him to agree that the popular vote winner should be awarded the presidency in the event of an electoral college tie (Humphrey told him to get lost). In 1976, very modest swings in Ohio and Hawaii would have given Ford the electoral college even though Carter was decisively, if narrowly, ahead in the popular vote. See Lawrence D. Longley with Neal R. Peirce, *The Electoral College Primer*, 2nd ed. (1996; New Haven, CT: Yale University Press, 1999); and Jack N. Rakove, "The E-College in the E-age," in *The Unfinished Election of 2000*, ed. Rakove (New York: Basic Books, 2001), 201–34.

39. Gary Gregg, "Keep Electoral College for Fair Presidential Votes," *Politico*, December 5, 2012.

2: SLAVERY AND THE SYSTEM

1. E.E. Schattschneider, *The Semisovereign People: A Realist's View of Democracy in America* (New York: Holt, Rinehart, and Winston, 1960), 100.

2. See, for example, Catherine Drinker Bowen, *Miracle at Philadelphia* (Boston: Little Brown, 1966); and Max Farrand, *The Framing of the Constitution of the United States* (New Haven, CT: Yale University Press, 1913).

3. Quoted in Richard Hofstadter, *The American Political Tradition* (New York: Knopf, 1948), 6.

4. Gerry quoted in Alexander Keyssar, *The Right to Vote: The Contested History of Democracy in the United States* (New York: Basic Books, 2000), 23.

5. Ibid., 49.

6. See, for example, Daniel J. Boorstin, who writes, "The most obvious peculiarity of our American Revolution is that, in the modern European sense of the word, it was hardly a revolution at all." Boorstin, *The Genius of American Politics* (Chicago: University of Chicago Press, 1953), 68.

7. See Bowen, *Miracle at Philadelphia*, 192–94; and Farrand, *Framing of the Constitution*, 163.

8. "White supremacy" line from Michael Lind, "75 Stars: How to Restore Democracy in the U.S. Senate (and End the Tyranny of Wyoming)," *Mother Jones*, January–February 1998; Robert Dahl, *How Democratic Is the American Constitution?* (New Haven, CT: Yale University Press, 2002).

9. For further discussion of this, see Garry Wills, *"Negro President"* (New York: Houghton Mifflin, 2003).

10. See Jack N. Rakove, "The E-College in the E-age," in *The Unfinished Election of 2000*, ed. Rakove (New York: Basic Books, 2001), 201–34.

11. Adams and Pickering quoted in Wills, *"Negro President"*, 1–2.

12. Leonard Richards, *The Slave Power: The Free North and Southern Domination, 1780–1860* (New Orleans: Louisiana State University Press, 2000), 62.

13. Bowen, *Miracle at Philadelphia*, 4.

14. See George Bancroft, *History of the United States of America, from the Discovery of the Continent* (New York: D. Appleton & Co., 1892), 6:292–367.

15. Michael Schudson, *The Good Citizen: A History of American Civic Life* (Cambridge, MA: Harvard University Press, 1999), 202.

16. Gore Vidal, *Perpetual War for Perpetual Peace* (New York: Nation Books, 2002), 70.

17. Samuel P. Huntington, *Political Order in Changing Societies* (New Haven, CT: Yale University Press, 1968), 98.

18. Ibid., 106.

19. Account taken from Robert V. Remini, *The Election of Andrew Jackson* (Philadelphia: Lippincott, 1963); and Sean Wilentz, *Andrew Jackson* (New York: Henry Holt, 2005).

20. For a discussion of Jackson and Protestant fundamentalism, see Anatol Lieven, *America Right or Wrong: An Anatomy of American Nationalism* (New York: Oxford University Press, 2004).

21. Michael Kazin, *The Populist Persuasion* (New York: Basic Books, 1995), 21.

22. Parton and Abernethy quoted in *Jacksonian Democracy: Myth or Reality?*, ed. James L. Bugg Jr. (New York: Holt, Rinehart and Winston, 1962).

23. Alexis de Tocqueville, *Democracy in America* (New York: Penguin Books, 1984), 158.

24. See Frances Fox Piven and Richard A. Cloward, *Why Americans Still Don't Vote and Why Politicians Want It That Way* (Boston: Beacon Press, 2000), 47–49.

3: PATRONAGE, LIQUOR, AND GRAFT: THE ASCENT OF MACHINE POLITICS

1. *Plunkitt of Tammany Hall*, recorded by William L. Riordan (New York: McClure Press, 1905), 56–57.

2. Quoted in Joseph P. Harris, *Election Administration in the United States* (Washington, DC: Brookings Institution 1934), 318.

3. Much of the following is taken, except where indicated, from Alexander B. Callow, *The Tweed Ring* (New York: Oxford University Press, 1966); M.R. Werner, *Tammany Hall* (Garden City, NY: Doubleday, 1928); and D.W. Brogan, *Politics in America* (New York: Harper, 1954).

4. Quoted in John I. Davenport, *The Election and Naturalization Frauds in New York City, 1860–1870* (New York: self-published, 1894).

5. See, for example, Carl Bode, *Maryland: A Bicentennial History* (New York: W.W. Norton, 1978), 99.

6. Defined in "The Mystery of Iniquity: A Passage of the Secret History of American Politics," in *American Review: A Whig Journal of Politics, Literature, Art, and Science* (New York: Wiley and Putnam, 1845), 1:562.

7. Early history of voting taken from Eldon C. Evans, *A History of the Australian Ballot System in the United States* (Chicago: University of Chicago Press, 1917).

8. This and many subsequent instances itemized in Chester H. Rowell's 1901 report for the House of Representatives, *A Historical and Legal Digest of All the Contested Election Cases in the House of Representatives of the United States from the First to the Fifty-Sixth Congress, 1789–1901* (Westport, CT: Greenwood Press, 1976).

9. Harris, *Election Administration*, 316.

10. On the early history of New York and the benefits of the spoils system for the working class, see Fred J. Cook, *American Political Bosses and Machines* (New York: Franklin Watts, 1973).

11. Natasha Geiling, "The (Still) Mysterious Death of Edgar Allan Poe," *Smithsonian*, October 7, 2014; William T. Bandy, "Dr. Moran and the Poe-Reynolds Myth," *Myths and Reality* (Baltimore: The Edgar Allan Poe Society, 1987), 26–36.

12. Quoted in Arthur M. Schlesinger Jr., *The Age of Jackson* (Boston: Little, Brown, 1945), 310.

13. For a discussion of the spoils system, see, for example, Hugh Brogan, *Penguin History of the United States of America* (1985; London: Penguin Books, 1990), 267–70.

14. *Plunkitt of Tammany Hall*, 51.

15. Quoted in Cook, *American Political Bosses.*

16. Brogan, *Politics in America.*

17. Quoted in Callow, *Tweed Ring*, 10, 12.

18. Quoted in Harris, *Election Administration*, 318.

19. Lawrence Goodwyn, *Democratic Promise: The Populist Moment in America* (New York: Oxford University Press, 1976), 6.

20. Quoted in Evans, *History of the Australian Ballot System*, 11.

21. Lincoln Steffens, *The Shame of the Cities* (1904; New York: Peter Smith, 1948), 70.

22. *Plunkitt of Tammany Hall*, 55.

23. Quoted in ibid., 139.

24. Quoted in Harris, *Election Administration*, 321.

4: THE THEFT OF THE CENTURY

1. Louis W. Koenig, "The Election That Got Away," *American Heritage* 11, no. 6 (1960): 4–7.

2. The account in this chapter draws principally on Roy Morris Jr., *Fraud of the Century: Rutherford B. Hayes, Samuel Tilden, and the Stolen Election of 1876* (New York: Simon & Schuster, 2003); Eric Foner, *Reconstruction: America's Unfinished Revolution, 1863–1877* (New York: Harper & Row, 1988); Koenig's brief summary (1960); Sidney I. Pomerantz's chapter in *The History of American Presidential Elections*, ed. Arthur M. Schlesinger Jr. (New York: Chelsea House, 1971); and the opening chapter of C. Vann Woodward, *Origins of the New South, 1877–1913* (Baton Rouge: Louisiana State University Press, 1951), 1–22.

3. Quoted in Morris, *Fraud of the Century*, 10.

4. Quoted in Ari Hoogenboom, *The Presidency of Rutherford B. Hayes* (Lawrence: University Press of Kansas, 1988), 26.

5. Quoted in Foner, *Reconstruction*, 571.

6. Supreme Court of the United States, *Civil Rights Cases*, 109 U.S. 3, decided October 16, 1883.

7. Quoted in Morris, *Fraud of the Century*, 153.

8. Quoted in C. Vann Woodward, *The Burden of Southern History* (Baton Rouge: Louisiana State University Press, 1960), 95.

9. Quoted in Mark W. Summers, *The Era of Good Stealings* (New York: Oxford University Press, 1993), 289.

10. Quoted in Morris, *Fraud of the Century*, 190.

11. Quoted in ibid., 174.

12. Cronin story detailed in the *New York Times* column "Political Intelligence" of January 4, 1877.

13. Quoted in Morris, *Fraud of the Century*, 235.

14. Quoted in Koenig, "Election That Got Away."

15. William C. Rehnquist, *Centennial Crisis: The Disputed Election of 1876* (New York: Knopf, 2004).

16. After Rehnquist's death in 2005, public records requests revealed a memo from then FBI director William Webster reporting that Republican lawyers, apparently

including Rehnquist, challenged black and Hispanic voters in line at a polling station to read an excerpt from the U.S. Constitution out loud. Many were deterred. Only after Democratic poll watchers complained and a scuffle broke out did Rehnquist leave. Detailed in Tova Andrea Wang, *The Politics of Voter Suppression* (Ithaca, NY: Cornell University Press, 2012), 44–50.

5: THE 1896 WATERSHED AND THE PARADOX OF REFORM

1. Quoted in Ralph G. Martin, *The Bosses* (New York: G.P. Putnam, 1964), 64.

2. Francis Parkman, "The Failure of Universal Suffrage," *North American Review*, July–August 1878.

3. Alexander Winchell, "The Experiment of Universal Suffrage," *North American Review*, February 1883.

4. Discussed in Frances Fox Piven and Richard A. Cloward, *Why Americans Still Don't Vote and Why Politicians Want It That Way* (Boston: Beacon Press, 2000), 4, 87.

5. John I. Davenport, *The Election and Naturalization Frauds in New York City, 1860–1870* (New York: self-published, 1894), 3.

6. Cited in Eric Foner, *Reconstruction: America's Unfinished Revolution, 1863–1877* (New York: Harper & Row, 1988), 587.

7. Eldon C. Evans, *A History of the Australian Ballot System in the United States* (Chicago: University of Chicago Press, 1917), 13.

8. Quoted in V.O. Key, *Southern Politics in State and Nation* (New York: Vintage, 1949), 553.

9. Cecilia Rasmussen, "L.A. Then and Now: When Voters Were Identified by Goiters, Missing Fingers and Tattoos," *Los Angeles Times*, September 14, 2003.

10. Louis Hartz, *The Liberal Tradition in America* (New York: Harcourt Brace, 1955).

11. Piven and Cloward, *Why Americans Still Don't Vote*, 34. See also E.E. Schattschneider, *The Semisovereign People: A Realist's View of Democracy in America* (New York: Holt, Rinehart, and Winston, 1950), which makes the argument at book length.

12. Discussed in Hugh Brogan, *Penguin History of the United States of America* (1985; London: Penguin Books, 1990), 411–15.

13. William Graham Sumner, *What Social Classes Owe to Each Other* (New York: Harper, 1883).

14. See Evans, *History of the Australian Ballot System*; and Joseph P. Harris, *Election Administration in the United States* (Washington, DC: Brookings Institution, 1934).

15. Quoted in J. Morgan Kousser, *The Shaping of Southern Politics* (New Haven, CT: Yale University Press, 1974), 52.

16. George Gunton, "Should Voting Be Compulsory?," *Social Economist*, September 1892, reprinted in *Gunton's Magazine, 1892* (London: Forgotten Books, 2013), 149.

17. Quoted in Evans, *History of the Australian Ballot System*, 25.

18. This was also the period in which Albany redrew the municipal boundaries of New York City to include the outer boroughs and so dilute Tammany Hall's Manhattan power base. (See Piven and Cloward, *Why Americans Still Don't Vote*, 80.) In New Jersey, the state legislature passed stringent restrictions on voter registration that applied in the state's seven largest cities only. See Alexander Keyssar, "The Right to Vote and Election 2000," in *The Unfinished Election of 2000*, ed. Jack N. Rakove (New York: Basic Books, 2001), 75–103.

19. J. Morgan Kousser, *The Shaping of Southern Politics* (New Haven, CT: Yale University Press,1974).

20. Keyssar, "Right to Vote and Election 2000."

21. Kousser, *Shaping of Southern Politics*, 55.

22. Alexander B. Callow, *The Tweed Ring* (New York: Oxford University Press, 1966), 209.

23. Lincoln Steffens, *The Shame of the Cities* (1904; New York: Peter Smith, 1948), 73.

24. Louise Overacker, *Money in Politics* (New York: Macmillan, 1932), 31–34.

25. V.O. Key, *Southern Politics in State and Nation* (New York: Vintage, 1949), 458.

26. Evans, *History of the Australian Ballot System*, 49.

27. Overacker, *Money in Politics*.

28. Quoted in Keyssar, "Right to Vote and Election 2000."

29. Quoted in William Gillette, *The Right to Vote: Politics and the Passage of the Fifteenth Amendment* (Baltimore: Johns Hopkins Press, 1965), 59.

30. Ibid., 88.

31. For further discussion of these issues, see Kousser, *Shaping of Southern Politics*; and C. Vann Woodward, *The Burden of Southern History* (Baton Rouge: Louisiana State University Press, 1960).

32. More on the run-up to 1896 in Lawrence Goodwyn, *Democratic Promise: The Populist Moment in America* (New York: Oxford University Press, 1976); Michael Kazin, *The Populist Persuasion* (New York: Basic Books, 1995); and Walter Dean Burnham, *Critical Elections and the Mainsprings of American Politics* (New York: Norton, 1970).

33. Figures from Piven and Cloward, *Why Americans Still Don't Vote*, 65–66.

34. More on the Progressive Era in Richard Hofstadter, *The Age of Reform* (New York: Knopf, 1955); Robert H. Wiebe, *The Search for Order, 1877–1920* (New York: Hill and Wang, 1967); Lawrence Lessing, *Republic, Lost: How Money Corrupts Congress—and a Plan to Stop It* (New York: Twelve, 2011); and Brogan, *Penguin History of the United States*.

35. Charles Seymour and Donald Paige Frary, *How the World Votes: The Story of Democratic Development in Elections* (Springfield, MA: C.A. Nichols, 1918), 12–13.

36. See, e.g., William Chafe, *The American Woman: Her Changing Social, Economic, and Political Roles, 1920–1970* (New York: Oxford University Press, 1972).

37. See Kevin Phillips, *William McKinley* (New York: New Press, 2003).

38. Quoted in Martin, *Bosses*, 65.

39. Lawrence Goodwyn, *The Populist Moment: A Short History of the Agrarian Revolt in America* (New York: Oxford University Press, 1978), 280.

40. Quoted in C. Vann Woodward, *The Strange Career of Jim Crow*, 3d ed. (New York: Oxford University Press, 1974), 63.

6: THE LONG AGONY OF THE DISENFRANCHISED SOUTH

1. W.E.B. Du Bois, *Black Reconstruction in America* (New York: Harcourt, Brace, 1935), 30.

2. Quoted in Francis Butler Simkins, *Pitchfork Ben Tillman* (Baton Rouge: Louisiana State University Press, 1944), xxiv.

3. Harry Hayden, *The Story of the Wilmington Rebellion* (Wilmington, NC: self-published, 1936), 23. Available through the excellent East Carolina University website on Wilmington, "Politics of a Massacre: Discovering Wilmington 1898," http://core.ecu.edu/umc/wilmington (accessed August 2015).

4. Except where indicated, the account of the Wilmington massacre is drawn from H. Leon Prather Sr., *We Have Taken a City: Wilmington Racial Massacre and Coup of 1898* (Cranbury, NJ: Fairleigh Dickinson University Press, 1984); and David S. Cecelski and Timothy B. Tyson, eds., *Democracy Betrayed: The Wilmington Race Riot of 1898 and Its Legacy* (Chapel Hill: University of North Carolina Press, 1998).

5. The text of Felton's speech and Manly's response are reproduced in the North Carolina Department of Cultural Resources' *1898 Wilmington Race Riot Report*, compiled in 2006 and available at http://www.history.ncdcr.gov/1898-wrrc/report/report.htm.

6. W.A. Dunning, "The Undoing of Reconstruction," *Atlantic Monthly*, July 1901.

7. Quoted in J. Morgan Kousser, *The Shaping of Southern Politics* (New Haven, CT: Yale University Press, 1974), 209.

8. Quoted in C. Vann Woodward, *Origins of the New South, 1877–1913* (Baton Rouge: Louisiana State University Press, 1951), 55.

9. Quoted in Kousser, *Shaping of Southern Politics*, 48.

10. Quoted in J. Morgan Kousser, *Colorblind Injustice: Minority Voting Rights and the Undoing of the Second Reconstruction* (Chapel Hill: University of North Carolina Press, 1999), 25.

11. See Dunning, "Undoing of Reconstruction."

12. Quoted in Kousser, *Shaping of Southern Politics*, 140.

13. Quoted in Richard Wormser, *The Rise and Fall of Jim Crow* (New York: St. Martin's Press, 2003), 70.

14. Details on Mississippi constitution from V.O. Key, *Southern Politics in State and Nation* (New York: Vintage, 1949), 533–54.

15. Tillman and Glass quoted in Woodward, *Origins of the New South*, 333.

16. Both stories from Steven F. Lawson, *Black Ballots: Voting Rights in the South, 1944–1969* (New York: Columbia University Press, 1976), 86, 88.

17. Quoted in Woodward, *Origins of the New South*, 327.

18. Quoted in Kousser, *Shaping of Southern Politics*, 70.

19. Quoted in Orville Vernon Burton's expert report on behalf of the plaintiffs in the 2013 Texas voter ID case, *Texas League of Young Voters Education Fund and Imani Clark v. State of Texas*, case no. 2:13-cv-00263; report furnished by Burton.

20. Figures from Dunning, "Undoing of Reconstruction."

21. Legal history from Pamela Karlan, "Equal Protection: *Bush v. Gore* and the Making of a Precedent," in *The Unfinished Election of 2000*, ed. Jack N. Rakove (New York: Basic Books, 2001), 159–200

22. Long material from T. Harry Williams, *Huey Long* (New York: Knopf, 1969).

23. Lawson, *Black Ballots*, xv.

24. Talmadge and Bilbo, quoted in ibid., 99, 103.

25. Roosevelt and Truman material from Lawson, *Black Ballots*; and C. Vann Woodward, *The Strange Career of Jim Crow*, 3d ed. (New York: Oxford University Press, 1974).

26. Quoted in Woodward, *Strange Career of Jim Crow*, 132.

27. Nixon's attitude changed somewhat after the 1968 presidential campaign, when his Southern strategy began focusing on attracting the support of white Southerners dismayed and disaffected by the successes of the civil rights movement.

28. Figures from Frances Fox Piven and Richard A. Cloward, *Why Americans Still Don't Vote and Why Politicians Want It That Way* (Boston: Beacon Press, 2000), 111–15.

29. Described in Tova Andrea Wang, *The Politics of Voter Suppression* (Ithaca, NY: Cornell University Press, 2012).

30. The historian Stanley L. Kutler, for example, described the VRA as "sweeping, almost revolutionary." See Kutler, *The Wars of Watergate: The Last Crisis of Richard Nixon* (1990; New York: W.W. Norton, 1992), 17. For a detailed description of the act's passage and subsequent history, see Ari Berman, *Give Us the Ballot: The Modern Struggle for Voting Rights in America* (New York: Farrar, Straus and Giroux, 2015).

31. In Alabama, the Voting Rights Act spurred a jump in black registration from 19 percent to 52 percent. In Mississippi, it went from 7 percent to 60 percent. See Kousser, *Colorblind Injustice*, 55.

32. Hatcher's 1967 campaign, and that of Curt Stokes in Cleveland, is recounted in detail in Frances Fox Piven, Lorraine C. Minnite, and Margaret Groarke, *Keeping Down the Black Vote: Race and the Demobilization of American Voters* (New York: New Press, 2009).

33. For a detailed account of the early attempts to roll back the VRA, including attempts made by a young John Roberts as a member of the Reagan-era Department of Justice, see Berman, *Give Us the Ballot*, 65–99, 121–58.

34. See, for example, Kousser, *Colorblind Injustice*.

35. Clinton's vision of a more corporate, business-friendly Democratic Party led by

its centrist Democratic Leadership Council wing (Clinton had been the DLC chair before running for president) was directly at odds with his reputation as "America's first black president"—a white Southerner who knew how to win over black constituencies.

36. The district in question was North Carolina's 12th congressional district, defended at the time by Democrats because they had drawn it; in the 2011 round of redistricting, described in chapter 13, the Democrats cried foul because this time the Republicans had drawn a similarly misshapen district, and for very similar reasons— to pack the black vote.

37. Figures from the Sentencing Project. Archive and latest figures at www .sentencingproject.org.

38. See "Democracy Imprisoned: A Review of the Prevalence and Impact of Felony Disenfranchisement Laws in the United States" (report prepared by multiple advocacy organizations including the ACLU, Sentencing Project, NAACP, and the Lawyers' Committee for Civil Rights Under Law, submitted to the United Nations Human Rights Committee, September 2013).

39. Christopher Uggen and Jeff Manza, "Democratic Contraction? The Political Consequences of Felon Disenfranchisement in the United States," *American Sociological Review* 67 (2002): 777–803.

40. Data cited in Michelle Alexander, *The New Jim Crow: Mass Incarceration in the Age of Colorblindness* (New York: The New Press, 2010, 2012), 180.

41. Eric Lotke and Peter Wagner, "Prisoners of the Census: Electoral and Financial Consequences of Counting Prisoners Where They Go, Not Where They Come From," *Pace Law Review* 24 (2004): 587.

42. Alexander, *New Jim Crow*.

43. See, e.g., the NAACP/People for the American Way Foundation report *The Long Shadow of Jim Crow: Voter Intimidation and Suppression in America Today* (Summer 2004), available at www.pfaw.org or www.naacp.org.

44. Supreme Court of the United States, *Shelby County, Alabama, Petitioner v. Eric H. Holder, Jr., Attorney General et al.*, No. 12-96, argued February 27, 2013, decided June 25, 2013.

7: CHICAGO: THE *OTHER* KIND OF MOB RULE

1. Estes Kefauver, *Crime in America* (Garden City, NY: Doubleday, 1951), 88.

2. Quoted in Benjamin C. Bradlee, *Conversations with Kennedy* (New York: W.W. Norton, 1984), 79.

3. This account largely taken from John Landesco, *Organized Crime in Chicago* (Chicago: University of Chicago Press, 1968).

4. James L. Merriner, *Grafters and Goo Goos: Corruption and Reform in Chicago, 1833–2003* (Carbondale: Southern Illinois University Press, 2004), 111.

5. See Joseph P. Harris, *Election Administration in the United States* (Washington,

DC: Brookings Institution, 1934), 353–54; and Adam Cohen and Elizabeth Taylor, *American Pharaoh: Mayor Richard J. Daley: His Battle for Chicago and the Nation* (New York: Little, Brown, 2000), 129, 138.

6. More on Crowe and the politics of the period in Douglas Bukowski, *Big Bill Thompson, Chicago and the Politics of Image* (Chicago: University of Illinois Press, 1998).

7. Quoted in Harris, *Election Administration*, 353.

8. Quoted in Merriner, *Grafters and Goo Goos*, 124.

9. Quoted in ibid., 129.

10. See Lyle W. Dorsett, *The Pendergast Machine* (New York: Oxford University Press, 1968); and Kefauver, *Crime in America*.

11. Kefauver, *Crime in America*.

12. Baltimore material from Sherry Bebitch Jeffe, who grew up there. Author interview, 2005.

13. Charles Edward Merriam, *Chicago: A More Intimate View of Urban Politics* (New York: Macmillan, 1929), 33.

14. Ibid., 22.

15. See Cohen and Taylor, *American Pharaoh*, 129.

16. Edmund F. Kallina Jr., *Courthouse over White House: Chicago and the Presidential Election of 1960* (Orlando: University of Central Florida Press, 1988), 11.

17. Kefauver, *Crime in America*.

18. Merriner, *Grafters and Goo Goos*, 169.

19. Account taken from Kallina, *Courthouse over White House*; Cohen and Taylor, *American Pharaoh*; and Seymour Hersh, *The Dark Side of Camelot* (New York: Little, Brown, 1997). See also David Greenberg, "Was Nixon Robbed? The Legend of the Stolen 1960 Presidential Election," *Slate*, October 16, 2000.

20. Account of Mazo's research from Greenberg, "Was Nixon Robbed?" Mazo himself wrote an account of the election in Earl Mazo and Stephen Hess, *Nixon: A Political Portrait* (New York: Harper & Row, 1968).

21. *Tribune* reporting examined in Greenberg, "Was Nixon Robbed?"; and Cohen and Taylor, *American Pharaoh*, 272.

22. Recount in state's attorney race sought by Republican candidate Ben Adamowski discussed in Greenberg, "Was Nixon Robbed?"

23. Hersh, *Dark Side of Camelot*, 137–39.

24. Ibid., 210.

25. Judith Campbell Exner, *My Story* (New York: Grove Press, 1977), 194.

26. Quoted in Cohen and Taylor, *American Pharaoh*, 265.

27. Juliet Eilperin and Matthew Vita, "GOP Leaders Back Plan to Block Gore," *Washington Post*, November 23, 2000.

28. See Anthony Summers, *The Arrogance of Power: The Secret World of Richard Nixon* (New York: Viking Penguin, 2000), 310.

29. Nixon's memoirs quoted in Stanley L. Kutler, *The Wars of Watergate* (1990; New York: Norton, 1992), 198.

30. Senate Select Committee on Presidential Campaign Activities, Final Report (1974).

31. The phrase was first used by Ronald Ziegler, the White House press secretary, in a briefing to reporters three days after the Watergate burglars were caught in the act and arrested.

32. From a roundtable discussion with network news anchors on January 4, 1971, quoted in Carl Bernstein and Bob Woodward, *All the President's Men* (New York: Simon & Schuster, 1974), 129.

33. H.R. Haldeman, *The Haldeman Diaries: Inside the Nixon White House* (New York: Berkley Books, 1994), 355.

34. H.R. Haldeman, with Joseph DiMona, *The Ends of Power* (New York: Times Books, 1978), 60.

35. Summers, *Arrogance of Power*, 407–8.

36. Quoted in Bernstein and Woodward, *All the President's Men*, 128. The shock factor, only twelve years after the Chicago mess, appears to have had a class component—gangsters and ward heelers were understandable, but operatives educated at Ivy League schools or the University of Southern California were not. (Segretti was part of a USC political crowd known as Trojans for Representative Government; other members included such Watergate figures as White House press secretary Ron Ziegler; appointments secretary Dwight Chapin; and Gordon Strachan, the White House liaison to Nixon's reelection committee.) The shock also had a component of presidential propriety. It was one thing to unleash the electoral hounds of hell far from Washington, another to do so from inside the White House.

37. See Summers, *Arrogance of Power*, 404–6. See also the three-hour PBS special *George Wallace: Settin' the Woods on Fire* (2000).

38. Seymour Hersh, "Nixon's Last Cover-Up," *New Yorker*, December 14, 1992. The man behind both the intelligence gathering on Teddy Kennedy and the Arthur Bremer job was former CIA operative E. Howard Hunt. Hunt and his fellow White House Plumber G. Gordon Liddy coordinated the Watergate break-in.

39. Quoted in Kallina, *Courthouse over White House*, 104.

8: THE FALLACY OF THE TECHNOLOGICAL FIX

1. David F. Noble, *America by Design: Science, Technology, and the Rise of Corporate Capitalism* (New York: Knopf, 1977), xvii.

2. Rebecca Mercuri, "Corrupted Polling," *Communications of the ACM* 36 (November 1993).

3. Account of the Ron Budd/Jim Fair scandals taken from Philip Morgan, "Tampa's Believe It or Not!," *Tampa Bay Tribune*, September 10, 2002; Howard Troxler, "Elections Scandal No Stranger to Tampa Bay," *St. Petersburg Times*, December 20, 2000; Christopher McDougall, "The Clan Behind the Curtain," *Philadelphia*, May 2001; and Jim Sebesta, author interview, 2005.

4. Bob Varni, author interview, 2005.

5. AVM history recounted in Steve Halvonik, "He Found Success in Doomed Company," *Pittsburgh Post-Gazette*, April 24, 1996.

6. McDougall, "Clan Behind the Curtain."

7. Varni, author interview.

8. See McDougall, "Clan Behind the Curtain"; and summary in *United States v. Ransom F. Shoup II*, U.S. Court of Appeals, Third Circuit, 79-1391 (1979).

9. Roy Lawyer material from Mark J. Kurlansky, "Honest: Vote Machines Can Be a Difficult Sell," *Chicago Tribune*, November 29, 1985.

10. *Behind the Freedom Curtain* was kept for years by the Prelinger Archive, now viewable (as of June 2015) on YouTube.

11. This and other details from the Louisiana secretary of state's highly informative website, http://www.sos.la.gov/ElectionsAndVoting/ReviewAdministrationAnd History/Pages/default.aspx.

12. Joseph P. Harris, *Election Administration in the United States* (Washington, DC: Brookings Institution, 1934), 255.

13. Lewis Mumford, *Technics and Civilization* (New York: Harcourt Brace, 1934), 215.

14. Quoted in Michael Finnegan et al., "A 'Modern' Democracy That Can't Count Votes," *Los Angeles Times*, December 11, 2000.

15. Emile "Peppi" Bruneau, author interview (2005).

16. Michael Ian Shamos, "Electronic Voting—Evaluating the Threat," paper delivered at the Third Conference on Computers, Freedom and Privacy, Burlingame, CA, March 1993, published by Computer Professionals for Social Responsibility.

17. Sebesta, author interview.

18. Bruneau, author interview.

19. The Jerry Fowler story is told, remarkably, in the highly informative, warts-and-all history section of the Louisiana secretary of state's website.

20. Quoted in George Olsen, "Professor Emeritus of Political Science, Joseph Harris, Dies," *Daily Californian*, February 13, 1985.

21. Biographical details from Joseph P. Harris with Harriet Nathan, *Professor and Practitioner: Government, Election Reform and the Votomatic* (Berkeley: University of California Press, 1983); and Bill Rouverol, author interview (2004).

22. Varni, author interview.

23. Rouverol, author interview.

24. Column by Drew Pearson and Jack Anderson, "Computer's Voting Mistakes," appeared around the country on December 11, 1968.

25. See Ronnie Dugger, "Counting Votes," *New Yorker*, November 7, 1988.

26. Sebesta, author interview. Sebesta said he worked with HP on the project.

27. See Bob Drummond, "Diebold Learns What Edison Knew: Voting Machine Sales Are Tough," *Bloomberg News*, September 1, 2004.

28. Detailed in Roy G. Saltman, *Effective Use of Computing Technology in Vote-Tallying* (final project report for National Bureau of Standards, March 1975).

29. Quoted in Dugger, "Counting Votes."

30. Ibid.

31. Michael Ian Shamos, *The Votomatic Election System: An Evaluation*, prepared for the Pennsylvania Bureau of Elections, Pittsburgh, 1980.

32. Quoted in David Burnham, "Computerized Systems for Voting Seen as Vulnerable to Tampering," *New York Times*, July 29, 1985.

33. Churchill's January 15, 1990, letter to Danny Lee McDonald of the FEC.

34. Federal Election Commission, *Performance and Test Standards for Punchcard, Marksense, and Direct Recording Electronic Voting Systems* (Washington, DC: 1990).

35. Described in Dugger, "Counting Votes." In court, Peggy Miller denied going into the computer cage at all on election night, and Steve Miller denied taking computer-sized cards out of his pockets. Their lawyers said the evidence against them was uncorroborated.

36. Dallas election material from ibid.; Saltman, *Accuracy, Integrity and Security*; and Terry Elkins's papers, provided to author by her friend Eva Waskell of Votewatch.

37. Quoted in Saltman, *Accuracy, Integrity and Security*.

38. Quoted in ibid.

39. Burnham's 1987 letter to Lance J. Hoffman of George Washington University.

40. Mack-MacKay race summarized in Jake Tapper, *Down and Dirty: The Plot to Steal the Presidency* (New York: Little, Brown, 2001), 404–5; William Trombley, "Programming Errors Often Blamed: Accurate Vote Tally with Computers Can Be Elusive," *Los Angeles Times*, July 3, 1989; and Russ Smith, "Votescam 2000: The Real Scandal Is the Voting Machines Themselves," *New York Press*, December 19, 2000.

41. MacKay said this in an interview with Carl Bernstein for the now-defunct website voter.com, quoted by Tapper, *Down and Dirty*, and Russ Smith in the *New York Press*.

42. Post by Peter G. Neumann at the online forum "The Risks Digest," run by the ACM (Association for Computer Machinery) Committee on Computers and Public Policy, November 15, 1988, available (as of July 2015) at http://catless.ncl.ac.uk/Risks /7.78.html.

43. Quoted in Trombley, "Programming Errors Often Blamed."

44. ECRI report, "An Election Administrator's Guide to Computerized Voting Systems" (Plymouth Meeting, PA, 1988).

45. Quoted in a February 26, 1990, letter from Mae Churchill to John Surina, FEC staff director.

46. Quoted in Rebecca Mercuri, "The Business of Elections," paper delivered at the Third Conference on Computers, Freedom and Privacy, Burlingame, CA, March 1993, published by Computer Professionals for Social Responsibility.

47. See, for example, Richard Stengel, "The Man Behind the Message: If Anyone

Can Build a Better Candidate, It Is Roger Ailes," *Time*, August 22, 1988.

48. Many years later, Sununu described how he used the power of his office to award low-digit New Hampshire "Live Free or Die" license plates, which had been out of circulation for a few years and were hotly sought after, to Republicans hesitating between Bush and Dole. "The promise of a low-digit license plate was a very effective tie-breaker," Sununu wrote in *The Quiet Man* (New York: Broadside Books, 2015).

49. See, for example, James M. Collier and Kenneth F. Collier, *Votescam: The Stealing of America* (New York: Victoria House, 1992), which spawned many similar voting-related conspiracy theories.

50. Ken Thompson, "Reflections on Trusting Trust," *Communication of the ACM* 27, no. 8 (August 1984).

51. Saltman, *Accuracy, Integrity and Security*.

52. Varni, author interview.

53. Rebecca Mercuri, author interview (2005).

54. Rouverol, author interview.

9: DEMOCRACY'S FRANGIBLE CONNECTIONS: FLORIDA 2000

1. Quoted in Ronnie Dugger, "Counting Votes," *New Yorker*, November 7, 1988.

2. Quoted in Michael Finnegan et al., "A 'Modern' Democracy That Can't Count Votes," *Los Angeles Times*, December 11, 2000.

3. The Gorton-Cantwell recount was widely covered at the time. See, e.g., Dionne Searcey, "Recount Without Rancor," *Washington Post*, November 30, 2000; and Helen Dewar, "Cantwell Senate Victory Over Gorton Upheld," *Washington Post*, December 2, 2000.

4. Jeff Greenfield, *Oh Waiter! One Order of Crow!* (New York: Putnam, 2001).

5. These and other details of election night in Austin taken from author's firsthand experience.

6. See, for example, Andrew Gumbel, "At Home with the Family Bush, America's Dynasty (Still) in Waiting," *The Independent*, November 9, 2000.

7. The events of November–December 2000 were exhaustively covered in the media at the time. Among the better book-length accounts are Jake Tapper, *Down and Dirty: The Plot to Steal the Presidency* (New York: Little, Brown, 2001); and Jeffrey Toobin, *Too Close to Call: The Thirty-Six-Day Battle to Decide the 2000 Election* (New York: Random House, 2001).

8. On John Ellis's role on election night, see David W. Moore, *How to Steal an Election: The Inside Story of How George Bush's Brother and Fox Network Miscalled the 2000 Election and Changed the Course of History* (New York: Nation Books, 2006), 1–6.

9. U.S. Commission on Civil Rights, *Voting Irregularities in Florida During the 2000 Presidential Election* (Washington, DC: June 2001).

10. Henry E. Brady of Berkeley did the initial analysis within days of the election. It was later written up in full. See Henry E. Brady et al., "Law and Data: The Butterfly Ballot Episode," *Political Science & Politics* 34, no. 1 (2001).

11. Figures taken from Tapper, *Down and Dirty*, 65.

12. Quoted in Greenfield, *Oh Waiter!*.

13. Few issues about the Florida fight have been obfuscated and misunderstood more than the media consortium data. Both the *New York Times* and *Washington Post* led their stories of November 12, 2001, with the misleading suggestion that the data upheld Bush's victory. See Dan Keating and Dan Balz, "Florida Recounts Would Have Favored Bush," *Washington Post*, November 12, 2001; and Ford Fessenden and John M. Broder, "Study of Disputed Florida Ballots Finds Justices Did Not Cast the Deciding Vote," *New York Times*, November 12, 2001. The *Times* story took fifteen paragraphs and more than nine hundred words to get to the key point: "An approach Mr. Gore and his lawyers rejected as impractical—a statewide recount—could have produced enough votes to tilt the election his way, no matter what standard was chosen to judge voter intent." The Associated Press was less misleading in its news lede: "A vote-by-vote review of untallied ballots in the 2000 Florida presidential election indicates George W. Bush would have narrowly prevailed in the partial recounts sought by Al Gore, but Gore might have reversed the outcome—by the barest of margins—had he pursued and gained a complete statewide recount." But the most salient news point was also buried far down in the story: "In the review of all the state's disputed ballots, Gore edged ahead under all six scenarios for counting all undervotes and overvotes statewide." The Florida newspapers did a better job, notably the *Orlando Sentinel*, which had made much of the early investigative running into the suppressed recounts in predominantly Republican counties. The *Sentinel's* headline on Jeff Kunerth's story of November 12, 2001: "Gore Could Have Overtaken Bush Under New State Counting Rules." The *St. Petersburg Times* also did better: see Steve Bousquet and Thomas C. Tobin, "Without Overvotes Gore Was Doomed; Thousands of Votes Were Rejected Because of Extra Marks Emphasizing the Voters' Real Choice," *St. Petersburg Times*, November 12, 2001. The full story of the votes hidden in the eighteen Republican counties is told in Toobin, *Too Close to Call*, 66.

14. David Barstow and Don Van Natta Jr., "How Bush Took Florida: Mining the Overseas Absentee Vote," *New York Times*, July 15, 2001.

15. "Overvotes Cost Gore the Election," *Palm Beach Post*, March 19, 2001.

16. The content of the e-mails was erased by Harris's office, supposedly because of a technical error that arose when she ordered a change of operating systems. The substitute operating system, however, was *older* than the one it replaced. See Ann Louise Bardach, "Hoodwinked: Why Is Florida's Voting System So Corrupt?," *Slate*, August 24, 2004.

17. See, e.g., Scott Gold, "Suit Alleges Vote Fraud in Martin County, Fla.," *Los Angeles Times*, December 2, 2000. Republican officials admitted giving preferential treatment to their party's operatives, but prevailed in court.

18. Carollo-Suarez controversy described in Toobin, *Too Close to Call*, 141.

19. See, for example, Andrew Gumbel, "Something Rotten in the State of Florida," *The Independent*, September 29, 2004, which drew on information and legal documents from the ACLU and NAACP.

20. The Sentencing Project and Human Rights Watch, *Losing the Vote: The Impact of Felony Disenfranchisement Laws in the United States* (Washington, DC/New York: 1998).

21. Ion Sancho, author interview, 2004.

22. Quoted in Democratic Investigative Staff, House Committee on the Judiciary, "How to Make Over One Million Votes Disappear: Electoral Sleight of Hand in the 2000 Presidential Election," August 20, 2001, 5.

23. Ion Sancho, author interview, 2006. See also Andrew Gumbel, "Guardian of the Ballot Box," *The Nation*, October 19, 2006.

24. The phrase was coined by GOP lawyer Jason Unger, quoted in Tapper, *Down and Dirty*, 301.

25. DeLay quoted in ibid., 216. Horowitz line from David Horowitz, "Al Gore Has Poisoned the Body Politic—for Generations to Come," *Jewish World Review*, December 5, 2000. Norquist and Will quoted in Stephen Braun, "Conservatives Dust Off Impeachment Outrage," *Los Angeles Times*, November 23, 2000.

26. Racicot and Smith quoted in Tapper, *Down and Dirty*, 204–12.

27. Photograph shown to author by Ion Sancho, 2006. See also Gumbel, "Guardian of the Ballot Box."

28. Timothy Downs, Chris Sutter, and John Hardin Young, *The Recount Primer* (Washington, DC: Sautter Communications, 1994).

29. Quoted in Tapper, *Down and Dirty*, 326.

30. See, e.g., Richard Perez-Peña, "Military Ballots Merit a Review, Lieberman Says," *New York Times*, November 20, 2000.

31. Joe Lieberman, press briefing, Capitol Hill, December 5, 2000.

32. "Irreparable harm" line from Justice Antonin Scalia's concurring opinion upholding the stay requested by the Bush camp of the recounts ordered by the Florida Supreme Court (December 9, 2000). The decision itself is U.S. Supreme Court, *George W. Bush et al. v. Albert Gore, Jr. et al.*, 00-949 (December 12, 2000). For a comparison to *Dred Scott* and much other discussion, see, e.g., Larry D. Kramer, "The Supreme Court in Politics," in *The Unfinished Election of 2000*, ed. Jack N. Rakove (New York: Basic Books, 2001), 105–58; Arthur J. Jacobson and Michael Rosenfeld, eds., *The Longest Night: Polemics and Perspectives on Election 2000* (Berkeley: University of California Press, 2002); or Vincent Bugliosi, *The Betrayal of America* (New York: Thunder's Mouth Press, 2001).

33. Quoted in Braun, "Conservatives Dust Off Impeachment Outrage."

34. Democratic Investigative Staff, House Committee on the Judiciary, "How to Make Over One Million Votes Disappear."

35. Voting Technology Project, "Voting—What Is, What Could Be," CalTech/MIT, July 1, 2001.

36. This and "vote whore" story in Finnegan et al., "'Modern' Democracy That Can't Count Votes."

37. See, e.g., Dan Keating, "Lost Votes in N.M. a Cautionary Tale," *Washington Post*, August 22, 2004.

38. Author interviews with Mike Laurance, Al Solis, and Bill Wheeler of the Doña Ana County Republican Party, 2005, and Chuck Davis and Bill Barnhouse of the county Democratic Party, 2005.

39. Results viewed on New Mexico secretary of state's website in 2005; results apparently no longer viewable in 2015.

10: MIRACLE CURE

1. Quoted in Marc Caputo, "Voting Machines Headed to Online Auction," *Palm Beach Post*, August 30, 2001.

2. David Jefferson, "A Response to the 'Election Center,'" posted at the Verified Voting website July 20, 2003, but no longer available there.

3. Quoted in Jake Tapper, *Down and Dirty: The Plot to Steal the Presidency* (New York: Little, Brown, 2001), 123.

4. See, e.g., Scott Gold, "Floridians Watch Touch-Screen Ballots in Action," *Los Angeles Times*, April 10, 2001.

5. Farhad Manjoo, "The Case for Electronic Voting," Wired News, November 14, 2000.

6. Laurie Koch Thrower and Imran Ghori, "Glitch Slows Touch Voting: San Bernardino County, Whose Voters Used Paper Ballots, Finished Tallying Its Votes Two Hours Ahead of Riverside County," *Riverside Press Enterprise*, November 9, 2000.

7. Burks letter to Townsend, November 9, 2000, obtained by author. The official tally before the machines went down had Burks leading John Bailey by 319 votes with just three out of seventy-eight precincts still to be tallied. Bailey ended up winning by 146 votes.

8. Townsend letter to Burks, December 5, 2000, obtained by author.

9. See, e.g., Andrew Gumbel, "Something Rotten in the State of Florida," *The Independent*, September 29, 2004.

10. See, e.g., Meghan Meyer, "Wellington Candidate Sues, Seeks New Vote," *Palm Beach Post*, April 9, 2002; Jennifer Peltz, "Elections Chief Defends New Vote System," *Orlando Sun Sentinel*, April 10, 2002; and, if findable, Wyatt Olson's terrific cover feature for *New Times Palm Beach*, "Out of Touch: You Press The Screen. The Machine Tells You That Your Vote Has Been Counted. But How Can You Be Sure," April 24, 2003.

11. Charlotte Danciu, author interview, 2004.

12. Experts who had written extensively on the subject at the time include Rebecca Mercuri (whose website www.notablesoftware.com archives many of their writings), David Dill, Peter Neumann, Doug Jones, and others. See also Roy G. Saltman, *Accuracy, Integrity, and Security in Computerized Vote-Tallying* (Gaithersburg, MD:

National Bureau of Standards,1988); Shamos, "Electronic Voting—Evaluating the Threat," paper delivered at the Third Conference on Computers, Freedom and Privacy, Burlingame, CA, March 1993, published by Computer Professionals for Social Responsibility; and the Voting Technology Project paper "Residual Votes Attributable to Technology: An Assessment of the Reliability of Existing Voting Equipment," CalTech/MIT, March 2001.

13. Governor's Select Task Force on Election Procedures, Standards and Technology, "Revitalizing Democracy in Florida," March 1, 2001.

14. Gumbel, "Something Rotten in the State of Florida;" Olson, "Out of Touch"; and "Lobbyist Made Money from Touch Screen Sales," *Associated Press*, October 6, 2002. Mortham acknowledged receiving a commission fee but said she did nothing improper and was not involved in an FAC decision to endorse ES&S voting machinery.

15. Lida Rodriguez-Taseff, author interview, 2004.

16. Cotter quoted in "Florida County Finds 100,000 Lost Votes," Associated Press, November 7, 2002.

17. Lamone material taken from legal papers in lawsuit filed against her by Linda Schade of True Vote Maryland and others, still viewable as of 2015 at the website www.SaveOurVotes.org.

18. Tom Iler, author interview, 2005.

19. Quoted in the "Recommendation of the Election System Evaluation Committee," sent to the Maryland Department of Management and Budget, October 24, 2001, obtained by author.

20. Documentation provided to author by Roxanne Jekot.

21. Theft disclosed by Kathy Rogers, head of the state elections division, to Georgia lawyer Sarah Shalf, per an e-mail from Shalf to other activists dated September 27, 2004; Rogers also discussed the theft with international election monitors in Georgia at the time, per another e-mail from Roxanne Jekot to activists dated September 22, 2004.

22. Letter from GTA's Gary Powell obtained by author.

23. Denis Wright, author interview, 2004.

24. Analysis by Charles Bullock of the University of Georgia, first reported in the *Baltimore City Paper*; Bullock, author interview, 2004.

25. Phone calls and a February 17, 2005, author letter to Judge Dwayne D. Forehand of Dooly County went unanswered.

26. Saltman, *Accuracy, Integrity, and Security*, 1988.

27. Rodriguez-Taseff, author interview, 2004.

28. On HAVA, see, e.g., Daniel P. Tokaji, "Early Returns on Election Reform: Discretion, Disenfranchisement, and the Help America Vote Act," *George Washington Law Review* 73, no. 5/6 (2005); or Leonard M. Shambon, "Implementing the Help America Vote Act," *Election Law Journal* 3, no. 3 (2004).

29. Bill Jones story detailed in Andrew Gumbel, "Down for the Count," *Los Angeles City Beat*, June 24, 2004.

30. Andrew Gumbel, "All the President's Votes?," *The Independent*, October 14, 2003.

31. The prices were almost certainly inflated. Jeremiah Akin, an anti-touchscreen activist in Riverside County, calculated he could go to a retail computer chain and pick out the component parts to run DRE software for $600–$800 per unit. Bob Varni, the Votomatic salesman from the 1960s and early 1970s, thought he could pull a system together for about $100 a unit and saw no reason why Diebold and Sequoia should be charging more than $500–600 (author interviews, 2004).

32. Conny McCormack, author interview, 2004.

33. HAVA's woes details in the USCCR report "Is America Ready to Vote?," 2004.

34. Quoted in Richard L. Hasen, *The Voting Wars: From Florida 2000 to the Next Election Meltdown* (New Haven, CT: Yale University Press, 2012), 130.

35. Shambon, "Implementing the Help America Vote Act."

36. Andrew Gumbel, "US Heading for Another Election Fiasco as Reforms Fail," *The Independent*, April 22, 2004.

37. See, e.g., Bev Harris, *Black Box Voting: Ballot Tampering in the 21st Century* (Renton, WA: Talion, 2004).

38. Julie Carr Smyth, "Voting Machine Controversy," *Cleveland Plain Dealer*, August 28, 2003.

39. Rebecca Mercuri, author interview 2003.

40. Shown to author by Adina Levin of the Texas ACLU.

41. Adina Levin, author interview, 2004.

42. See Kim Zetter, "How E-Voting Threatens Democracy," Wired News, March 29, 2004.

43. Aviel D. Rubin, Dan S. Wallach, Tadayoshi Kohno, and Adam Stubblefield, *Analysis of an Electronic Voting System*, Johns Hopkins University Information Security Institute Technical Report TR-2003-19, July 23, 2003, updated in *IEEE Symposium on Security and Privacy 2004*, IEEE Computer Society Press, May 2004.

44. David Jefferson, testimony before the California Secretary of State's Voting Systems and Procedures panel, April 22, 2004 (author present).

45. Diebold later retracted the spokesman's comments and substituted them with a much more cautious statement. Controversy summarized in Dale Keiger, "E-lective Alarm," *Johns Hopkins*, February 2004.

46. Rubin was attacked for failing to take account of security procedures in polling stations and the safeguards they might provide against vulnerabilities, and for his own personal ties to VoteHere, a software company in direct competition with Diebold that had appointed him to its technical advisory board.

47. See Bill Poovey, "E-Vote Machine Certification Criticized," Associated Press, August 23, 2004. Material also based on author interviews with David Dill, Kim Alexander, and Rebecca Mercuri, 2004. The Election Assistance Commission, which took on oversight responsibilities, later criticized one of the labs, Ciber, and its license subsequently expired. Two other testing labs, Wyle and SysTest, are still in business as of August 2015, but under different names.

48. In early 2004, the *Philadelphia Inquirer* unearthed an IRS filing showing that

the center had received annual donations of $10,000 from Sequoia over a four-year period. The center's executive director, R. Doug Lewis, acknowledged the payments, saying he had received other donations from ES&S and "probably" from Diebold as well. He didn't show any sign of embarrassment about these ties. See Linda K. Harris, "Group that Called Electronic Vote Secure Got Makers' Aid," *Philadelphia Inquirer*, March 25, 2004. At a national conference of county registrars in Washington in August 2004, the Election Center put on a welcome reception sponsored by Diebold, a graduation luncheon and awards ceremony sponsored by ES&S, and a dinner cruise on the Potomac and "monuments by night" tour co-sponsored by Sequoia (per the Election Center website at the time).

49. Author interview with senior federal voting standards official, who could not be named because he was still working for the government at the time, 2005. One example of software that did not meet the 2002 standards was the WinEDS program widely used in Sequoia's tabulation software, written in Visual Basic, a language known for its vulnerability to virus writers.

50. Quoted in Zetter, "How E-Voting Threatens Democracy."

51. E-mails obtained by author, 2004.

52. SAIC, *Risk Assessment Report: Diebold AccuVote-TS Voting System and Processes* report prepared for Maryland Department of Management and Budget, September 2, 2003.

53. Raba Technologies, *Trust Agent Report: Diebold AccuVote-TS Voting System* report prepared for Maryland General Assembly Department of Legislative Services, January 20, 2004.

54. Quoted in Zetter, "How E-Voting Threatens Democracy."

55. Paul Franceus, quoted in Stephanie Desmon, "Md. Computer Testers Cast a Vote: Election Boxes Easy to Mess With," *Baltimore Sun*, January 30, 2004.

56. State of Maryland State Board of Elections, "Response to: Department of Legislative Services Trusted Agent, Report on Diebold AccuVote-TS Voting System," January 29, 2004, cited in litigation initiated by Linda Schade.

57. Martha Ezzard, "Georgia's Voting System a Keeper," *Atlanta Journal Constitution*, October 7, 2003.

58. R. Doug Lewis, Testimony for U.S. Senate Hearings on Disasters and Special Elections, Senate Judiciary Committee, Subcommittee on Constitution, September 9, 2003.

59. The Diebold fiasco was amply documented by the California secretary of state's office at the time. Major reports include the Ad Hoc Touch Screen Task Force Report, July 1, 2003, the Report on the March 2, 2004 Primary Election, April 20, 2004, and the Staff Report on the Investigation of Diebold Election Systems Inc., April 20, 2004. The quote is from assistant secretary of state Marc Carrel, from a Voting Systems and Procedures Panel hearing in Sacramento on April 22, 2004, attended by author.

60. Urosevich was speaking at the same Voting Systems and Procedures Panel hearing attended by author, April 21, 2004.

61. Help America Vote Act (2002), 42 U.S.C.A. §§ 15301–15545.

62. Bills were introduced by Rush Holt in the House and by Hillary Clinton and Bob Graham in the Senate.

63. See Andrew Gumbel, "The Coming Ballot Meltdown," *The Nation*, June 28, 2006.

64. See Lawrence Norden and Christopher Famighetti, *America's Voting Machines at Risk* (New York: Brennan Center for Justice, 2015).

65. McCormack, author interview.

66. See Gumbel, "Down for the Count."

67. Paul Krugman, "Fear of Fraud," *New York Times*, July 27, 2004.

68. Documents obtained by a public records request initiated by Art Cassel.

69. Mischelle Townsend, author interview, 2004.

11: ELECTION 2004: THE SHAPE OF THINGS TO COME

1. Bess McElroy, author interview, 2004.

2. See my own reporting in "Something Rotten in the State of Florida," *The Independent*, September 29, 2004; and also Bob Herbert's *New York Times* op-eds "Suppress the Vote?," August 16, 2004, "Voting While Black," August 20, 2004, and "A Chill in Florida," August 23, 2004.

3. Quoted in Herbert, "Voting While Black."

4. Joe Egan, author interview, 2004.

5. John-Thor Dahlburg, "Orlando Mayor Back After 40 Days in Political Wilderness," *Los Angeles Times*, May 1, 2005.

6. Quoted in Rich Mckay, "Dyer Supporters Rally to Protest Indictment," *Orlando Sentinel*, March 17, 2005.

7. From an August 2003 cabinet meeting at which Tunnell's appointment was confirmed. Transcript obtained by civil rights lawyer Kevin Wood and shared with author. Tunnell was forced to resign from the FDLE in 2006 after he compared Barack Obama, then a U.S. senator, to Osama bin Laden in the midst of a controversial, race-tinged murder investigation he was conducting. See Marc Caputo and Mary Ellen Klas, "Fla. Top Cop Resigns Post Under Cloud," *Miami Herald*, April 21, 2006.

8. Mark Schlueb, "Grand Jury Tells Orlando to End Paid Campaigning," *Orlando Sentinel*, September 1, 2004.

9. Steve Clelland, author interview, 2004.

10. Gumbel, "Something Rotten in the State of Florida."

11. Ibid. See also Brendan Farrington, "Florida Sets Touch-Screen Recounts Rule," Associated Press, October 15, 2014.

12. Robert Wexler, author interview, 2004.

13. Blackwell's actions were widely reported at the time, e.g., in Paul Farhi, "In Fierce Contest for Ohio Vote, Secretary of State Feels Scrutiny," *Washington Post*, October 27, 2004.

14. Geoff Dougherty, "Dead Voters on Tolls, Other Glitches Found in 6 Key States," *Chicago Tribune*, December 4, 2004.

15. "Democrats Blast GOP Lawmaker's 'Suppress the Detroit Vote' Remark," Associated Press, July 21, 2004. The senator, John Pappageorge, later said he'd been taken out of context.

16. Based on my own reporting in Little Haiti in 2004.

17. The acceptance rate ranged from about 8 percent in Oklahoma to about 77 percent in Ohio and Colorado. From an Electionline.org report on the 2004 election, released in December 2004 but no longer available through the organization's website.

18. See, e.g., Farhad Manjoo, "Sproul Play," *Salon*, October 21, 2004.

19. Michael Riley, "Election Tactics Push Envelope," *Denver Post*, October 24, 2004.

20. Ibid.

21. Dave Umhoefer and Greg J. Borowski, "City, County Spar over Ballot Supply," *Milwaukee Journal Sentinel*, October 13, 2004.

22. Teresa James, *Caging Democracy: A 50-Year History of Partisan Challenges to Minority Voters* (Washington, DC: Project Vote, 2007).

23. The Voting Rights Act (1965) made it illegal to discriminate overtly against African Americans; the National Voter Registration Act (1993) made it illegal to single out voters for the express purpose of disenfranchising them. The problem with both laws is that they deal with intent, not outcomes—hence repeated calls down the years for a specific anti-caging law that would not give vote-caging managers wiggle room to claim they were acting in good faith to weed out fraud and illegality, as they invariably do.

24. In Ohio, an appellate court ruling banning use of the caging lists was issued within hours of the poll opening. See James, *Caging Democracy*. Three days earlier, assistant attorney general Alex Acosta, the head of the Justice Department's civil rights division, wrote a letter to the judge supporting the challenge lists as an acceptable way "to strike a balance between ballot access and ballot integrity." The letter came to light only in 2007. See Greg Gordon, "Ex-Justice Official Accused of Aiding Scheme to Scratch Minority Voters," McClatchy, June 24, 2007.

25. Richard Rubin and Binyamin Appelbaum, "Needed: Voting Machines," *Charlotte Observer*, November 4, 2004.

26. The limit in New York State was three minutes; in Ohio, five minutes. Enforcement of these limits varied but was noted, for example, in Franklin County, Ohio, covering Columbus. See, e.g., Geoff Dutton, "Suburbs Were Busiest, Even with More Machines," *Columbus Dispatch*, November 5, 2004.

27. Detailed in John Conyers, *What Went Wrong in Ohio* (Chicago: Chicago Review Press, 2005).

28. The exit polls by Mitofsky International showing Kerry ahead in many of the battleground states, including Ohio, were subject to intense scrutiny. Polling experts (author spoke to David W. Moore of Gallup and Rebecca Mercuri in 2004) faulted Mitofsky for sampling on a statewide basis, not county by county, and for assuming that high turnout would translate to a surge for Kerry. In fact, many rural counties

in southern Ohio saw a big surge in turnout among Republicans—something the pollsters had not anticipated or picked up on in their sampling.

29. Greg Palast, "Kerry Won," TomPaineDispatch.com, November 4, 2004.

30. Quoted in Richard Leiby, "Reliable Source," *Washington Post*, November 4, 2004.

31. CNN, "Officials Discuss How to Delay Election Day," July 12, 2004.

32. Author interviews with Palm Beach County activists Echo Steiner and Susan Van Houten and LePore's successful challenger Arthur Anderson, 2004. See also John Lantigua and Jane Musgrave, "Exclusion from Absentee-Vote Recount Angers Democrats," *Palm Beach Post*, September 2, 2004.

33. Erica Solvig and Dan Horn, "Warren Co. Defends Lockdown Decision," *Cincinnati Enquirer*, November 10, 2004.

34. Terrorism invoked as a reason not to release key election-related materials in a letter from Kathy Rogers, Georgia's state elections director, and provided to author by Roxanne Jekot.

35. Andrew Gumbel, "America's Next Election Nightmare," *Huffington Post*, September 27, 2005.

36. Author interview with election observer and activist Jeremiah Akin, 2004.

37. Associated Press, "More than 4,500 North Carolina Votes Lost Because of Mistake in Voting Machine Capacity," November 4, 2004.

38. Kim Alexander, author interview, 2004.

39. Gail Collins, "Public Interest: Thanksgiving 2000," *New York Times*, November 22, 2000.

40. Of the many accounts of the Rossi-Gregoire standoff, see, e.g., Richard L. Hasen, *The Voting Wars: From Florida 2000 to the Next Election Meltdown* (New Haven, CT: Yale University Press, 2012), 57–58, 149–55.

41. Rebecca Cook, "King County Recount Puts Gregoire on Top, Democrats Say," Associated Press, December 21, 2004.

42. McKay considered a fraud investigation but concluded there was no evidence anyone had deliberately cast an illegal ballot. See David Bowermaster, "McKay 'Stunned' by Report on Bush," *Seattle Times*, March 13, 2007.

43. Edward Epstein, "Boxer Delays Presidential Vote Count with Protest," *San Francisco Chronicle*, January 7, 2005. Observation of Cheney from author watching Senate vote on television.

12: THE 3 PERCENT SOLUTION

1. Dissenting opinion in Seventh Circuit Court of Appeals, *Ruthelle Frank et al. v. Walker*, 14-2058 and 14-2059, decided October 14, 2014.

2. Joshua Green, "Karl Rove in a Corner," *The Atlantic*, November 2004.

3. Quoted in ibid.

4. First quote from "Bond Alleges Voter Fraud in Missouri," *PBS*, November 9,

2000; and second from Jeffrey Toobin, "Poll Position: Is the Justice Department Poised to Stop Voter Fraud—or to Stop Voters Voting?," *New Yorker*, September 20, 2004.

5. Kevin Murphy, "Ashcroft to Fortify Voting Rights Enforcement," Knight-Ridder, March 6, 2001.

6. Joe Rich, author interview, 2008.

7. From an op-ed written by Royal Masset on the website Quorum and reprinted in the *Houston Chronicle* under the title "A Republican, His Mother and Voter ID," April 24, 2007.

8. Taken from the Justice Department's website, www.justice.gov. See "Prepared Remarks of Attorney General John Ashcroft," Voting Integrity Symposium, Washington, DC, October 8, 2002.

9. Von Spakovsky's rise chronicled in Andrew Gumbel, "Justice, Bush-Style," *The Nation*, October 20, 2008. The relevant sections of HAVA are 42 U.S.C.A. § 15483(b) and (d)(2)(B).

10. See, e.g., Kevin Drum, "The Dog That Voted and Other Election Fraud Yarns," *Mother Jones*, July–August 2012.

11. John Feehery, author interview, 2015.

12. Justin Levitt, *The Truth About Voter Fraud* (New York: Brennan Center for Justice, 2007).

13. One comprehensive analysis of the numbers, based on census data and opinion polling, is the Brennan Center for Justice's November 2006 survey "Citizens Without Proof: A Survey of Americans' Possession of Documentary Proof of Citizenship and Photo Identification." It put the number without ID at 11 percent of the adult population, or more than 20 million people.

14. Even where the state offers an alternate ID free of charge—as they all have since the Georgia law was modified in 2006—there are often steep costs attached to obtaining the underlying documentation, e.g., a replacement birth certificate. For further discussion, see, for example, Tova Andrea Wang, *The Politics of Voter Suppression* (Ithaca, NY: Cornell University Press, 2012); or Lorraine C. Minnite, *The Myth of Voter Fraud* (Ithaca, NY: Cornell University Press, 2011).

15. Kristen Mack, "In Trying to Win, Has Dewhurst Lost a Friend?," *Houston Chronicle*, May 18, 2007.

16. Martin Wiskcol, "Armey Wants to Transform Congressional GOP," *Orange County Register*, September 2, 2010.

17. See Scott Horton, "Vote Machine," *Harper's*, March 2008; and Jon K. Lauck, *Daschle vs. Thune: Anatomy of a High-Plains Senate Race* (Norman: University of Oklahoma Press, 2007). Daschle's campaign had its own dirty laundry, and he ended up losing by 4,500 votes.

18. The campaign was widely covered at the time. On collective bargaining rights, see, e.g., David Firestone, "Homeland Security Fight Returns to the Fore," *New York Times*, October 16, 2002. For Cleland's own account, see Max Cleland with Ben Raines, *Heart of a Patriot: How I Found the Courage to Survive Vietnam, Walter Reed and Karl Rove* (New York: Simon & Schuster, 2009), 187–200.

19. See, e.g., Jeffrey Gettleman, "With Two Candidates Claiming Victory, Legislature May Decide Alabama Governor's Race," *New York Times*, November 7, 2002.

20. James H. Gundlach, "A Statistical Analysis of Possible Electronic Ballot Stuffing: The Case of the Baldwin County, Alabama Governor's Race in 2002," presentation at the Annual Meeting of the Alabama Political Science Association, Troy, AL, April 11, 2003. Alabama subsequently changed its election law to allow for manual recounts in close races.

21. The opposition researcher, Republican lawyer Jill Simpson, later went public. See "Did Ex-Alabama Governor Get a Raw Deal?," *60 Minutes*, February 21, 2008. Rove has denied knowing her.

22. Don Siegelman, author interview, 2012. See Andrew Gumbel, "Former Governor Don Siegelman Lobbies for Presidential Pardon at DNC," *The Guardian*, September 5, 2012. The prosecutor was Leura Canary, who was married to Republican operative Bill Canary. Canary has denied reports that he deliberately set his wife and another federal prosecutor on Siegelman's tail; Rove was asked on ABC's *This Week* if he had been in touch with the Justice Department about the Siegelman case and did not explicitly deny it; see David Corn, "On the Siegelman Scandal, Rove Offers a Very Suspicious Non-Denial Denial," *Mother Jones*, May 26, 2008.

23. Fred Barnes, "The (Finally) Emerging Republican Majority," *Weekly Standard*, October 27, 2003.

24. Memo made public by Dan Eggen, "Justice Staff Saw Texas Districting as Illegal," *Washington Post*, December 2, 2005. The leak led to a nasty internal investigation at the Justice Department, leading to a number of career lawyers in the voting section quitting. See Gumbel, "Justice, Bush-Style."

25. Rich, author interview.

26. See Gumbel, "Justice, Bush-Style." When Tanner's remarks were made public, they precipitated his resignation.

27. Timeline of the Georgia law detailed in Shannon McCaffrey, "Despite Voter ID Law, Minority Turnout Up in Georgia," *Atlanta Journal-Constitution*, September 3, 2012.

28. Commission on Federal Election Reform, *Building Confidence in U.S. Elections* (Washington, DC: Center for Democracy and Election Management, 2005). Carter-Baker was cited in the Supreme Court ruling (see note 31) but not in the Appeals Court ruling penned by Posner (see note 30).

29. See, e.g., Stephanie Mencimer, "How Conservative Judges Are Using Jimmy Carter to Screw Over Minority Voters," *Mother Jones*, October 7, 2014. By 2013, Carter had either extricated himself from James Baker's clutches or seen the light, or both. See Sean Sullivan, "Jimmy Carter: Think of How King Would Have Reacted to Voter I.D. Laws," *Washington Post*, August 28, 2013.

30. U.S. Court of Appeals Seventh Circuit, *William Crawford et al. v. Marion County Election Board et al*, 06-2218 and 06-2317, decided January 4, 2007.

31. Supreme Court of the United States, *Crawford v. Marion County Election Board*, 07-21 and 07-25, decided April 28, 2008. Years later, Stevens appears to have had a change of heart about voter ID, telling a Senate Rules Committee hearing that

"excessive" photo ID requirements "never made any sense." See Stephen Spaulding, "Justice Stevens Rips Citizens United, But Disagrees with Hillary Clinton's Litmus Test," *Huffington Post*, May 22, 2015.

32. See Lorraine Minnite, *The Politics of Voter Fraud* (Washington, DC: Project Vote, 2007).

33. Gumbel, "Justice, Bush-Style."

34. See, e.g., Alex Koppelman, Mark Follman, and Jonathan Vanian, "How U.S. Attorneys Were Used to Spread Voter-Fraud Fears," *Salon*, March 21, 2007. The full name of ACORN is the Association of Community Organizations for Reform Now.

35. Schlozman e-mails cited in U.S. Department of Justice, Office of the Inspector General/Office of Professional Responsibility, *An Investigation of Allegations of Politicized Hiring and Other Improper Personnel Actions in the Civil Rights Division*, June 2, 2008, released publicly January 13, 2009.

36. Author interviews with Rich, David Becker, and Toby Moore, 2008.

37. Schlozman was appointed through a loophole in the USA Patriot Act and was not confirmed by the Senate. See, e.g., Art Levine, "The Republican War on Voting," *American Prospect*, March 19, 2008.

38. The Ohio furor and its origins are traced in Joe Mahr, "Voter Fraud Case Traced to Defiance County Registrations Volunteer," *Toledo Blade*, October 19, 2004. Many more allegations can be found in American Center for Voting Rights Legislative Fund, "Vote Fraud, Intimidation & Suppression in the 2004 Presidential Election," July 21, 2005. More on ACORN and ACVR in Richard L. Hasen, *The Voting Wars: From Florida 2000 to the Next Election Meltdown* (New Haven, CT: Yale University Press, 2012), 50–72.

39. See Office of the Inspector General, "An Investigation into the Removal of Nine U.S. Attorneys in 2006," U.S. Department of Justice, September 2008.

40. Quoted in Dahlia Lithwick, "Nuts about ACORN," *Slate*, October 16, 2008.

41. Quoted in Andrew Gumbel, "Protect This Election," *The Nation*, October 22, 2008.

42. Supreme Court of the United States, *Citizens United v. Federal Election Commission*, 08-205, decided January 21, 2010.

43. Lawrence Lessig, *Republic, Lost: How Money Corrupts Congress—and a Plan to Stop It* (New York: Twelve, 2011), 244.

44. Data from the American National Election Studies project at the University of Michigan, cited in ibid.

45. Feingold has used the term since at least 1999, when he said it in an acceptance speech for a Profile in Courage award from the John F. Kennedy Presidential Library. On Sanders, see, e.g., Jordain Carney, "Bernie Sanders to Fight for Campaign Finance Reform," *The Hill*, August 4, 2015. Abramoff quoted in Dana Milbank, "Jack Abramoff's Atonement," *Washington Post*, February 6, 2012. Rubenstein quoted in Michael Lewis, "The Access Capitalists," *New Republic*, October 18, 1993. Long quoted in John H. Cushman Jr., "Russell B. Long, 84, Senator Who Influenced Tax Laws," *New York Times*, May 11, 2003.

46. Quoted in John Nichols and Robert W. McChesney, *Dollarocracy: How the Money and Media Election Complex Is Destroying America* (New York: Nation Books, 2013), 17. The quote—"those who own the country ought to govern it"—is not directly from Jay or Hamilton but comes from a contemporary Philadelphia newspaper summarizing their views in admittedly scathing terms. It was also picked up, however, in a biography of Jay by his son. See William Jay, *The Life of John Jay* (New York, J. & J. Harper, 1833), 70.

47. For example, in 1887, the former president Rutherford B. Hayes described money in politics as "the giant evil and danger in this country, the danger which transcends all others." Quoted in Nichols and McChesney, *Dollarocracy*, 20.

48. Tilman Klumpp, Hugo M. Mialon, and Michael A. Williams, "The Business of American Democracy: Citizens United, Independent Spending, and Elections," working paper, University of Alberta, 2014, due to be published in the *Journal of Law and Economics*, 2015.

13: POPE AND ABBOTT: THE NEW RELIGION OF BUYING AND SUPPRESSING VOTES

1. Yelton interviewed on *The Daily Show*, Comedy Central, October 23, 2013.

2. Narrative of 2010 election from Chris Kromm, "Art Pope's Big Day: Republican Benefactor Fueled GOP Capture of NC Legislature," *Facing South*, Institute of Southern Studies, November 4, 2010, updated November 29, 2010; and Jane Mayer, "State for Sale," *New Yorker*, October 10, 2011.

3. The Dickson ad was paid for by her opponent, who had received campaign contributions from Pope and other Pope family members. Pope publicly decried the ad, but Dickson argued in the *New Yorker* that he bore "some responsibility" because of where he'd put his money.

4. For Pope's interview on the Raleigh TV station WRAL, see "GOP Donor Spent Heavily on Legislative Races," WRAL, November 12, 2010.

5. Both *Shaw v. Reno* (1993) and *Shaw v. Hunt* (1996) (see chapter 7) were North Carolina cases and focused on the troublesome 12th electoral district, which would be gerrymandered again.

6. The Republican money trail is tracked brilliantly in Olga Pierce, Justice Elliott, and Theodoric Meyer, "How Dark Money Helped Republicans Hold the House and Hurt Voters," *ProPublica*, December 21, 2012.

7. Comparison of Democratic and Republican redistricting and double bunking from author interview with Bob Hall of Democracy North Carolina, 2015.

8. See, e.g., Christopher Ingraham, "America's Most Gerrymandered Districts," *Washington Post*, May 15, 2014. Three of his top ten are in North Carolina. The districts Ingraham highlights have nicknames including "praying Mantis" and "Goofy kicking Donald Duck."

9. Sam Wang, "The Great Gerrymander of 2012," *New York Times*, February 3, 2013.

10. E-mail obtained by *ProPublica* and quoted in Pierce, Elliott, and Meyer, "How

Dark Money Helped Republicans." Hofeller said the plan in North Carolina's first congressional district was to "incorporate all the significant concentrations of minority voters in the northeast."

11. Bob Hall, "Voting Rights & Fair Elections," Democracy North Carolina briefing paper for the North Carolina NAACP, February 8, 2014.

12. See, e.g., RSLC head Chris Jankowski's interview with Rachel Maddow, "GOP Seeks to Rig Presidential Race on Model of Congressional Gerrymandering," *The Rachel Maddow Show*, MSNBC, January 15, 2013.

13. Republicans got on board with early voting when they realized they benefited from it as much as Democrats did in the 2002 election. Democrats, and a small number of Republicans, consented to same-day registration only if it was restricted to the early voting period, when ballots were not secret but could be traced back to individual voters (like absentee ballots), and if voters produced ID to prove their identity. Casting out-of-precinct provisional ballots was rejected by the state supreme court in 2005 as unconstitutional, but reinstated after lawmakers were presented with evidence of clear racial disparities as a result of scrapping it and rewrote the law to overcome the court's objections. Per Bob Hall of Democracy North Carolina, who lobbied extensively for these reforms; author interview, 2015.

14. Figures taken from Wang, "Great Gerrymander of 2012."

15. Jack Hawke, "McCrory's Election Performance Defended," *Carolina Journal Online*, November 21, 2008.

16. Bob Hall, author interview, 2015.

17. John Davis, "North Carolina Governor's Race Is McCrory's to Lose: Democrats Are Not Structurally Capable of Rescuing Dalton," John Davis Consulting, July 11, 2012, www.johndavisconsulting.com.

18. "Democracy Undone by Ending Funding for NC Court Races," *Raleigh News & Observer*, June 14, 2014.

19. Quoted in Matea Gold, "In N.C., Conservative Donor Art Pope Sits at Heart of Government He Helped Transform," *Washington Post*, July 19, 2014.

20. From the complaint in *NC NAACP v. McCrory*, case no. 1:13-cv-658.

21. Tom Apodaca quoted in "NC Voter ID Bill Moving Ahead with Supreme Court Ruling," WRAL TV, June 25, 2013.

22. Quoted in a news release from the Advancement Project, "Federal Trial against North Carolina Voter Suppression Law Starts July 13, Followed by Mass March for Voting Rights," July 8, 2015.

23. Still viewable, as of July 2015, at the Civitas website, http://www.nccivitas.org /moralmonday/.

24. Sue Sturgis, "Art Pope–Funded Group Launches Database Targeting Moral Monday Arrestees," *Facing South*, June 19, 2013.

25. The Supreme Court did not explicitly offer this reason, but it came up in the briefs and was consistent with the so-called Purcell principle arising from a 2006 case in Arizona. See Richard L. Hasen, "Reining in the Purcell Principle," University of

California, Irvine School of Law Research Paper No. 2015-05, May 8, 2015, due out in the *Florida State University Law Review*, 2015.

26. Anne Blythe, "Federal Trial Set to Start over NC's Election Law," *Raleigh News & Observer*, July 11, 2015.

27. Isela Gutierrez and Bob Hall, *Alarm Bells from Silenced Voters* (Durham: Democracy North Carolina, 2015).

28. From the North Carolina NAACP website.

29. Lisa Worf, "NC General Assembly Approves Tweaks to Photo ID Voting Law," WFAE Charlotte, June 18, 2015.

30. William Barber of the North Carolina NAACP said, "Today, the General Assembly is more committed to protecting . . . symbols of a pro-slavery, white supremacist, segregationist past than they are to protecting people who are living right now." Press release, NAACP, July 24, 2015.

31. Hall, author interview. See also Press Millen, "Why NC Lawmakers Caved on Voter ID," *Raleigh News & Observer*, June 23, 2015.

32. Details taken from lawsuit *Veasey v. Perry*, case no. 2:13-cv-00193, filed in U.S. District Court in Corpus Christi in 2013, and the court's opinion, filed October 9, 2014.

33. Todd Smith, author interview, 2015.

34. Chad Dunn, author interview, 2015.

35. Martinez-Fischer, cited in Judge Nelva Gonzales Ramos's opinion in *Veasey v. Perry*.

36. For numbers from 2008, see Ross Ramsey, "The Case of the Missing Democratic Voters," *Texas Tribune*, February 14, 2014; and Susan Minushkin and Mark Hugo Lopez, *The Hispanic Vote in the 2008 Democratic Presidential Primaries* (Washington, DC: Pew Research Center, 2008).

37. See Alexa Ura, "GOP Hopefuls Eyeing the Texas Hispanic Vote," *Texas Tribune*, January 25, 2015; and Alexa Ura, "For Abbott, a Balancing Act of Far Right and Hispanics," *Texas Tribune*, December 7, 2014.

38. In his *Years of Lyndon Johnson: The Path to Power* (1982; New York: Knopf, 2002), 718, Robert Caro cites John Gunther on San Antonio politics in the 1940s: "The way to play politics in San Antonio is to buy, or try to buy, the Mexican vote. . . . An honest Mexican is one who stays bought."

39. Quoted in Orville Vernon Burton's expert report on behalf of the plaintiffs in the Texas voter ID case *Veasey v. Perry*; report provided to the author.

40. Figure on Hispanic voter turnout in 2012 from Ura, "For Abbott." Historical detail from Judge Ramos's opinion in *Veasey v. Perry*.

41. Greg Abbott, "Let's Stamp Out Voter Fraud in Texas," March 1, 2006, still available (as of 2015) on the Texas attorney general's website, www.texasattorneygeneral.gov.

42. Wayne Slater, "Few Texas Voter-Fraud Cases Would Have Been Prevented by Photo ID Law, Review Shows," *Dallas Morning News*, September 9, 2013.

43. Details of suit from Campaign Legal Center website, www.campaignlegalcenter .org. See also Ralph Blumenthal, "Texas Democrats File Suit Against Voting Fraud Law," *New York Times*, September 23, 2006.

44. Quoted in Steven Rosenfeld, "Vote By Mail, Go to Jail," *Texas Observer*, April 18, 2008.

45. James Drew, "Abbott's Houston Raid Didn't End with Arrests, but Shut Down Voter Drive," *Dallas Morning News*, August 30, 2014. Abbott denied having personal knowledge of the raid, and his office scoffed at the suggestion that it was politically motivated. The group had been targeted by Tea Party activists, in part because the head of its parent organization, Texans Together, had filed a complaint leading to the indictment of Houston congressman and former House chief whip Tom DeLay on corruption charges.

46. Gallegos story told in Richard L. Hasen, *The Voting Wars: From Florida 2000 to the Next Election Meltdown* (New Haven, CT: Yale University Press, 2012), 42–43.

47. Texas Republicans led by Dan Patrick eventually lobbied to have the two-thirds rule overturned altogether. See, e.g., the editorial "Nuclear Option, Texas Senate–Style?," *Dallas Morning News*, January 14, 2014.

48. Quotes and details of the passage of the law taken from Judge Ramos's opinion in *Veasey v. Perry*.

49. Smith, author interview.

50. Greg Abbott, "Obama's Scheme to Take over Texas," *Washington Times*, July 30, 2013.

51. Data from National Conference of State Legislatures website, www.ncsl.org.

52. Quoted in Ethan Magoc, "Flurry of Voter ID Laws Tied to Conservative Group ALEC," *NBC/News21*, August 21, 2012.

53. Discussed in Gary May, *Bending Toward Justice: The Voting Rights Act and the Transformation of American Democracy* (New York: Basic Books, 2013), 237–54.

54. Michael Van Sickler, "Gov. Rick Scott Delivers Mea Culpa on Voter Purge," *Miami Herald*, October 6, 2013.

55. See, e.g., "Teacher Says No Way to Comply with Florida's Voting Law," Associated Press, November 1, 2011. The head of the Florida League of Women Voters explained why she was suspending her registration drives in Deirdre Macnab, "Newly Registered Voters in Florida Could Become an Endangered Species," *TC Palm*, November 28, 2011.

56. O'Brien's comments were captured on video and posted to YouTube; see Brian Beutler, "NH GOP Seeks to Disenfranchise Students Who 'Just Vote Their Feelings,'" *Talking Points Memo*, March 7, 2011. Preisse quoted in Darrel Rowland, "Fight over Poll Hours Isn't Just Political," *Columbus Dispatch*, August 19, 2012.

57. They cite, for example, Shannon McCaffrey, "Despite Voter ID Law, Minority Turnout Up in Georgia," *Atlanta Journal-Constitution*, September 3, 2012.

58. Nate Silver, "Measuring the Effects of Voter Identification Laws," *New York Times*, July 15, 2012.

59. GAO, *Issues Related to State Voter Identification Laws* (September 2014, revised February 27, 2015).

60. On Brownback and Tillis, see, e.g., Elizabeth Drew, "Big Dangers for the Next Election," *New York Review of Books*, May 21, 2015.

61. The earlier case, which laid much of the groundwork for *Shelby*, was *N.W. Austin v. Holder* (2009).

62. Another example: in late 2015, Alabama closed thirty-one DMV offices, many in black-majority counties, making it harder for voters without driver's licenses to obtain the photo ID now required to vote. See Ari Berman, "Alabama, Birthplace of the Voting Rights Act, Is Once Again Gutting Voting Rights," *The Nation*, October 1, 2015.

14: THE SUPER-RICH AND THE DEMOCRATIC FUTURE

1. E.E. Schattschneider, *The Semisovereign People: A Realist's View of Democracy in America* (New York: Holt, Rinehart and Winston, 1960), 120.

2. Rebecca Ballhaus, Beth Reinhard, and Christopher S. Stewart, "Billionaires Put Their Stamp on 2016 Presidential Campaigns," *Wall Street Journal*, July 31, 2015.

3. Martin Gilens and Benjamin I. Page, "Testing Theories of American Politics: Elites, Interest Groups, and Average Citizens," *Perspectives on Politics* 12, no. 3 (September 2014): 564–81.

4. Discussed further in Andrew Gumbel, "Silicon Valley's Brave New Economic Order," *Pacific Standard*, March 3, 2015.

5. Benjamin I. Page, Larry M. Bartels, and Jason Seawright, "Democracy and the Policy Preferences of Wealthy Americans," *Perspectives on Politics* 11, no. 1 (March 2013): 51–73.

6. For analysis of the prosecution end of this, see Jed S. Rakoff, "The Financial Crisis: Why Have No High-Level Executives Been Prosecuted?," *New York Review of Books*, January 9, 2014.

7. Figures from a study conducted by the New America Foundation's Lee Drutman and cited in Darrell West, *Billionaires: Reflections on the Upper Crust* (Washington, DC: Brookings Institution Press, 2014), 9.

8. See, for example, the Pew Research poll, "Public Knowledge of Current Affairs Little Changed by News and Information Revolutions," Pew Research Center, April 15, 2007, available at www.people-press.org.

9. Quoted in Martin Schram, *Speaking Freely: Former Members of Congress Talk about Money in Politics* (Washington, DC: Center for Responsive Politics, 1995), 42.

10. On AIPAC's influence on Congress, see John Mearsheimer and Stephen Walt, "The Israel Lobby," *London Review of Books*, March 23, 2006. On the NRA, see Alan Berlow and Gordon Witkin, "Gun Lobby's Money and Power Still Holds Sway over Congress," Center for Public Integrity, May 1, 2013, updated May 13, 2013. An interesting discussion on countering the power of lobbies in the Internet age is Lorelei Kelly, "How Groups Like the NRA Captured Congress—and How to Take It Back," *The Atlantic*, March 7, 2013.

11. Seymour Martin Lipset, "Some Social Requisites of Democracy: Economic Development and Political Legitimacy," *American Political Science Review* 53 (1959).

12. The leading economic researchers into inequality in the United States are

Emmanuel Saez at Berkeley and Thomas Piketty. See, e.g., Thomas Piketty and Emmanuel Saez, "Income Inequality in the United States, 1913–1998," *Quarterly Journal of Economics* 118, no. 1 (2003): 1–41. A useful and updated summary of their findings is, as of 2015, at the website Inequality.org. For another useful analysis of the same data from a political science perspective, see Charles Noble, "What John Kerry Won't Say about the 'Two Americas,'" *Logos* 3, no. 4 (Fall 2004).

13. Andrea Ichino, Loukas Karabarbounis, and Enrico Moretti, "The Political Economy of Intergenerational Income Mobility," *Economic Inquiry* 49, no. 1 (January 2011): 47–69.

14. Ricardo's famous model of comparative advantage in international trade assumed capital was immobile. See David Ricardo, *On the Principles of Political Economy and Taxation* (London: John Murray, 1817).

15. Ben Brody, "How John Oliver Transformed the Net Neutrality Debate Once and for All," Bloomberg News, February 26, 2015. According to the Center for Responsive Politics, five former FCC officials worked for Comcast alone, as of 2014. See Robbie Feinberg, "The Comcast-FCC Revolving Door," *OpenSecretsblog*, Center for Responsive Politics, April 18 2014. The FCC chair, Tom Wheeler, was also a former telecommunications industry lobbyist.

16. Barack Obama interviewed by Jon Stewart on *The Daily Show*, Comedy Central, July 21, 2015.

17. A rundown of these studies, including two by the University of Maryland's Program on International Policy Attitudes (since renamed the Program for Public Consultation), can be found in Chris Mooney, *The Republican Brain: The Science of Why They Deny Science and Reality* (New York: Wiley, 2012), 147–68.

18. Study results discussed in Kevin Charles Redmon, "American Voters: Plenty of Opinions, But Without a Clue," *Pacific Standard*, November 5, 2012.

19. Amy Chozick, "Hillary Clinton Says G.O.P. Rivals Try to Stop Young and Minority Voters," *New York Times*, June 4, 2015; Ed Pilkington, "Hillary Clinton: Republicans Warning of Election Fraud Are 'Fear-Mongering,'" *The Guardian*, August 6, 2015.

20. See, for example, the work of President Obama's Presidential Commission on Election Administration, co-chaired by Bob Bauer and Ben Ginsberg; the Carter-Baker National Commission on Federal Election Reform from 2005; the Constitution Project's Forum on Election Reform; the Brennan Center for Justice's many position papers, especially on registration; the CalTech/MIT Voting Technology Project on machines; the California Voter Foundation; Fairvote.org; and others.

21. Lawrence Lessig, *Republic, Lost: How Money Corrupts Congress—and a Plan to Stop It* (New York: Twelve, 2011), 265–72.

22. Brennan Center proposals summarized in its "Fact Sheet: Voter Registration for the 21st Century," July 10, 2015.

23. Nevada adopted a version of "none of the above" in 1978. California had a ballot initiative on the question in 2000, which failed, in part because it was restricted to a few high-profile races.

24. More at the National Popular Vote website, www.nationalpopularvote.com.

25. The leading proponent of this form of reform is Rob Richie's Fairvote.org.

26. From the Carter Center's mission statement.

INDEX

Publishing in the Public Interest

Thank you for reading this book published by The New Press. The New Press is a nonprofit, public interest publisher. New Press books and authors play a crucial role in sparking conversations about the key political and social issues of our day.

We hope you enjoyed this book and that you will stay in touch with The New Press. Here are a few ways to stay up to date with our books, events, and the issues we cover:

- Sign up at www.thenewpress.com/subscribe to receive updates on New Press authors and issues and to be notified about local events
- Like us on Facebook: www.facebook.com/newpressbooks
- Follow us on Twitter: www.twitter.com/thenewpress

Please consider buying New Press books for yourself; for friends and family; or to donate to schools, libraries, community centers, prison libraries, and other organizations involved with the issues our authors write about.

The New Press is a 501(c)(3) nonprofit organization. You can also support our work with a tax-deductible gift by visiting www.thenewpress.com/donate.